The Kennedy Years

text prepared under the direction of

HAROLD FABER
Day National News Editor
The New York Times

with contributions by

John Corry
Paul Greenfeder
Lee Kanner
Alvin Shuster
Warren Weaver Jr.

introduction by Tom Wicker

contributing photographer

George Tames
The New York Times

THE

text by
THE NEW YORK TIMES

photographs by
JACQUES LOWE
and others

KENNEDY YEARS

THE VIKING PRESS   **NEW YORK**

Contents

ACKNOWLEDGMENTS

Of the many individuals whose efforts have gone into the making of this book, special thanks are due to the following:

For THE NEW YORK TIMES:

The reporters, copy readers and editors of The New York Times, whose news reports formed the basis for the text of this book; especially helpful were articles by Russell Baker, William M. Blair, Wallace Carroll, Robert Doty, Leo Egan, John Fenton, Max Frankel, M. S. Handler, Marjorie Hunter, William Jorden, Paul Kennedy, E. W. Kenworthy, Clayton Knowles, Arthur Krock, W. H. Lawrence, Anthony Lewis, Drew Middleton, John D. Morris, James Reston, Nan Robertson, Harold Schonberg, Claude Sitton, C. L. Sulzberger, Tad Szulc, Seymour Topping, Tom Wicker and Richard Witkin.

Michael O'Keefe, picture research and assistance.

For JACQUES LOWE:

Nira Lowe.

George Kampos and Terri Hyman, research and assistance.

Sol Blackman of Hoffman Laboratories, black and white prints; Jerry Wind of Langen and Wind, color prints.

The Kennedy Years

Introduction

Millions of words, thousands of articles and scores of books have been written about the life and death of John F. Kennedy. One of the articles, written shortly after the assassination, was published in Times Talk, the house organ of The New York Times. It was written by Tom Wicker, White House correspondent for The Times, who had been assigned to the Kennedy Administration from the beginning, to tell his colleagues how he covered the assassination. Here is his story:

I think I was in the first press bus. But I can't be sure. Pete Lisagor of The Chicago Daily News says he *knows* he was in the first press bus and he describes things that went on aboard that didn't happen on the bus I was in. But I still *think* I was in the first press bus.

I cite that minor confusion as an example of the way it was in Dallas in the early afternoon of Nov. 22. At first no one knew what happened, or how, or where, much less why. Gradually, bits and pieces began to fall together and within two hours a reasonably coherent version of the story began to be possible. Even now, however, I know no reporter who was there who has a clear and orderly picture of that surrealistic afternoon; it is still a matter of bits and pieces thrown hastily into something like a whole.

It began, for most reporters, when the central fact of it was over. As our press bus eased at motorcade speed down an incline toward an underpass, there was a little confusion in the sparse crowds that at that point had been standing at the curb to see the President of the United States pass. As we came out of the underpass, I saw a motorcycle policeman drive over the curb, across an open area, a few feet up a railroad bank, dismount and start scrambling up the bank.

Jim Mathis of The Advance (Newhouse) Syndicate went to the front of our bus and looked ahead to where the President's car was supposed to be, perhaps ten cars ahead of us. He hurried back to his seat.

"The President's car just sped off," he said. "Really gunned away." (How could Mathis have seen that if there had been another bus in front of us?)

But that could have happened if someone had thrown a tomato at the President. The press bus in its stately pace rolled on to the Trade Mart, where the President was to speak. Fortunately, it was only a few minutes away.

At the Trade Mart, rumor was sweeping the hundreds of Texans already eating their lunch. It was the only rumor that I had ever *seen*; it was moving across that crowd like a wind over a wheatfield. A man eating a grapefruit seized my arm as I passed. "Has the President been shot?" he asked.

"I don't think so," I said. "But something happened."

With the other reporters—I suppose 35 of them—I went on through the huge hall to the upstairs press room. We were hardly there when Marianne Means of Hearst Headline Service hung up a telephone, ran to a group of us and said: "The President's been shot. He's at Parkland Hospital."

One thing I learned that day; I suppose I already knew it, but that day made it plain. A reporter must trust his instinct. When Miss Means said those eight words—I never learned who told her—I knew absolutely they were true. Everyone did. We ran for the press buses.

Again, a man seized my arm—an official-looking man.

"No running in here," he said sternly. I pulled free and ran on. Doug Kiker of The Herald Tribune barreled head-on into a waiter carrying a plate of potatoes. Waiter and potatoes flew about the room. Kiker ran on. He was in his first week with The Trib, and his first Presidential trip.

I barely got aboard a moving press bus. Bob Pierrepoint of C.B.S. was aboard and he said that he now recalled having heard something that could have been shots—or firecrackers, or motorcycle backfire. We talked anxiously, unbelieving, afraid.

Fortunately again, it was only a few minutes to Parkland Hospital. There, at its emergency entrance, stood the President's car, the top up, a bucket of bloody water beside it. Automatically, I took down its license number—GG300 District of Columbia.

The first eyewitness description came from Senator Ralph Yarborough, who had been riding in the third car of the motorcade with Vice President and Mrs. Johnson. Senator Yarborough is an east Texan, which is to say a Southerner, a man of quick emotion, old-fashioned rhetoric.

"Gentlemen," he said, pale, shaken, near tears. "It is a deed of horror."

The details he gave us were good and mostly—as it later proved—accurate. But he would not describe to us the appearance of the President as he was wheeled into the hospital, except to say that he was "gravely wounded." We could not doubt, then, that it was serious.

I had chosen that day to be without a notebook. I took notes on the back of my mimeographed schedule of the two-day tour of Texas we had been so near to concluding. Today, I cannot read many of the notes; on Nov. 22, they were as clear as 60-point type.

A local television reporter, Mel Crouch, told us he had seen a rifle being withdrawn from the corner fifth-floor or sixth-floor window of the Texas School Book Depository. Instinct again—Crouch sounded right, positive, though none of us knew him. We believed it and it was right.

Mac Kilduff, an assistant White House press secretary in charge of the press on that trip, who was to acquit himself well that day, came out of the hospital. We gathered round and he told us the President was alive. It wasn't true, we later learned; but Mac thought it was true at that time, and he didn't mislead us about a possible recovery. His whole demeanor made plain what was likely to happen. He also told us—as Senator Yarborough had—that Gov. John Connally of Texas was shot, too.

Kilduff promised more details in five minutes and went back into the hospital. We were barred. Word came to us second-hand—I don't remember exactly how—from Bob Clark of A.B.C., one of the men who had been riding in the press "pool" car near the President's, that he had been lying face down in Mrs. Kennedy's lap when the car arrived at Parkland. No signs of life.

That is what I mean by instinct. That day, a reporter had none of the ordinary means or time to check and double-check matters given as fact. He had to go on what he knew of people he talked to, what he knew of human reaction, what two isolated "facts" added up to in sum—above all on what he felt in his bones. I knew Clark and respected him. I took his report at face value, even at second-hand. It turned out to be true. In a crisis, if a reporter can't trust his instinct for truth, he can't trust anything.

When Wayne Hawks of the White House staff appeared to say that a press room had been set up in a hospital classroom at the left rear of the building, the group of reporters began struggling across the lawn in that direction. I lingered to ask a motorcycle policeman if he had heard on his radio anything about the pursuit or capture of the assassin. He hadn't, and I followed the other reporters.

As I was passing the open convertible in which Vice President and Mrs. Johnson and Senator Yarborough had been riding in the motorcade, a voice boomed from its radio:

"The President of the United States is dead. I repeat—it has just been announced that the President of the United States is dead."

There was no authority, no word of who had announced it. But—instinct again—I believed it instantly. It sounded true. I knew it was true. I stood still a moment, then began running.

Ordinarily, I couldn't jump a tennis net if I'd just beaten Gonzales. That day, carrying a briefcase and a typewriter, I jumped a chain fence looping around the drive, not even breaking stride. Hugh Sidey of Time, a close friend of the President, was walking slowly ahead of me.

"Hugh," I said, "the President's dead. Just announced on the radio. I don't know who announced it but it sounded official to me."

Sidey stopped, looked at me, looked at the ground. I couldn't talk about it. I couldn't think about it. I couldn't do anything but run on to the press room. Then I told others what I had heard.

Sidey, I learned a few minutes later, stood where he was a minute. Then he saw two Catholic priests. He spoke to them. Yes, they told him, the President was dead. They had administered the last rites. Sidey went on to the press room and spread that word, too.

Throughout the day, every reporter on the scene seemed to me to do his best to help everyone else. Information came only in bits and pieces. Each man who picked up a bit or a piece passed it on. I know no one who held anything out. Nobody thought about an exclusive; it didn't seem important.

After perhaps ten minutes when we milled around in the press room—my instinct was to find the new President, but no one knew where he was—Kilduff appeared red-eyed, barely in control of himself. In that hushed classroom, he made the official, the unbelievable announcement. The President was dead of a gunshot wound in the brain. Lyndon Johnson was safe, in the protective custody of the Secret Service. He would be sworn in as soon as possible.

Kilduff, composed as a man could be in those circumstances, promised more details when he could get them, then left. The search for phones began. Jack Gertz, traveling with us for A.T.&T., was frantically moving them by the dozen into the hospital but few were ready yet.

I wandered down the hall, found a doctor's office, walked in and told him I had to use his phone. He got up without a word and left. I battled the hospital switchboard for five minutes and finally got a line to New York—Hal Faber on the other end, with Harrison Salisbury on an extension.

They knew what had happened, I said. The death had been confirmed. I proposed to write one long story, as quickly as I could, throwing in everything I could learn. On the desk, they could cut it up as they needed—throwing part into other stories, putting other facts into mine. But I would file a straight narrative without worrying about their editing needs.

Reporters always fuss at editors and always will. But Salisbury and Faber are good men to talk to in a crisis. They knew what they were doing and realized my problems. I may fuss at them again sometime, but after that day my heart won't be in it. Quickly, clearly, they told me to go ahead, gave me the moved-up deadlines, told me of plans already made to get other reporters into Dallas, but made it plain they would be hours in arriving.

Salisbury told me to use the phone and take no chances on a wire circuit being jammed or going wrong. Stop reporting and start writing in time to meet the deadline, he said. Pay anyone $50 if necessary to dictate for you.

The whole conversation probably took three minutes. Then I hung up, thinking of all there was to know, all there was I didn't know. I wandered down a corridor and ran into Sidey and Chuck Roberts of Newsweek. They'd seen a hearse pulling up at the emergency entrance and we figured they were about to move the body.

We made our way to the hearse—a Secret Service agent who knew us helped us through suspicious Dallas police lines—and the driver said his instructions were to take the body to the airport. That confirmed our hunch, but gave me, at least, another wrong one. Mr. Johnson, I declared, would fly to Washington with the body and be sworn in there.

We posted ourselves inconspicuously near the emergency entrance. Within minutes, they brought the body out in a bronze coffin.

A number of White House staff people—stunned, silent, stumbling along as if dazed—walked with it. Mrs. Kennedy walked by the coffin, her hand on it, her head down, her hat gone, her dress and stockings spattered. She got into the hearse with the coffin. The staff men crowded into cars and followed.

That was just about the only eye-witness matter that I got with my own eyes that entire afternoon.

Roberts commandeered a seat in a police car and followed, promising to "fill" Sidey and me as necessary. We made the same promise to him and went back to the press room.

There, we received an account from Julian Reed, a staff assistant, of Mrs. John Connally's recollection of the shooting. Most of his recital was helpful and it established the important fact of who was sitting in which seat in the President's car at the time of the shooting.

The doctors who had treated the President came in after Mr. Reed. They gave us copious detail, particularly as to the efforts they had made to resuscitate the President. They were less explicit about the wounds, explaining that the body had been in their hands only a short time and they had little time to examine it closely. They conceded they were unsure as to the time of death and had arbitrarily put it at 1 P.M., C.S.T.

Much of their information, as it developed later, was erroneous. Subsequent reports made it pretty clear that Mr. Kennedy probably was killed instantly. His body, as a physical mechanism, however, continued to flicker an occasional pulse and heartbeat. No doubt this justified the doctors' first account. There also was the question of national security and Mr. Johnson's swearing-in. Perhaps, too, there was a question about the Roman Catholic rites. In any case, until a later doctors' statement about 9 P.M. that night, the account we got at the hospital was official.

The doctors hardly had left before Hawks came in and told us Mr. Johnson would be sworn in immediately at the airport. We dashed for the press buses still parked outside. Many a campaign had taught me something about press buses and I ran a little harder, got there first and went to the wide rear seat. That is the best place on a bus to open up a typewriter and get some work done.

On the short trip to the airport, I got about 500 words on paper—leaving a blank space for the hour of Mr. Johnson's swearing-in, and putting down the mistaken assumption that the scene would be somewhere in the terminal. As we arrived at a back gate along the airstrip, we could see Air Force One, the Presidential jet, screaming down the runway and into the air.

Left behind had been Sid Davis of Westinghouse Broadcasting, one of the few reporters who had been present for the swearing-in. Roberts, who had guessed right in going to the airport when he did, had been there too and was aboard the plane on the way to Washington.

Davis climbed on the back of a shiny new car that was parked near where our bus halted. I hate to think what happened to its trunk deck. He and Roberts—true to his promise—had put together a magnificent "pool" report on the swearing-in. Davis read it off, answered questions and gave a picture that so far as I know was complete, accurate and has not yet been added to.

I said to Kiker of The Trib: "We better go write. There'll be phones in the terminal." He agreed. Bob Manning, an ice-cool member of the White House transportation staff, agreed to get our bags off the press plane, which would return to Washington as soon as possible, and put them in a nearby telephone booth.

Kiker and I ran a half-mile to the terminal, cutting through a baggage-handling room to get there. I went immediately to a phone booth and dictated my 500-word lead, correcting it as I read, embellishing it too. Before I hung up, I got Salisbury and asked him to cut into my story whatever the wires were filing on the assassin. There was no time left to chase down the Dallas police and find out those details on my own.

Dallas's Love Field has a mezzanine running around its main waiting room; it is equipped with

Tom Wicker.

The Times national copy desk.

writing desks for travelers. I took one and went to work. My recollection is that it was then about 5 P.M. New York time.

I would write two pages, run down the stairs, across the waiting room, grab a phone and dictate. Miraculously, I never had to wait for a phone booth or to get a line through. Dictating, I would throw in items I hadn't written, sometimes whole paragraphs. It must have been tough on the dictating room crew.

Once, while in the booth dictating, I looked up and found twitching above me the imposing mustache of Gladwin Hill. He was the first Times man in and had found me right off; I was seldom more glad to see anyone. We conferred quickly and he took off for the police station; it was a tremendous load off my mind to have that angle covered and out of my hands.

I was half through, maybe more, when I heard myself paged. It turned out to be Kiker, who had been separated from me and was working in the El Dorado room, a bottle club in the terminal. My mezzanine was quieter and a better place to work, but he had a TV going for him, so I moved in too.

The TV helped in one important respect. I took down from it an eye-witness account of one Charles Drehm, who had been waving at the President when he was shot. Instinct again: Drehm sounded positive, right, sure of what he said. And his report was the first real indication that the President probably was shot twice.

Shortly after 7 P.M., New York time, I finished. So did Kiker. Simultaneously we thought of our bags out in that remote phone booth. We ran for a taxi and urged an unwilling driver out along the dark airstrip. As we found the place, with some difficulty, an American Airlines man was walking off with the bags. He was going to ship them off to the White House, having seen the tags on them. A minute later and we'd have been stuck in Dallas without even a toothbrush. (Somewhere in the excitement, I did lose a raincoat, replacement value $35; Mr. Garst please note.)

Kiker and I went to The Dallas News. The work wasn't done—I filed a number of inserts later that night, wrote a separate story on the building from which the assassin had fired, tried to get John Herbers, Don Janson, Joe Loftus on useful angles as they drifted in. But when I left the airport, I knew the worst of it was over. The story was filed on time, good or bad, complete or incomplete, and any reporter knows how that feels. They couldn't say I missed the deadline.

It was a long taxi ride to The Dallas News. We were hungry, not having eaten since an early breakfast. It was then that I remembered John F. Kennedy's obituary. Last June, Hal Faber had sent it to me for updating. On Nov. 22, it was still lying on my desk in Washington, not updated, not rewritten, a monument to the incredibility of that afternoon in Dallas.

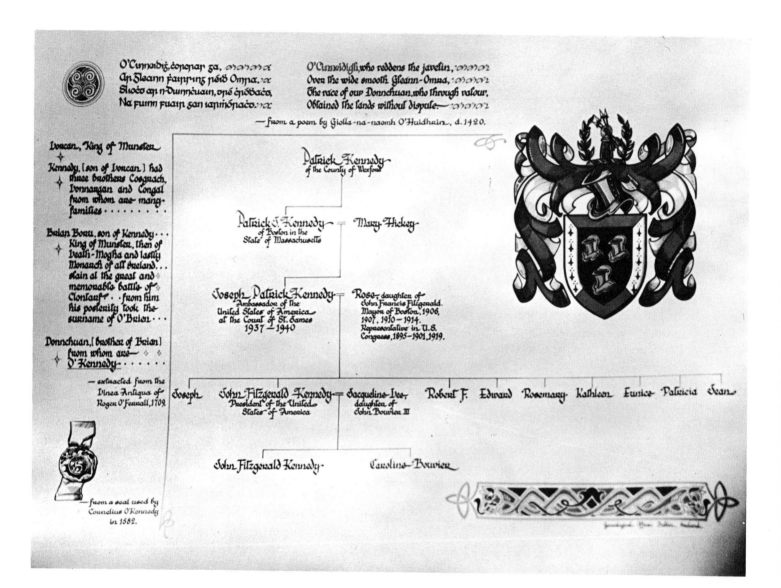

The Kennedy family tree, hand-lettered on parchment and presented
to the White House by a County Wexford relative of the President.

FAMILY

On the morning of Wednesday, May 30, 1917, the front page of The New York Times was devoted to articles about the war which the United States had entered less than two months earlier. The main story was:

PLOTTERS HERE
AGAINST DRAFT
UNDER WATCH

The activities of the various organizations and individuals in New York City opposed to the enforcement of the Selective Draft Act are under investigation by the Federal and local authorities . . .

War news continued heavy on the inside pages. Some weddings and social notes were discreetly displayed on a back page. Ignored was the birth of John Fitzgerald Francis Kennedy in Brookline, Mass., the previous day. It was one of the few important events in his life that The Times failed to record.

John F. Kennedy was the second child and second son of Joseph Patrick Kennedy and Rose Fitzgerald Kennedy, both of whose grandparents were Irish immigrants, and both of whose fathers were political powers in the Irish wards of Boston. If Patrick J. Kennedy and John F. (Honey Fitz) Fitzgerald were toilers in the same political vineyard, they had little else in common until the marriage of their children. So dissimilar were their personalities and modes of operation that only the harsh practicalities of politics kept their mutual dislike and antagonism from erupting more frequently.

Patrick J. Kennedy (son of another Patrick who lacked the initial) was born in 1862, the fourth and last child of parents who emigrated to America during the devastating potato famine of the 1840's. Tall, handsome, reserved, ambitious, Patrick J. early displayed the first signs of the Kennedy determination to progress and prosper. Starting out as a dock worker, he accumulated enough capital to open a saloon. It proved his springboard to financial success. He expanded and diversified, adding more saloons, retail and wholesale liquor businesses, a coal company and, finally, a bank that later would serve to catapult his son Joseph into his first prominence.

Along with his modest accumulation of wealth, the industrious Patrick J. began to hoard the influence that proved invaluable to the early political career of his grandson. He was State Representative five times, State Senator, Fire Commissioner, Election Commissioner, Street Commissioner, a member of the informal —and not infrequently vilified—"Board of Strategy," that select group of hard-bitten Irish leaders who daily decided Boston's political destiny. Patrick J. accomplished much until his death in 1929, but he never tried to scale the wall that separated the political Irish from the proper Bostonians. But his son Joseph did, in vain. His grandson John never tried; he didn't have to.

At the turn of the century, if "Sweet Adeline" was a gushy sentimental song to most of the country, to Boston it was more. There it was irrevocably linked to Honey Fitz, a bouncy, cheerful, loquacious mite of an extrovert (5 feet 2 inches tall). It was his campaign theme and he would sing it at the drop of his inevitable top hat, anywhere, any time. Honey Fitz used the sticky notes of the song to climb the political ladder. (His opponents often hinted that more crass things stuck to the fingers of the dapper Fitz, but in an era when graft and corruption prevailed in the big cities, this charge hardly aroused the electorate.) He adroitly managed to get himself elected a councilman, an alderman, state legislator, U. S. Representative (twice) and Mayor of Boston. Naturally, he served on the Board of Strategy. Not so naturally, "Sweet Adeline" turned sour in 1922 and he lost a race for Governor of Massachusetts.

To the voters, Honey Fitz presented an image that bordered dangerously on the buffoonish. Still, he was shrewd enough and tough enough to survive being orphaned at 16 and to claw his way up in the jungle politics of his day. He was also astute enough to give his beautiful daughter Rose the kind of education needed to attract a college man for a husband. Honey Fitz, who was born only a year later than Patrick J., survived him by many years. He lived until 1950, long enough to assist his grandson in getting elected to the House of Representatives.

The quiet resolution to succeed evident in Patrick J. Kennedy burgeoned in his dynamic son Joseph. As a Harvard student, Joe Kennedy vowed to make his first million before he was 35. He achieved that goal without undue strain and went on to amass one of the largest fortunes in the country, variously estimated at from $300 million to $500 million. Savagely competitive, never satisfied with anything less than perfection or first place in any venture or activity, however slight, he swept to success in the financial and business world.

It all began with a minor coup at the family's Columbia Trust Company. Joseph Kennedy borrowed $45,000, and, after a proxy fight, gained control of the bank. In doing so he became, at 25, the country's youngest bank president—a fact duly noted in the nation's press. Mr. Kennedy went on to make his enormous fortune "in a very roundabout way," as forecast in the 1908 Boston Latin School yearbook. A Times article put it this way:

> World War I found him [Mr. Kennedy] associated with the late Charles M. Schwab, the self-made millionaire head of Bethlehem Steel.
> At war's end Mr. Kennedy plunged into Wall Street. He started out in the amusement industry, piling up millions in various film and theater operations. He ran stock pools. He branched out into liquor and, with the repeal of Prohibition, got a firm grip on the import to the United States of Scotch whiskies, He spread out into real estate.

His stanchest admirers would be hard put to find a milder description of Mr. Kennedy's real estate deals and wild stock market speculations and killings. Many of the market practices he employed in the Terrible Twenties were outlawed with the advent of the Securities and Exchange Commission. Ironically, Mr. Kennedy was named to be the commission's first chairman by President Roosevelt, whose election he strongly supported in 1932. He turned a controversial appointment into a resounding success, making the agency one of the New Deal's most effective regulatory instruments.

Mr. Kennedy also served, with lesser success, as chairman of the Maritime Commission and, after backing Roosevelt for a second term, as Ambassador to the Court of St. James's, until his isolationist views forced his resignation. He never ran for political office. Whether he had such ambitions for himself is still in dispute; there is no dispute concerning the overweening political ambitions he had for his children, particularly for his first son, Joseph Jr.

There were nine Kennedy children (six of whom survive), and the financier, although frequently absent from home, played a dominant role in their upbringing. A Times article reported:

> As his fortune grew, Mr. Kennedy turned the drive and perfectionism of his character toward his clanlike family, inculcating it with a fierce kind of intrafamily competitiveness and combativeness against the outside world.
> The slogan of the Kennedy family was "Second best is a loser." To encourage independence in his family, Mr. Kennedy settled on each of the children a $1,000,000 trust fund. As Mr. Kennedy put it, he wanted each child to be able to look at him—if he wished —and tell him to go to hell, that he would follow his own way.

It is doubtful whether any of the Kennedy children exercised that prerogative. A clan can have only one leader—and Mr. Kennedy was it, autocratic, imperious and sometimes an anomaly.

Of Jack Kennedy's eight brothers and sisters, only one, his older brother Joe, apparently had any influence on him greater than that generated by the usual sibling relationships. Joe was two years older, heavier, stronger, better-looking, more athletic and, many believed, more intelligent. He was the heir apparent to the dynastic rule and first choice for the high elective office Mr. Kennedy set as the ultimate goal of his family.

During the elder Kennedy's many absences on business, Joe assumed the mantle of father. Quick-tempered, domineering, like his father, he ruled the roost with an iron hand—and fist. The other children passively bowed to his dictates, but not Jack. The Times described his stubborn resistance in this fashion:

> All through childhood and early adolescence Joseph Jr. and John fought. The outcome was inevitable—John was smaller, slimmer and less developed than his brother. But still the boys fought. Their younger brother Robert remembered years later how he and his sisters had cowered in an upstairs room while the two boys fought below.

The rivalry between the brothers was more than physical. Joe, an outstanding athlete and a top student, cast a huge shadow. Jack, following in his footsteps at Choate and Harvard, could not begin to shake off that shadow until after Joe died on Aug. 12, 1944, on an experimental bomber mission.

When the father was present to keep the peace, the family dinner table abounded with lively talk about politics and world affairs, talk stimulated and welcomed by Mr. Kennedy. Any of the children could participate, as long as he or she had questions to ask or opinions to voice. During the dinner discussions, Mr. Kennedy often expressed his disdain for businessmen, whom he had so easily bested on Wall Street and in the board room. As a corollary, he emphasized to his children again and again the importance of public service as a way of life.

The Kennedys were a devout family, but Mr. Kennedy left the religious training of his children to his church and his wife. He opposed parochial-school education for his sons, he has been quoted as saying, because he considered it more important for them to broaden their horizons by attending secular schools. Jack Kennedy, therefore, with the exception of a year at Canterbury—a preparatory school at New Milford, Conn.—never attended Catholic institutions.

The boy's education began at Brookline's Dexter School. He switched to the Riverdale Country Day School in New York when the family moved there in 1926 because of Mr. Kennedy's increasing financial activities. Many years later Jack was vaguely recalled by his teachers as likable, polite, moderately studious and, not unexpectedly, hot-tempered.

At some time during this period the elder Kennedy bought an 11-bedroom brick house in nearby Bronxville and moved his still-expanding family into it. Also during this period he received from Jack, whom he restricted, as he did all his children, to a limited allowance, the following letter:

A Plea for a raise
By Jack Kennedy
Dedicated to my father,
Mr. J. P. Kennedy

Chapter I

My recent allowance is 40¢. This I used for areoplanes and other playthings of my childhood but now I am a scout and I put away my childish things. Before I would spend 20¢ of my 40¢ allowance and in five minutes I would have empty pockets and nothing to gain and 20¢ to lose. When I am a scout I have to buy canteens, haversacks, blankets, search-lidgs, poncho things that will last for years and I can always use it while I cant use a cholcolote marshmellow sunday with vanilla ice cream and so I put in my plea for a raise of thirty cents for me to buy scout things and pay my own way more around.

Finis
John Fitzgerald Francis
Kennedy

He obviously thought the rare use of his confirmation name would add weight to his fiscal plea. Whether it succeeded is not known.

Jack's year at Canterbury was cut short by an emergency appendicitis operation and his convalescence, the first of many illnesses to plague him during his life. In the fall, despite a seeming reluctance to attend a school where he faced the challenge of emulating his brother Joe's enviable record, he transferred to Choate, at Wallingford, Conn.

The years spent at Choate must have somewhat disappointed his father. Jack's grades were average (Joe's were superior); he failed to make the varsity football squad (Joe was a star); he was admonished by the authorities for the many innocent boyish pranks in which he was involved with his friends, Lemoyne Billings and Ralph Horton. But he did make the cheering squad and for two years was a competent business manager of the yearbook.

The Kennedy brothers, John (in circle) and Joseph Jr. (in square), and classmates at the Dexter School, Brookline, Mass., in 1927.

By the time Jack graduated from Choate in 1935 at 18, the last of the nine Kennedy children had been born. After Joe and Jack came four girls: Rosemary, born in 1919; Kathleen, 1920; Eunice, 1921; Patricia, 1924. Robert F. followed in 1925; another girl, Jean, in 1928; and Edward (Teddy), in 1932. [Rosemary, born with a handicap, now lives in an institution, which explains the intense Kennedy efforts to help retarded children. Kathleen married the Marquess of Hartington in 1944, lost him the same year in a World War II battle, and herself died in a plane crash four years later. Eunice is the wife of Sargent Shriver, head of the Peace Corps; Patricia of Peter Lawford the actor; Jean of Stephen Smith, who manages the financial affairs of the Kennedy family. Robert, who skillfully assisted his brother in all his political races and directed the 1960 Presidential campaign, was appointed Attorney General of the United States. Edward is the junior Senator from Massachusetts.]

Young Jack's latent resentment at having to compete against Joe's scholastic and athletic record surfaced with his graduation from Choate. Since Mr. Kennedy was a Harvard graduate and Joe was making a name for himself there, it seemed natural that Jack should go to Cambridge. He insisted, however, on applying to Princeton, as were Billings and Horton.

Displeased by the decision, Mr. Kennedy nevertheless acquiesced. Then came another of the almost baffling moves characteristic of Joseph Kennedy. He dispatched Jack to London that summer to study under Harold Laski, the renowned socialist theorist, at the London School of Economics. Earlier Joe Jr. had studied with him, winning high praise for his grasp of the alien left-wing concepts.

LEFT: Jack Kennedy at 16, a reserve lineman on the Choate football team. RIGHT: With classmates Ralph Horton (left) and Lemoyne Billings (center), at Princeton in 1935.

Mr. Kennedy's motive for sending his sons to London was a logical extension of his attitude on secular education. He wanted his sons, he explained patiently to friends, to understand the philosophy of those opposing the free enterprise system, which he ardently advocated. Only by gaining a full comprehension of socialist theories could they effectively defend capitalism, he reasoned. It was an unusual attitude for the average millionaire to take, but Mr. Kennedy was far from the average. Unfortunately, the plan went awry. Before young Jack had a real opportunity to study with Mr. Laski he was stricken with an attack of jaundice and had to be rushed home. In December, after a late start at Princeton, jaundice struck again, and he left for Arizona to recover his health.

Jack Kennedy never returned to Princeton. In the fall of 1936 he enrolled at Harvard. Some reports say he finally yielded to his father's wishes; others say it was his own decision. Whatever the reason, he was, at long last, a Harvard undergraduate—as his father had desired.

The Kennedy family in 1938, at their home in Bronxville; seated (from left), Eunice, Jean, Edward (on his father's lap), Joseph Kennedy, Patricia, Kathleen; standing, Rosemary, Robert, John, Mrs. Kennedy, Joseph Jr.

THE WAR

John Kennedy's career at Harvard was marked by an accident and a late-blooming interest in foreign affairs, stimulated by a trip to Europe and his father's appointment as Ambassador to Britain. Too slight for the varsity fooball team, John managed to win a place on the scrubs; in a practice scrimmage he suffered a spinal injury that years afterward endangered his political career and his life. He did excel in swimming, and with brother Joe he won the intercollegiate sailing title; he was to be grateful for these two skills in the coming war.

Academically, it was a different story—at first. His record during his first two years at Harvard was undistinguished. He got slightly better than a C average as a freshman and about the same as a sophomore. In those days of ferment on the campus, when students were stirred by the New Deal at home and the rise of Fascism abroad, Kennedy was curiously apolitical.

Then a European visit in the summer of 1937 with Lemoyne Billings stirred his interest in foreign affairs; this interest grew during a leave of absence from Harvard in the second semester of his junior year. He spent six months as an office boy in the American embassies of London and Paris, to ascertain whether he wanted a diplomatic career. A Times dispatch from London on Feb. 13, 1939, quoted Mrs. Kennedy as saying that "it was Mr. Kennedy who thought of John's making the experiment."

His proximity to the diplomatic maneuverings before and after the outbreak of war (two days after hostilities began, Mr. Kennedy sent his 22-year-old son to Glasgow to aid the American survivors of the torpedoed British liner *Athenia*) undoubtedly influenced his choice of a senior thesis.

That last year at Harvard verged on brilliance. The Times, on Nov. 23, 1963, looked back:

> For the first time he demonstrated intellectual drive and vigor. He was determined to be graduated with honors and took extra work in political science toward this end. His grades improved to a B average.
>
> But his principal achievement of the year was the writing of a thesis, "Appeasement at Munich." In it, his basic point was:
>
> Most of the critics have been firing at the wrong target. The Munich Pact itself should not be the object of criticism but rather the underlying factors such as the state of British opinion and the condition of Britain's armaments which made "surrender" inevitable.

In June 1940, Kennedy was graduated from Harvard *cum laude* in political science, his thesis having earned *magna cum laude*. That same thesis was published as a book with a new title suggested by Arthur Krock of The Times, "Why England Slept." In the introduction, Henry R. Luce, editor of Time magazine, said, "If John Kennedy is characteristic of the younger generation—and I believe he is—many of us would be happy to have the destinies of this Republic handed over to his generation at once." A book review in The Times on Aug. 3, 1940, said:

> Mr. Kennedy has made a careful analysis from the records that are available. His factual and unemotional approach to the problem is praiseworthy, and his conclusion ought to be weighed carefully in this country. The new publishing firm of Wilfred Funk, Inc., has made an excellent choice for its first book.

War talk was in the air. Like most young men who were graduated from college in 1940, Kennedy found it difficult to settle on a civilian career. He decided to enter Yale Law School, abruptly changed his mind and entered Stanford University's graduate business school, dropped out after six months and left on a long tour of South America. But, on Oct. 30, 1940, while he was still at Stanford, this item appeared:

While Ambassador Joseph P. Kennedy was telling a radio audience last night that he and Mrs. Kennedy had given "nine hostages to fortune," a dispatch revealed that John Kennedy, one of the nine, had become No. 18 on Palo Alto, Calif., draft board rolls. Mr. Kennedy, whose serial number is 2,748, is a graduate student at Stanford University.

It would be many months, however, before he could serve in the armed forces. First came rejections by both the Army and Navy because of his weak back, then a rigorous period of self-conditioning to strengthen it and, ultimately, a commission by the Navy in September, 1941. After Pearl Harbor, Kennedy had to invoke his father's connections to shake loose from the frustrating desk jobs he had been

LEFT: Arriving in England, July 1938: Ambassador Kennedy with sons Jack and (right) Joseph Jr.

OPPOSITE: Ambassador and Mrs. Kennedy at the American Embassy in London, 1938.

OVERLEAF: A dance at the Embassy in London, shortly after Jack's 21st birthday.

given. The Navy, taking into consideration his experience with small craft, transferred him to a torpedo boat training station.

In March 1943, Lieutenant (j.g.) Kennedy received orders to proceed to the Solomon Islands in the Pacific, where American forces were making their first desperate counterattacks against the Japanese. It took him a month to reach the Solomons because of a low transportation priority, weeks more to receive his first command—PT-109.

Kennedy and his crew patrolled often and long during the next few months, but saw little action except against low-flying enemy planes. Then, on Aug. 2, shortly after midnight, PT-109 led two other boats into dangerous Blackett Strait, about 40 miles from their Rendova base. On Aug. 20, three weeks later, the following appeared on Page 1 of The Times:

Lieutenant (j.g.) Kennedy (right) with his PT boat crew "somewhere in the South Pacific," July 1943.

KENNEDY'S SON IS HERO IN PACIFIC
AS DESTROYER SPLITS HIS PT BOAT

A UNITED STATES TORPEDO BOAT BASE, New Georgia, Aug. 8 (Delayed)—Out of the darkness, a Japanese destroyer appeared suddenly. It sliced diagonally in two the PT boat skippered by Lieut. (j.g.) John F. Kennedy, son of the former American Ambassador in London, Joseph P. Kennedy.

Crews of two other PT boats, patrolling close by, saw flaming high octane gasoline spread over the water. They gave up "Skipper" Kennedy and all his crew as lost that morning of Aug. 2.

But Lieutenant Kennedy, 26, and ten of his men were rescued today from a small coral island deep inside Japanese-controlled Solomon Islands territory and within range of enemy shore guns.

Two men died instantly in the ramming. Without Kennedy's leadership, at least a third, possibly all, would have perished. In the darkness enveloping the shark-ridden waters, Kennedy, who had escaped injury except for a severe jolt to his back, rallied his men around the PT hulk still afloat. They clung to it hour after hour until it turned turtle. Kennedy then led his men to an island three miles distant; swimming breaststroke, he himself towed an injured crewman by clamping the man's life jacket straps between his teeth.

On the first night, Kennedy swam and drifted for hours in nearby Ferguson Passage, vainly searching for a friendly craft. The effort left him exhausted and ill. His executive officer, George Ross, made the same fruitless attempt while Kennedy shifted his hungry and thirsty crew to another island; he and Ross wearily swam to a third glob of land, Cross Island, where they discovered a native dugout canoe and some abandoned Japanese food and water. He almost drowned twice, once alone and once with Ross. Finally he was sighted by natives and he scratched on a coconut husk the message, "NAURU ISL NATIVE KNOWS POSIT HE CAN PILOT 11 ALIVE NEED SMALL BOAT KENNEDY."

That did it. On the sixth morning he and Ross were awakened on Cross Island by four natives, one of whom spoke English and said, "I have a letter for you, sir." The letter was from an Australian coast watcher, one of a band of intrepid men who worked behind enemy lines. The machinery for the rescue of PT-109's haggard crew had begun to grind.

The rescue also marked the virtual end of Kennedy's war service. Despite his protests, the Navy shipped him to the States in December. The aggravation of his back injury, a siege of malaria and a drop in weight to 125 pounds were too much to overcome. In the spring of 1944, still ailing, he entered Chelsea Naval Hospital near Boston for a disk operation on his back. But the Navy had not forgotten him. On June 12, 1944, The Times carried this dispatch:

> WASHINGTON, June 11—The Navy and Marine Corps Medal has been awarded to Lieut. John F. Kennedy, son of Joseph P. Kennedy, former United States Ambassador to Great Britain, for "extremely heroic conduct" when his PT boat was cut in two and sunk by a Japanese destroyer, the Navy said tonight.

With his health still far from robust, Kennedy was mustered out of service. Ahead of him, a new civilian life opened.

June 1944, after his Pacific ordeal: receiving the Navy and Marine Corps Medal from Captain Frederic L. Conklin.

Voting, with his grandparents, John F. (Honey Fitz) and Mrs. Fitzgerald, in the Massachusetts primary, June 19, 1946. Kennedy himself was a candidate for the House of Representatives.

CONGRESS

Did John F. Kennedy enter politics of his own volition after his brother's death in the war? Or did his father's aspirations for his family force the decision? Two contradictory quotations appeared in The Times. Here is the father (in a 1957 interview):

> "I got Jack into politics. I was the one. I told him Joe was dead and that it was therefore his responsibility to run for Congress. He didn't want to do it. He felt he didn't have the ability and he still feels that way. But I told him he had to do it."

And here is the son (while a Senator):

> "Just as I went into politics because Joe died, if anything happened to me tomorrow, my brother Bobby would run for my seat in the Senate. And if Bobby died Teddy would take over for him."

Again, in explaining that he had terminated a brief journalism career after the war because he found it too "passive," Kennedy was quoted:

> "We all liked politics, but Joe seemed a natural to run for office. Obviously you can't have a whole mess of Kennedys asking for votes. So when Joe was denied his chance, I wanted to run and was glad I could."

Who or what was the catalyst may never be resolved, but there is no doubt about the first political item involving Kennedy. It appeared in The Times on April 10, 1946, and said:

> BOSTON, April 9—Nomination papers for John F. Kennedy, son of Joseph P. Kennedy, former Ambassador to Great Britain, for the Democratic nomination in the 11th Congressional District, were being circulated today. The papers were taken out by two Charlestown residents, but Mr. Kennedy said the action was without his consent. The district is now represented by Mayor James M. Curley of Boston.

Thirteen days later, Kennedy formally announced his candidacy, and joined a primary fight. He faced nine rivals, with the winner certain of election to the House in the fall because of perennial Republican shortcomings in a working-class district.

Kennedy had to overcome a number of serious obstacles. He was virtually unknown except through his family's reputation; he had never lived in the area (he had, in fact, to establish what amounted to a beachhead residency to qualify); he was a Harvard graduate; he had a wealthy father. In his favor were his grandfathers' political prestige and connections, his war record, his family's social standing, and, paradoxically, his father's wealth.

Kennedy set a pattern for future campaigns in that first uphill battle. Of course, he embellished, refined and polished the technique until it sparkled like a diamond in 1960, but, basically, it varied little. He began running early and strong, finished late and stronger. He surrounded himself with college and wartime friends (John Droney, Paul B. Fay, Lemoyne Billings, Ralph Horton, Torbert H. Macdonald and Timothy J. Reardon Jr., among others). The entourage was spiced by seasoned professionals provided by his father and Honey Fitz, but they soon melted away, disgruntled by Kennedy's increasing reliance on the "amateurs."

Kennedy was slow in hitting his campaign stride; he found the rough working crowd of the district a world he had never known. But until he organized himself, there were always members of the ubiquitous Kennedy clan, shaking hands, ringing doorbells, setting up house parties financed from the bottomless pit of Kennedy funds. His parents and sisters joined the reception line of the first of the famous teas at the Hotel Commander in Cambridge. It was the sole appearance of the former Ambassador in any of his son's campaigns; he early concluded that his own controversial background called for a discreet behind-the-scene role.

Kennedy ran mainly on his war record. He was an authentic war hero, a Boston Fitzgerald-Kennedy, and so, on June 19, 1946, in the third paragraph of a dispatch from Boston, The Times took note of a political upset:

> John F. Kennedy, son of Joseph P. Kennedy, former Ambassador to Great Britain, making his political debut, ran well ahead of nine rivals for the Democratic nomination in the 11th Congressional District.

How much the election cost is impossible to estimate, as it has been with all Kennedy campaigns. With his father's ambition and resources, money was something that could be tossed to the winds.

Kennedy served three terms in the House of Representatives—until his election to the Senate in 1952. He was a member of the District of Columbia Committee and the Education and Labor Committee. The Times offered this evaluation of Kennedy's record in the House:

> His record was not spectacular but his votes usually were on the liberal side.
> He demonstrated flashes of independence, such as in his refusal to kowtow to Representative John W. McCormack, long-time leader of the Massachusetts Democratic delegation.
> He also fought the American Legion for its opposition to housing projects, declaring that the [leadership of the] Legion "hasn't had a constructive thought since 1918."

There were instances during his House tenure when liberals looked askance at Kennedy. As an outspoken member of the Labor Committee, he raised some civil liberties eyebrows—and hackles— with his tactics during a labor racket inquiry. He opted for a balanced budget. He sought to tack on to a school aid bill an amendment that would have paid half the costs of bus service for private and parochial schools. He was the lone Democrat to vote for a losing Republican amendment to soften an excess profits tax bill. He opposed the traditional Democratic high farm price supports, a position he reversed as a Senator when jockeying for the post position began in 1960. All through the six years, however, his voting record was sufficiently "correct" not to alienate the influential labor leaders. One important reason was his opposition to the Taft-Hartley Act.

As early as 1948, after just two years in the House, Kennedy weighed and discarded the possibility of seeking Leverett Saltonstall's Senate seat. Then, on April 7, 1952, The Times carried this item:

> BOSTON, April 6—Representative John F. Kennedy, Democrat of Massachusetts, announced tonight that he would be a candidate for the Senate seat now held by Henry Cabot Lodge Jr., national chairman of General of the Army Dwight D. Eisenhower's Presidential campaign.

Kennedy had chosen a formidable opponent, but he conducted a formidable campaign. The Kennedy money, the Kennedy family, this time reinforced by wives and husbands of brothers and sisters, the Kennedy teas (one report insisted 50,000 women were entertained at 1,000 teas), the Kennedy good looks and charm and the Kennedy organizational skill inundated Lodge. Eisenhower carried Massachusetts by a plurality of 208,000, but Lodge lost to the 35-year-old Kennedy by 70,737. In 1958, when Kennedy had his eye on the White House and needed a smashing victory, he was re-elected by a record margin of 874,608 over a virtually unknown Republican lawyer, Vincent J. Celeste.

A proper evaluation of Kennedy's Senate career must consider the serious illness of 1954-55 that disabled him for seven months as an arbitrary dividing line. Until his hospitalization, despite a few speeches on regional industrial matters that he regarded as important, The Times files reveal he was involved in only one major issue—a foreign policy debate on Indochina. He himself touched off the debate by calling on France to promise independence to the people of Indochina to save the nation from falling into the hands of Communist-led rebels.

After his illness, it was a far different story.

Through the years, Kennedy had been troubled by spasmodic back pains. In 1954, the pain became so crippling he was forced to use crutches to move about. Drastic action had to be taken and, on Oct. 22, 1954, a Times article disclosed the decision:

> Senator John F. Kennedy, Democrat of Massachusetts, underwent a spinal operation yesterday at the Hospital for Special Surgery, 321 East 42nd Street, where his condition was reported as "good."

A month later he flew to his father's winter home in Palm Beach, and the "good" proved premature. A second operation was required and he returned to the hospital for surgery on Feb. 11. For the second time, he received the last rites of his Church; then again he flew south to convalesce. This time the operation was a success, and his ordeal of pain came gradually to an end.

Kennedy turned to writing during his recuperation as a form of therapy and as a means of combating enforced idleness. With some help from Theodore C. Sorensen, a brilliant Nebraska lawyer who was his chief assistant and researcher, he wrote "Profiles in Courage," a study of courageous United States Senators. The book was highly praised on its publication on Jan. 2, 1956; Charles Poore of The Times called it "splendidly readable." It became an immediate best-seller, and on May 6 of the following year it received the Pulitzer Prize for biography. But "Profiles in Courage" was more than a literary achievement. The Times later said:

> Many vehicles have launched public men onto the stage of national politics. But seldom has the instrument been a best-selling collection of historical biographies. But such was the case with John Kennedy.
> "Profiles in Courage" lifted him into a special category—a category of statesmanship and scholarship beyond the reach of most men in politics. It served a more subtle purpose as well. For in the process of writing about the great and brave men of American politics Mr. Kennedy acquired a stature and fiber of political philosophy that he had not had before.

Kennedy returned to the Senate on May 23, 1955. During his absence, the furor over Senator Joseph R. McCarthy's crusade against Communism had reached an acrimonious climax. On Dec. 2, 1954, the Senate voted, 67 to 22, to censure the Wisconsin Republican, thereby effectively checking his power. The issue of Kennedy's position on McCarthy would not die, however. The Times summarized it this way:

> Senator Kennedy had, in effect, evaded the McCarthy issue in his campaign of 1952. But now as the Wisconsin Senator's activities impinged more and more on the national scene and sentiment rose in the Senate for curbing Mr. McCarthy's activities, the question of Mr. Kennedy's position came to the fore.
> As the issue was drawn tighter Senator Kennedy continued to steer a cautious course in correspondence with his constituents and in public speeches.
> But the direct issue of Senate censure of Mr. McCarthy was building up rapidly. Mr. Kennedy decided to vote for censure—but on the narrow technical ground that Mr. McCarthy had jeopardized the dignity and honor of the Senate.

When the censure vote was taken, Kennedy was in the hospital, unable to vote. In 1958 Mrs. Franklin D. Roosevelt charged, however, that he had refused to take a stand on the issue; Washington wits said he had shown lots of profile, but little courage; in 1959 the satirists of the Washington Press Club taunted him at a Gridiron dinner:

> "Where were you, John,
> When the Senate censored Joe?"

But after 1955, Kennedy's prominence and stature increased rapidly. His speeches and activities received detailed coverage in the press. One of his major efforts, in domestic affairs, involved sponsor-

ship of a labor reform bill with Senator Irving M. Ives, a New York Republican. The measure brought Kennedy into direct confrontation with the Eisenhower Administration, which regarded it as too mild. The Senate approved the bill, 88 to 1, with Senator George W. Malone, Republican of Nevada, as the dissenter. On June 19, 1958, an editorial in The Times hailed it as a "triumph of moderation and a powerful blend of principle and political savvy." The bill died in the House.

Kennedy pressed the fight for labor reform in the next session of Congress. His bill again easily passed the Senate, 90 to 1, with Senator Barry M. Goldwater, the Arizona Republican, casting the negative vote. Again the pattern repeated itself; the measure encountered rough going in the House, which approved the more restrictive Landrum-Griffin version. The two bills were reconciled after intricate parliamentary maneuverings, but Kennedy requested that his name be kept off the measure because

A hearing of the McClellan Committee on Improper Activity in Labor and Management, 1957; Senator Kennedy in right foreground, with Robert Kennedy, the Committee's chief counsel, hidden from camera, on his right. Dave Beck, Teamsters president, is testifying (left).

of the changes. The final compromise antagonized labor, but Kennedy's efforts in striving for moderation were commended. On Sept. 4, 1959, a Times editorial said:

> The joint conference committee of the Senate and House has done a conspicuous service to the public—and to honest, democratic unionism—in sweating out a labor reform bill. The job of "reconciling" the provisions of the Kennedy Senate bill and the Landrum-Griffin House measure was one of the most formidable in Congressional history. It called for twelve days of the utmost skill in the art of compromise—which the committee chairman, Senator Kennedy, outstandingly provided.

Other domestic issues were not neglected by Kennedy. He spoke out on defense, oil and wool import curbs, civil rights, mail subsidies, foreign aid, immigration, aid to cities, education. He led a losing struggle to repeal the student loyalty oath. He was a member of a committee to study election gifts. He headed a panel that selected five outstanding Senators of the past for the Senate's own Hall of Fame—Henry Clay, Daniel Webster, John C. Calhoun, Robert M. La Follette and Robert A. Taft.

Foreign affairs occupied more and more of Kennedy's attention after his unsuccessful attempt for the Democratic Vice-Presidential nomination in 1956. (See page 54.) Among the topics of his speeches: Algeria, the Mideast, Tunisia, India, the defense of Quemoy (attacking Eisenhower policy), Africa, colonial policy, nuclear testing, disarmament and the lack of leadership in Washington.

The speech on Algeria in the Senate on July 2, 1957, brought Kennedy instantaneous world-wide recognition—a great deal of it unfavorable. Allan Nevins, in "The Strategy of Peace," a collection of Kennedy's major addresses, observed that "no speech on foreign affairs by Mr. Kennedy attracted more attention at home and abroad."

Algerian nationalists had been engaged, since 1954, in a war for independence from France. In his address, Kennedy echoed his 1954 Indochina theme when he said:

"I am submitting today a resolution which I believe outlines the best hopes for peace and settlement in Algeria. It urges, in brief, that the President and Secretary of State be strongly encouraged to place the influence of the United States behind efforts, either through the North Atlantic Treaty Organization or the good offices of the Prime Minister of Tunisia and the Sultan of Morocco, to achieve a solution which will recognize the independent personality of Algeria and establish the basis for a settlement interdependent with France and the neighboring nations."

The speech aroused angry French resentment and wide criticism at home. Among the critics was The Times, which in an editorial on July 3 said:

> Senator Kennedy has probably added fuel to a raging fire with his speech and resolution yesterday suggesting that the United States use its good offices to solve the Algerian problem. It took courage—perhaps rashness—to present a case so critical of French policies. As a Democrat and a Senator he is certainly entitled to criticize our own Administration's policies on this issue, but considering the sensitivity, jealousy and distrust the French have shown of our motives, an intervention of this type is at the very least risky.

Predictably, France did not heed Kennedy's advice, but the "rashness" of his proposal served its purpose—to project the image of a statesman to the voters at home, an image that grew sharper in focus as the years went by, and contributed mightily toward bringing Kennedy to 1960 as one of the leading contenders for the Democratic Presidential nomination.

The Senator, seen for the first time in the rocking chair he made famous, in his office on Capitol Hill.

MARRIAGE

Once upon a time there was a beautiful young society girl who met a handsome young Congressman....

There is no better way to begin the fairy tale courtship of Jacqueline Lee Bouvier and John F. Kennedy. She was a striking young woman, with soft, abundant hair, modulated voice and an independent and inquisitive mind. She had been brought up in the social whirl of New York and Washington. She had been educated at the best of girls' schools, at Vassar, at the Sorbonne, and was soon to graduate from George Washington University. She was a good horsewoman; she swam well. She was, as Arthur Krock of The Times later characterized her, "a Beaux Arts type of girl, merry, arch, satirical, terribly democratic and, yes, brilliant."

Kennedy, by this time regarded as one of the nation's most eligible bachelors, was smitten with the dark slender girl at their first encounter at a dinner party in 1951. He pursued her, but his Senate campaign in Massachusetts cramped his ardor as swain. "He'd call me from some oyster bar up there, with a great clinking of coins, and ask me out to the movies the following Wednesday in Washington," Jackie recalled. Once the Senate victory was his, he renewed in earnest his courtship of Jackie, who despite her shyness had become an inquiring photographer for The Washington Times-Herald. On June 25, 1953, there appeared on the society page of The Times:

SENATOR KENNEDY
TO MARRY IN FALL

NEWPORT, R.I., June 24—Mr. and Mrs. Hugh D. Auchincloss of Hammersmith Farm and McLean, Va., have announced the engagement of Mrs. Auchincloss' daughter, Miss Jacqueline Lee Bouvier, to Senator John Fitzgerald Kennedy of Massachusetts, son of the former Ambassador to Great Britain and Mrs. Joseph P. Kennedy of Hyannis Port, Mass. The wedding will take place in September.

The first chapter of the romance ended happily on Sept. 12, 1953, at St. Mary's Roman Catholic Church in Newport. The 24-year-old society girl and the 36-year-old Senator were married there, with the Most Reverend Richard J. Cushing, then Archbishop of Boston and later a Cardinal, performing the ceremony. More than 800 prominent society and political figures crowded the church; more than 1,200 attended the reception at Hammersmith Farm, the 300-acre estate of the bride's mother and stepfather.

The wedding, one of society's most glamorous in years, was front-page news all over the country. The Times of Sept. 13 displayed a picture of the smiling couple cutting the wedding cake:

NEWPORT, R.I., Sept. 12—A crowd of 3,000 persons broke through police lines and nearly crushed the bride, Miss Jacqueline Lee Bouvier, when she arrived for her marriage here this morning to United States Senator John Fitzgerald Kennedy of Massachusetts. The throng had milled around St. Mary's Roman Catholic Church for more than an hour before the guests began to arrive. The ceremony far surpassed the Astor-French wedding of 1934 in public interest. The crowd pressed forward again as the couple left the church and posed briefly for photographers, Senator Kennedy with a grin on his face and the bride appearing a little startled.

Unlike the usual fairy tale, the second chapter of this one was marred by tragedy. Before and after the births of their children, Caroline, on Nov. 27, 1957, and John F. Jr., on Nov. 25, 1960, the couple lost two other infants. The first was a girl, dead at birth on Aug. 23, 1956; the second a son, Patrick Bouvier Kennedy, born on Aug. 7, 1963, dead two days later.

With Jacqueline Bouvier at Hyannis Port the summer before their marriage.

Fourth of July weekend, 1953, at Hyannis Port. ABOVE AND ON FOLLOWING PAGES: Touch football on the lawn with the young Kennedys and Jacqueline Bouvier; softball; sailing on Nantucket Sound; the Senator and his fiancée on the beach, and on the porch of the Joseph P. Kennedy house.

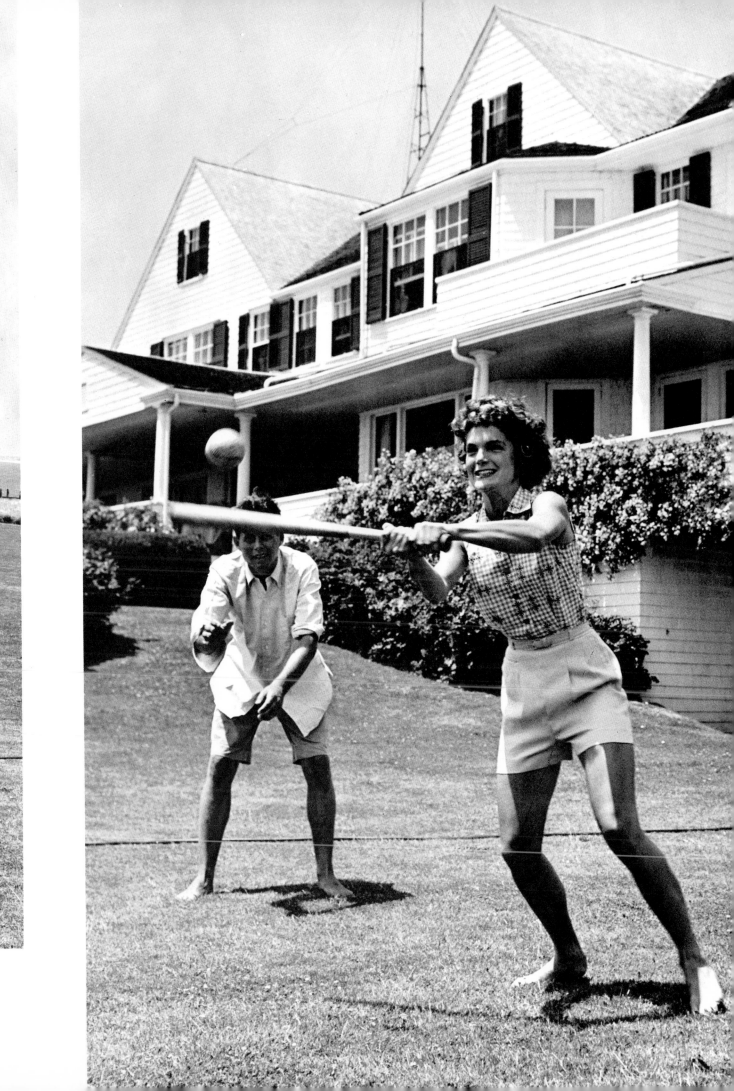

LEFT: The wedding party at Hammer-smith Farm, Newport, Sept. 12, 1953.
BELOW: The bride tosses her bouquet.

The Senator and Mrs. Kennedy at home in their house on N Street in Georgetown.

The Kennedys' first child, Caroline Bouvier, born
Nov. 27, 1957, at her christening. The then
Archbishop Richard Cushing of Boston (right)
performed the ceremony of baptism.

OPPOSITE: Posing with Caroline in the summer
of 1958. OVERLEAF: Jacqueline Kennedy at Hyannis Port; the Senator playing with his daughter in their Georgetown back yard.

Jacqueline Kennedy helps out in her husband's Senate office;
Kennedy in reading glasses, rarely worn for the camera.

DECISION TO RUN

Historians are already disputing the precise moment when John F. Kennedy decided that the Presidency of the United States was within his reach. Some historians insist the decision was implicit the day his father transferred his political ambitions from his fallen brother Joseph to him. Others believe it came later. Arthur Schlesinger Jr. has indicated that Kennedy set his sights on the White House during the "private crisis of identity" following his illness in 1954 and 1955.

These are conjectures, but with elements of fact, for many events obviously contributed to Kennedy's historic decision. One such event was his fight for the Democratic Vice-Presidential nomination in 1956. Kennedy reached the convention in mid-August of 1956 as a national figure, riding a minor boom for second place on the ticket. He and his aides felt that Adlai Stevenson, who would be renominated for the Presidency, would choose his running mate, but they were trying to make Kennedy a leading contender.

As early as the preceding June, Governors Abraham A. Ribicoff of Connecticut and Dennis J. Roberts of Rhode Island had urged his nomination at the annual Governors Conference. Ribicoff remained a leading New England force in the Kennedy drive through 1960, as did another Connecticut leader, John M. Bailey, Democratic State Chairman. It was Bailey who, in the 1956 Vice-Presidential effort, mailed to party leaders all over the nation the memorandum prepared for Kennedy on the Catholic vote. One section of that memorandum, referring to three political books by polling experts, said:

> The voter surveys of Lazarsfeld ("The People's Choice"), Lubell ("The Future of American Politics"), Bean ("How to Predict Elections") and others—as well as the statistics contained within on the 1928 election and the 1952 vote for Catholic candidates—all indicate that there is, or can be, such a thing as a "Catholic vote," whereby a high proportion of Catholics of all ages, residences, occupations and economic status vote for a well-known Catholic candidate or a ticket with a special Catholic appeal.

Stevenson had no opposition for the Presidential nomination in 1956. But, surprisingly, after his nomination he threw the choice of a Vice-Presidential candidate onto the floor of the convention. The heavy favorite was Senator Estes Kefauver of Tennessee, but the Kennedy workers spread quickly through the city, trying to find delegates and to convince them that Kennedy was their man. Kennedy, who had put Stevenson in nomination, stayed within range on an exciting but inconclusive first ballot. He surged ahead on the second ballot with 618 votes to Kefauver's 551½—within a few votes of victory. Then, unexpectedly, he faltered; delegates scrambled to shift to Kefauver, the tide turned. Disappointed, but with a grin, Kennedy moved to make the nomination unanimous. This is how The Times reported the result on Aug. 18:

KEFAUVER NOMINATED FOR VICE PRESIDENT; BEATS KENNEDY, 755½-589, ON SECOND BALLOT

CHICAGO, Aug. 17—Senator Estes Kefauver seized the Democratic Vice-Presidential nomination by an eyelash today.

The Tennessean edged out Senator John F. Kennedy of Massachusetts on the second ballot in an open floor fight to become the running mate of Adlai E. Stevenson of Illinois. Mr. Stevenson was renominated for the Presidency last night.

It was Kennedy's first political defeat, and yet it was not a defeat. Eisenhower-Nixon overwhelmed Stevenson-Kefauver in November. Because of Eisenhower's great popularity, Kennedy's presence on

Placing the name of Adlai E. Stevenson in nomination before
the Democratic National Convention, Chicago, Aug. 16, 1956.

the ticket would not have changed the result materially. As the first Catholic on a national ticket since Al Smith in 1928, Kennedy might have received the major blame for the loss, and hopes for a Catholic Presidential nominee might have been set back for years.

Kennedy avoided these pitfalls by his convention "defeat." And within days after the Democrats' November debacle, signs of his new stature appeared. An article in The Times on Nov. 11 viewed Kennedy as one of the party's rising young leaders and a possible 1960 Presidential candidate. On Nov. 14, The Times published a small but significant item:

> LOS ANGELES, Nov. 13—An early supporter of Franklin D. Roosevelt for President said today he was forming an association to acquaint California, Oregon and Washington Democratic voters "with the talents of Massachusetts United States Senator John F. Kennedy." Patrick J. Cooney, a lawyer, said that Mr. Kennedy "is sure to be heard from."

Indeed, Kennedy was to be heard from, both in Congress and outside it. He was given a seat on the all-important Senate Foreign Relations Committee despite the claims of Kefauver, who had four years' seniority over him. He made speeches all over the country; he began to bolster his national legislative record. As The Times analyzed it later:

> He criticized the level of ambassadorial appointments of the Eisenhower Administration. He backed aid for Poland and for India. He called for the independence of Algeria. He published incisive critiques of United States foreign policy in the quarterly, Foreign Affairs. He warned of a missile gap.
> In domestic policy he steered a difficult course. He compromised on features of civil rights legislation, drawing criticism from the left. He backed better budgeting and fiscal housekeeping. He fought for moderate labor reform.

On June 7, 1957, Kennedy, in an address before the Arkansas Bar Association in Little Rock, disclaimed any ambitions for 1960. This was the usual gambit that deceived no one versed in politics. Arthur Krock, in The Times of July 7, included Kennedy among three leading Democratic aspirants—Senators Lyndon B. Johnson of Texas and Hubert H. Humphrey of Minnesota being the other two.

Kennedy picked up momentum in 1958. Ribicoff, at the Governors Conference in Miami on May 18, announced again for him—this time for the Presidency. On Sept. 23, members of the Southern Governors Conference indicated that he appeared to be the section's favorite Democratic hopeful. With the November elections approaching, Kennedy, not too concerned about his own race for re-election, took time out to help other Democratic candidates. James Reston accompanied him to Parkersburg, W. Va., on one such trip. From there on Oct. 10, Reston reported:

> Senator John F. Kennedy of Massachusetts is quietly but diligently building support these days for the 1960 Democratic Presidential nomination.
> Though the voters are not even showing much interest as yet in the 1958 election, the handsome young New Englander was here today helping the West Virginia Democratic candidates in the hope that they will in turn help him two years from now.
> This is not a new adventure for Senator Kennedy. Ever since his strong bid for the Democratic Vice-Presidential nomination in 1956, he has been methodically going from one state to another, meeting the party leaders, speaking at party rallies and getting himself known.

Shortly after Kennedy's landslide re-election to the Senate, a poll of state Democratic chairmen put him in the lead for the 1960 nomination. Presidential politics now seemed to preoccupy him to an even greater extent. At this stage, he had a small but tightly organized political staff functioning for him. Besides his brother Bobby and other members of his family, the key men were: Ted Sorensen,

The Senator stands on a chair to address a labor meeting in Los Angeles.

who had become virtually a Kennedy alter ego; Torb Macdonald, by now United States Representative from Massachusetts; Lawrence F. O'Brien, a Boston political veteran; Ted Reardon; Kenneth P. O'Donnell, a Harvard football star and Boston political pro; and Francis X. Morrissey, another Boston pro.

Kennedy quickened his campaign in 1959, but could not avoid the Catholic question. There were important fences he had to mend: on McCarthyism (was he soft on that issue?), on farm policy (was he against high price supports?), on civil rights (was he too moderate? why was he a favorite in the South?), but the Catholic issue was paramount—and complex. James Reston, on the first day of 1959, explained it this way:

> The political implications of nominating a Roman Catholic for the Presidency are now coming increasingly to the fore in the capital. With Senator John F. Kennedy of Massachusetts quietly increasing his influence with Democratic politicians, what was primarily a matter of private speculation at the start of the year is now being openly debated from the public platform.
> The American Catholic Historical Association, for example, not only discussed "the Catholic question in Presidential campaigns" this week, but touched obliquely on one issue that has seldom been mentioned outside of private discussions of the 1960 campaign.
> This is not the usual issue of the dangers of alienating some non-Catholic voters by nominating a Catholic, but the opposite: namely, the dangers of alienating Catholic voters by passing over a popular Catholic candidate.

Kennedy's acknowledged leadership in the Democratic derby (Arthur Krock in The Times of Feb. 15 reported that his rivals were already thinking in terms of a "stop Kennedy" coalition) had turned the Catholic question into a two-edged sword. An article in the March 3 issue of Look magazine broadened the scope of the controversy. Kennedy was quoted as declaring that he strongly favored complete separation of church and state, was opposed to the use of Federal funds for the support of parochial or private schools, and to sending an Ambassador to the Vatican. Kennedy said:

"Without reference to the Presidency, I believe as a Senator that the separation of church and state is fundamental to our American concept and heritage and should remain so. There can be no question of Federal funds being asked for support of parochial or private schools. It's unconstitutional under the First Amendment as interpreted by the Supreme Court."

Catholic publications, including parish weeklies and national magazines, reacted strongly to the Kennedy stand. He was accused of overstating his case and of appeasing "professional critics" of his church to protect his political career. America, a Jesuit publication, suggested in an editorial that by answering Look's questions Kennedy had submitted to a religious test of his qualifications for office, a test specifically proscribed by the First Amendment.

The storm did not abate until March 10, when the following article appeared in The Times:

CUSHING DEFENDS KENNEDY'S VIEWS

BOSTON, March 9—Richard Cardinal Cushing of Boston came to the defense today of one of the most prominent members of the archdiocese, Senator John F. Kennedy of Massachusetts.

The Roman Catholic prelate said he could say without hesitation that Mr. Kennedy would fulfill his oath of public office in obedience to the highest standards of conscience.

Cardinal Cushing said it was "ridiculous" to ask questions about church and state relationships of a man who has been in public life as long as Mr. Kennedy. Moreover, it is "a great pity" that a man should have to answer questions about his religion, the cardinal asserted.

On a swing through the Northwest in 1959, Kennedy talks with a local backer on a tugboat in Oregon. OVERLEAF: One of the President's favorite pictures shows the lonely beginnings of his campaign for the nomination: a sparse turnout greets the Kennedys and Pierre Salinger (center) when they touch down at Portland, Ore., in the fall of 1959.

The Kennedys on a West Coast political tour in late 1959. ABOVE: Repeating the pledge
of allegiance in a high school auditorium. BELOW: Breakfast in a diner after early
Mass. OPPOSITE: The Senator speaking to a women's group in Washington.

A month later, however, Kennedy at a news conference in Milwaukee conceded that religion was a proper matter for discussion in political campaigns. "All questions that interest or disturb people should be answered," he said.

Questions were asked again, but not until late in November. They were stirred by a statement by the Roman Catholic Bishops of the United States opposing the use of public funds to promote artificial birth control at home and abroad. Kennedy's views on this were sought by James Reston in a telephone interview on Nov. 27. The Senator responded that he had felt long before the Bishops' statement that it would be a "mistake" for the United States to advocate birth control in other countries, that it was a decision for the nations concerned to make for themselves, but that, if he were elected President, he would resolve any such issue in accordance with his oath to do whatever was best for the United States.

ABOVE: Jackie charms an Oregon longshoreman.
RIGHT: Using a gesture now familiar, Kennedy talks
with students at Mills College, Oakland, Calif.

It remained for President Eisenhower to quiet this last controversy of 1959. On Dec. 2, he ruled out the use of foreign aid funds for the teaching of birth control in underdeveloped countries.

During all this furor, Kennedy's campaign continued. As late as the previous Feb. 22 he insisted he was "not a candidate at this time" and that the appropriate time to disclose any plans regarding the Presidential nomination would be in 1960. He adhered rigidly to his self-imposed timetable, never admitting he was running, never standing in one place.

In the spring and fall he made three-day swings through Wisconsin, appealing for the farm vote and denying that he was soft on McCarthyism. He toured Ohio for four days, Illinois for three. He addressed the United Automobile Workers convention in a bid for labor's support. He invaded Oregon in October 1959, for a political tour after admirers opened a campaign headquarters in Portland. By this time most political observers were convinced he was a candidate and that only the official announcement remained to be made.

On Oct. 28, according to Theodore H. White in "The Making of the President," a crucial meeting took place in the home of Robert Kennedy in Hyannis Port. Present were 16 persons and, Mr. White noted, "nine at least should be starred for the record, for it was these nine who together created and directed the machinery that was to give them, a year later, in this room, their victory." The nine were Kennedy and his brother Bobby, O'Donnell, O'Brien, Sorensen, Bailey, his brother-in-law Stephen Smith, Pierre Salinger, the San Francisco newspaperman who had become Kennedy's press secretary, and Louis Harris, the public-opinion analyst. The conference mapped out campaign strategy, selected primaries to enter and picked the date to announce Kennedy's candidacy.

On Dec. 17, the United Press International carried the text of a letter from Kennedy to party leaders disclosing that he would announce his candidacy for the Presidency on Jan. 2, 1960. The news created a sensation—but mainly in the Kennedy headquarters. How the letter had leaked out was lost in the confusion, but it was hurriedly explained that the Senator had not yet made up his mind and that the letter was one of many drafts being prepared to "cover all eventualities."

The explanation put a different perspective on the news, and most newspapers treated it humorously. The Times headline, which ran on Page 1, said:

KENNEDY'S OFFICE SNATCHES BACK
A HAT THAT BLEW INTO THE RING

On Jan. 2, 1960, three days after Humphrey entered the race as the first Democratic hopeful, Kennedy officially threw his hat into the ring, thus confirming what had been common gossip since 1956. The next day The Times made his announcement the lead story of the paper:

KENNEDY IN RACE;
BARS SECOND SPOT
IN ANY SITUATION

WASHINGTON, Jan. 2—Senator John F. Kennedy made it official today.

He told a news conference that he was a candidate for the Democratic Presidential nomination and was convinced that he could win both the nomination and the election.

At the same time Democratic leaders who believe that his following can be consolidated behind the Democratic ticket if Mr. Kennedy is given the Vice-Presidential nomination were given a sober warning.

If he is rejected for top place on the ticket, the Senator said, he will refuse to accept the Vice-Presidential nomination "under any condition."

As expected, he announced that he would enter the New Hampshire primary of March 8. He will announce his intentions about other primaries—in Wisconsin, Oregon, Nebraska, Indiana, Maryland, Ohio, Florida and California—within the next six weeks, he said.

Jan. 2, 1960: Senator Kennedy declares his candidacy for Democratic nomination for President of the United States.

THE PRIMARIES

It took John Kennedy just one day as a candidate to make his preconvention strategy clear; he planned to fight his way to the nomination through the primary elections.

On the Saturday morning after New Year's Day, timing his move for maximum publicity in the well-read Sunday papers, Kennedy formally announced he was running for the Presidency. On Sunday evening, he invited all comers to pit their vote-getting strength against his, state by state. The Times story said:

> WASHINGTON, Jan. 3—Senator John F. Kennedy of Massachusetts challenged his potential rivals for the Democratic Presidential nomination today to fight it out in the primaries.
>
> He said anyone who stayed out of the primaries did not deserve to be taken seriously by the Democratic convention next July. He specifically mentioned Senators Stuart Symington of Missouri and Lyndon B. Johnson of Texas as subject to his advice.
>
> So far only Senators Kennedy and Hubert H. Humphrey of Minnesota are announced Democratic candidates. Senator Kennedy said today that he thought they would eventually oppose each other in "two or three primaries."
>
> He said the inference to be drawn about someone who was reluctant to enter the race against the two of them was: "If he can't beat us, he can't beat Mr. Nixon in November."

There had never been any real question in Kennedy's mind that he would have to run in a series of primaries. Only by winning such state elections could he demonstrate to the leaders of the Democratic party that his youth, his Roman Catholic religion and his lack of national stature were not the serious handicaps some thought them to be.

Confident he could defeat all his rivals in open combat, Kennedy now tried to maneuver them into playing his game. Senator Humphrey, whose only chance for the nomination also lay along the arduous primary route, had already agreed. Announcing his candidacy four days before Kennedy, the Minnesotan had chosen four primaries: Wisconsin, the District of Columbia, Oregon and South Dakota—and he was to add a critical fifth, West Virginia.

Two days after Kennedy made his primary challenge, Governor Michael DiSalle gave him a big boost. He said he would run as a favorite son in the Ohio primary, pledging all the state's 64 delegates to Kennedy. Two days later, as promised, Kennedy formally entered the earliest Presidential primary, the March 8 contest in New Hampshire. No one, it appeared, .was eager to challenge the New Englander there.

Later in January, he entered the first contested primary. The Times said:

KENNEDY ANNOUNCES
ENTRY IN WISCONSIN

> MILWAUKEE, Jan. 21—Senator John F. Kennedy announced today his intention to enter the Wisconsin Presidential primary against Senator Hubert H. Humphrey. He also said he would enter the Nebraska primary.
>
> The decision on Wisconsin opened the way for the first direct test of strength by the two leading avowed contenders for the Democratic nomination. Senator Humphrey of Minnesota, who had previously announced that he would enter the Wisconsin contest, opened his campaign in Milwaukee last Monday.
>
> Senator Kennedy of Massachusetts said today that the outcome in Wisconsin would "indicate which way the convention will go."

Wisconsin was particularly challenging because it was—and is—the only "open" primary in the nation, an election in which members of one party can vote in the other party's primary if they want to. Since there was no Republican contest in 1960, large numbers of Wisconsin Republicans would probably "cross over" and choose between the two Democrats.

Humphrey, as a major political leader in the area, could naturally expect sympathetic support from his Middle Western neighbors. Kennedy, on the other hand, could test his vote-getting appeal among the Roman Catholics who make up nearly one-third of Wisconsin's population.

Less than two weeks later, Kennedy entered the Maryland primary, where opposition seemed unlikely. As he had in Nebraska, he tried to lure Stuart Symington, an undeclared candidate and former Baltimore resident, into open competition, but Symington did not respond.

Then came the most important announcement: Kennedy and Humphrey would cross swords again in May in West Virginia:

> WASHINGTON, Feb. 4—Senators John F. Kennedy of Massachusetts and Hubert H. Humphrey of Minnesota settled today on West Virginia for a new clash in their campaign for the Democratic Presidential nomination.
>
> Mr. Kennedy said he would enter the West Virginia Presidential primary May 10 and Indiana's May 3. He challenged Mr. Humphrey and all other Democratic aspirants to meet him in Indiana and elsewhere.
>
> Mr. Humphrey, through an aide, put up the $1,000 fee for filing in West Virginia. The primary outcome will not be binding on the state's delegates, who will have 25 votes in the nomination convention at Los Angeles in July.

Through February and on into early March, the focus of political attention was on Wisconsin. There Humphrey concentrated on issues—agriculture, social security, medical care and taxes—while Kennedy preferred to devote himself to personality campaigning, moving through the state with his wife and other members of his family.

Briefly in the first week of March, Kennedy made a three-day swing through New Hampshire on the eve of the primary there, although he had no real opposition in the popularity contest. His backers were interested in rolling up a Democratic vote that would compare favorably with Vice President Nixon's Republican New Hampshire total. The Times article on the results said:

KENNEDY MAKING A STRONG SHOWING IN NEW HAMPSHIRE

> CONCORD, N. H., March 9—New Hampshire voters gave a massive endorsement to Senator John F. Kennedy as the Democratic nominee in the nation's first Presidential primary yesterday.
>
> Returns early today showed that some Republicans, unable to cast official Democratic ballots, were writing in his name on the G.O.P. lists.
>
> Vice President Nixon appeared certain to exceed the total vote drawn by President Eisenhower in the 1956 primary. But the gap between Mr. Nixon and the Massachusetts Democrat was significantly narrower than the traditional Republican margin of 2 to 1 in this state. It was closer to 5 to 4.

When the New Hampshire tally was completed, Nixon had about 65,000 to 43,000 for Kennedy, but the Senator had received more than twice as many votes as any Democrat in the state's primary history. Republicans emphasized that Nixon had also broken a New Hampshire record by outdrawing President Eisenhower's 1956 vote of 56,500.

Back in Wisconsin, the candidate's brothers, Bobby and Ted, were speaking for him when Senate business or politicking in other states kept the Senator away. Humphrey was showing success with Negro voters and sharpening his claim that Kennedy's Congressional voting record had been indistinguishable from Nixon's.

Then a third Democratic Presidential candidate entered the lists.

SYMINGTON MAKES
PRESIDENTIAL BID

WASHINGTON, March 24—Senator Stuart Symington announced his candidacy for President today on a platform of national unity, "lasting peace and unparalleled progress."

The Missouri Democrat conceded that Senator John F. Kennedy of Massachusetts was now the front-runner for the Democratic Presidential nomination. But Mr. Symington said he was "in this campaign to win."

"And my number one goal is to unite this great country," he asserted.

His audience packed the large Senate caucus room where many investigations have been televised with Mr. Symington in the role of interrogator.

Symington said he would not compete in the primaries because their results did not reflect the voters' preferences as accurately as the convention itself. The Missouri Senator denied he had moved up his announcement time because Kennedy appeared to be pulling away in the Democratic contest.

The day after this announcement, a "Stop Kennedy" movement was organized by his rivals at a meeting of Democratic leaders from Middle Western states, a scant ten days before the Wisconsin primary. But a survey showed he had considerable convention support among those states, even then.

As the Wisconsin primary race went into the home stretch, the religious issue finally surfaced. Protestant ministers contended that a Catholic President could not properly respect the dividing line between his public duties and his religious convictions. The Senator's mother, Mrs. Rose Kennedy, argued the opposite thesis at closed meetings. Bare-headed and coatless, Kennedy trudged through the streets, extending his hand and saying, "My name is John Kennedy; I'm running for President." He publicly discouraged Wisconsin Catholics from supporting him solely because of their common faith. Humphrey, a Protestant, discounted the possibility of voting along religious lines and hammered away at his chief theme: that he had proved himself a more liberal Democrat than his opponent. On April 5 the results were:

KENNEDY BEATS HUMPHREY
IN HEAVY WISCONSIN VOTE;
NIXON DISPLAYS STRENGTH

MILWAUKEE, April 6—Senator John F. Kennedy of Massachusetts defeated Senator Hubert H. Humphrey of Minnesota in yesterday's Wisconsin Democratic Presidential primary.

Early today the 42-year-old Bostonian held a comfortable and growing lead over his Minnesota rival.

Vice President Nixon ran unopposed in the Republican column. He did not campaign in the state.

Returns from 3,039 of 3,455 precincts gave:

Kennedy (D)	389,417
Humphrey (D)	318,890
Nixon (R)	305,375

Kennedy ultimately got 56 per cent of the Democratic vote in the Wisconsin primary, but he knew the result was not conclusive. He had been expected to win more comfortably, with his impressive organization and extensive funds. To convince party leaders, he had to make a stronger showing.

Examination of the Wisconsin vote showed that Kennedy had drawn heavily in Roman Catholic communities, obviously attracting Republican as well as Democratic votes. While such power augured well for the Senator as a Presidential candidate, his backers feared the Wisconsin showing might tend to solidify Protestant opposition, highlight the religious issue and make Kennedy's nomination more difficult to achieve. "It means we have to do it all over again," Kennedy said dejectedly.

The nation's political interest now swung to West Virginia, the primary that had seemed unim-

PRECEDING PAGES: The Convair Caroline took the Kennedy team on many cross-country flights during 1960. With the Senator in the cabin, below, are Mrs. Kennedy and brother-in-law Stephen Smith.

OPPOSITE: On plane, en route to a speaking engagement in Nebraska.

portant when Kennedy and Humphrey entered it two months before. Here Roman Catholics made up less than 6 per cent of the population. If Kennedy could win decisively, he would go a long way toward disposing of the argument that Protestants would not vote for a Catholic Presidential candidate, an idea that had been imbedded in the public mind with the defeat of Alfred E. Smith by Herbert Hoover in 1928.

In West Virginia, supporters of all the other candidates swung behind Humphrey. The powerful United Mine Workers Union indicated dissatisfaction with Kennedy, who angrily charged that his opponents were "ganging up"; he asked voters if he had "lost this primary 42 years ago when I was baptized."

Less than three weeks before the West Virginia trial, Kennedy faced the religious issue squarely.

KENNEDY, BACKED BY HUMPHREY, HITS ISSUE OF RELIGION

WASHINGTON, April 21—Senator John F. Kennedy, in a massive assault on the religious issue in politics, today told a convention of newspaper editors:

"I am not the Catholic candidate for President."

Senator Hubert H. Humphrey, his opponent in the Democratic primary in West Virginia on May 10, went before the same group a few hours later and declared:

"I would not want to receive the vote of any American because my opponent or opponents worship in a particular church, whatever that church may be."

Kennedy's speech to the editors was serious and challenging, asking them to keep issues of religion in perspective and questioning conclusions that Wisconsin voters had divided along religious lines.

As the West Virginia date of May 10 grew nearer, both Kennedy and Humphrey stepped up their pace. The Massachusetts Senator laid the economic deprivation in much of the state at the doorstep of the Eisenhower Administration. The Minnesotan complained bitterly that his campaign did not enjoy the advantages afforded by his opponent's wealth. Kennedy enlisted Franklin D. Roosevelt Jr. to speak for him, as a symbol of the New Deal battle against depression.

The highly organized Kennedy forces, spending money freely, bought lots of television time; they emphasized Kennedy's war record and his PT-boat exploits; F. D. R. Jr. even went beyond the bounds of normal political commentary in charging that Humphrey had sought deferment from the armed forces in the war, a charge disavowed by Kennedy. For his part, Humphrey, politically money-poor and without an organization, stumped the state in a bus, criticizing lavish expenditures in the campaign.

Meanwhile, outside West Virginia both contestants picked up support. Kennedy won the uncontested Indiana primary, although his total vote ran 50,000 behind Vice President Nixon's. Humphrey swept the District of Columbia primary.

Six days before the West Virginia primary, the two candidates appeared together on statewide television for the first of what was to be a historic series of 1960 political debates. Although the influence of television in that state was doubtful, Kennedy, well briefed on local issues, was judged the more effective.

Both men campaigned down to the wire, and on May 10, with Humphrey favored to win, the West Virginians voted. The next day, The Times reported:

KENNEDY WINNER OVER HUMPHREY IN WEST VIRGINIA

CHARLESTON, W. Va., May 11 — Senator John F. Kennedy of Massachusetts won a smashing upset victory in yesterday's West Virginia Presidential preferential primary.

The Senator promptly forecast that he would be nominated at the Democratic National Convention, which starts July 11.

His "significant and clear-cut" victory was conceded at 1 A.M. Eastern standard time (2 A.M. New York time) by Senator Hubert H. Humphrey.

Senator Humphrey also announced that he would withdraw from the race for the Democratic Presidential nomination.

Stumping West Virginia in April 1960, Kennedy speaks to school children ranged on a hillside.

West Virginia had given Kennedy a 3-to-2 margin over his opponent, but it had given him much more. The primary established that the Massachusetts Catholic was a powerful enough candidate to win in a state where his religion could only have been a political handicap.

Now the Senator's bandwagon was moving, and lesser but important victories began to fall into place. On the day after West Virginia, Kennedy swept the Nebraska primary, capturing two-thirds of the state's 32 delegates. New York and New Jersey were then reported ready to deliver some 130 delegates. On May 17 the Maryland primary gave him 70 per cent of the vote and all 24 of the delegates.

Finally, on May 20, came the last of Kennedy's seven primaries: Oregon. There he faced a favorite son, Senator Wayne Morse, and for the first time Stuart Symington and Lyndon Johnson were on the ballot, too, although neither man campaigned. Through a rainy day and into the night, Oregon Democrats voted, and the next day Washington was impressed when it read the news:

KENNEDY'S DRIVE GAINS MOMENTUM IN OREGON SWEEP

WASHINGTON, May 21—Senator John F. Kennedy's bandwagon rolled more swiftly toward Los Angeles today on the strength of a seven-for-seven grand slam in the Democratic Presidential preferential primaries.

The Massachusetts Senator capped his series of popularity tests in Oregon yesterday, by apparently polling as many votes as his four rivals for the Democratic nomination combined.

He soundly trounced Senator Wayne Morse in his home state by about 3 to 2. The outcome forced Senator Morse's withdrawal from any pursuit of Democratic convention delegates.

It was a display of political popularity and power that could not fail to impress uncommitted Democratic delegations.

Vice President Nixon, whose unopposed march through the Republican primaries had given him the mouse's share of the publicity, reported now that he was "looking into" Kennedy's campaign spending in West Virginia. (It took the Justice Department until July 12, the day before the Democratic convention nominated, to announce that no Federal law had been violated in West Virginia.)

As May closed, Kennedy received his first endorsement from an international union, the Textile Workers of America. Then he came to the union's convention and sounded for the first time what was to become one of the major themes of his Presidential campaign:

KENNEDY CHARGES NATIONAL DECLINE

CHICAGO, June 2—Senator John F. Kennedy charged today that the Eisenhower Administration had failed to fulfill the nation's responsibilities as a world power during its eight-year tenure.

"I do not," he said, "underplay in any sense the mistakes that this Administration has made during the past month, during the past eight months and during the past eight years.

"But what I consider to be their chief responsibility has been that they have permitted the power and the strength of the United States to decline in relation to that of the Communist world.

"And," he went on, "they have permitted that when we represent the only great hope for freedom around the world."

Early in June the majority of the 51-member Michigan delegation swung into line behind Kennedy, and he stole a half-dozen more votes from under Lyndon Johnson's nose in New Mexico.

At a Michigan labor meeting he told reporters he was "positive" of winning the Democratic nomination. He predicted he would have more than 600 votes in the early balloting at Los Angeles of the 761 that would obtain the nomination. Actually, it would be three weeks later before Kennedy had 550 publicly guaranteed votes, but he was confident now of his growing power in undecided states.

In the long struggle from underdog to front-runner, Kennedy had relentlessly pursued his political ambitions at the expense, on many occasions, of his duties in the Senate. Less than a month before the convention, however, he took time for a major foreign policy speech on the Senate floor:

KENNEDY FAVORS
PEIPING CONTACTS

WASHINGTON, June 14—Senator John F. Kennedy suggested today that the next Administration should try to bring Communist China into the Geneva negotiations seeking a ban on nuclear tests.

The Massachusetts Democrat emphasized that he would not favor recognition of Red China without a genuine change in her belligerent attitude. But he told the Senate that a reassessment of the nation's policy on China should nevertheless be undertaken by the next President.

The present policy, he said, has "failed dismally" to weaken Communist rule on the mainland, to prevent steady growth of Communist strength there and to provide "real solutions to the problems of a militant China."

While Kennedy was presenting his foreign policy credentials before packed Senate galleries, his political strength was steadily building. New Jersey Democrats sent word they would be with him on the second ballot. New York delegates caucused and guaranteed him 87 of their 114 votes, with more probably to come. Having crisscrossed the country a half-dozen times since the Oregon primary for state political conventions and meetings with Democratic leaders, Kennedy made one last trip in late June. He flew to Iowa to accuse Nixon of failing to face the nation's farm problems directly, then on to Montana to speak to convention delegates and to send a message to the Governors' Conference at Glacier Park.

Every reachable political base having been touched, Kennedy flew back to Cape Cod for ten days' rest at Hyannis Port before the final fatal combat of the convention. As he vacationed there, Harry Truman made a last attempt to exert the political influence he had irretrievably lost when his Presidency ended eight years before. A Symington backer from the beginning, Truman called on Kennedy to withdraw in favor of "someone with the greatest possible maturity and experience." The former President resigned as a delegate in protest over "a prearranged affair." He proposed nine candidates besides Symington, three of whom were in their 40's and one younger than Kennedy (Orville Freeman). The Senator flew to New York for a retaliatory news conference in which he said the White House needed the "strength and health and vigor" of a young man. He refused to step aside and denied that his supporters had brought any "improper pressure" to bear on convention delegates.

A week before the delegates were to gather in Los Angeles, Lyndon Johnson's supporters proposed that all Democratic contenders take a physical examination; they claimed Kennedy suffered from Addison's disease, an adrenal deficiency.

Almost on the eve of the convention, another undeclared candidate formally joined the competition.

JOHNSON ENTERS
RACE OFFICIALLY,
SEES 500 VOTES

WASHINGTON, July 5—Senator Lyndon B. Johnson announced today that he was a candidate for the Democratic Presidential nomination.

Senator Johnson said he expected to go to the convention with more than 500 first-ballot votes against fewer than 600 for Senator John F. Kennedy of Massachusetts. The nomination requires 761.

The 51-year-old Texan, majority leader of the Senate, had been campaigning for weeks. So his announcement was no surprise to anyone.

But he carried off the ritual of making a formal declaration before television cameras, now standard procedure for Presidential aspirants, in the approved manner.

Except for Adlai Stevenson, more reluctant than ever, and Hubert Humphrey, lost over the rough primary course, the candidates were all now on hand. In a matter of days, the Democratic party in convention assembled would decide whether Kennedy's long, patient, mounting drive was to reward him with an ironic prize: another even tougher campaign.

CONVENTION

While Kennedy rested at Hyannis Port, preconvention activity began to stir on both sides of the continent. In Washington, Congress agreed to recess during July and the first week of August to clear time for the two party conventions. The Republicans, notably Vice President Nixon, argued against the recess. They contended that any session after the Presidential nominations would be dominated by politics and, since the Democrats controlled Congress, by Democratic politics. In Los Angeles, a campaign once again to renominate Adlai Stevenson finally began to take shape. A national office for the "draft Stevenson" forces was opened, and the two-time candidate's supporters were assigned space in convention headquarters as a recognized contingent.

Even as the first Democrats began to gather ten days before the convention, controversy arose. A Times story said:

BUTLER DENIES HE RIGGED CONVENTION FOR KENNEDY

LOS ANGELES, June 30—A bitter dispute flared today between the Democrats' national chairman, Paul M. Butler, and other party notables, especially former President Harry S. Truman.

Mr. Butler, opening his office at the Democratic National Convention headquarters here, expressed "bitter resentment" over allegations attributed to Mr. Truman and others that he had "rigged" the convention in favor of Senator John F. Kennedy of Massachusetts, the front-running candidate.

On the eighth floor of the Biltmore Hotel and in a cottage just outside the convention hall, the Kennedy forces set up their command posts. Installed for their private use was a telephone system connecting the candidate's hotel suite, his private apartment, the two headquarters, key points on the floor and, ultimately, roving floor agents with walkie-talkie sets. In over-all charge of the Massachusetts Senator's operation was his 34-year-old brother, Bobby. His chief lieutenants at the Biltmore were O'Donnell, O'Brien and Salinger. Ready for important duty among state delegations and on the convention floor were two veteran allies from Connecticut, John M. Bailey and Abe Ribicoff, backed by a corps of well-trained Massachusetts delegates.

Five days before the convention opened, Robert Kennedy told the press how his brother would have the nomination wrapped up by the day the delegates formally convened:

LOS ANGELES, July 6—Robert F. Kennedy predicted today that the outcome of the Democratic National Convention would be decided by noon Monday, five hours before it officially opens.

The prediction was made as persistent reports circulated here that Gov. Edmund G. Brown of California would announce his personal support of Senator John F. Kennedy of Massachusetts for the Presidential nomination before Monday.

By now, the problem facing the Kennedy team was clear. The Massachusetts Senator had 600 of the 761 votes he needed for the nomination all but locked up. For the rest he was looking to Iowa and Kansas, which were still behind their governors as favorite sons, and to five major uncommitted states: Pennsylvania, California, New Jersey, Minnesota and Illinois.

Under the Kennedy banner at Los Angeles: sister Eunice Shriver and sisters-in-law Joan and Ethel Kennedy.

Behind-the-scenes workers at the Convention: RIGHT: Steve Smith, with Mrs. Evelyn Lincoln, Kennedy's private secretary, in right foreground; CENTER: brother Teddy; FAR RIGHT: brother Bobby, chief of staff.

Pausing in Chicago on his way to the convention, just two days after announcing his own candidacy, Lyndon Johnson inquired rhetorically—and a little anxiously—whether the outcome at Los Angeles had "been determined somewhere in a back room, with the result only now being announced to the delegates." This was one of a series of statements of mounting bitterness the Texan was to make in the coming six days, as his political fortunes declined. That same day in the convention city, James Reston found Johnson the candidate up against long odds:

The Ardent Young Lover
and the Old Suitor

LOS ANGELES, July 7—Unless Lyndon Johnson can somehow persuade the North to secede from the Union between now and next Wednesday, his chances of being nominated for the Presidency are approximately nil.

All the angels of heaven and hell in Los Angeles could not persuade the governors of California, Pennsylvania and New Jersey or Their Honors, the Mayors of New York and Chicago, to vote for Ol' Lyndon.

They have decided, as the Republicans did with Senator Taft in 1940, '44, '48 and '52, that he can't win in their districts, and since most of them put winning and their districts above everything else, they are ruling him out.

Accordingly, if there is any contest ahead here in Los Angeles, it is not between Senator Kennedy and Senator Johnson, despite Johnson's impressive first-ballot strength, but between Senator Kennedy and Adlai Stevenson of Illinois.

82

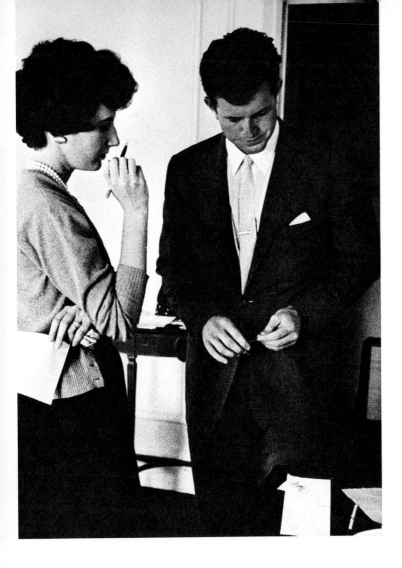 

As the preconvention weekend approached, the Kennedy strategists worked over the latest reports on their strength in the vital uncommitted delegations, in advance of the caucuses that would formally commit their votes.

KENNEDY FORCES
CLAIM NEW GAINS
IN 2 KEY STATES

LOS ANGELES, July 7—Senator John F. Kennedy's prospects for an early-ballot Presidential nomination mounted tonight on the strength of reports of impending breaks for him in the Pennsylvania and California delegations to the Democratic National Convention.

Now, the critical days of the convention had arrived, and Bobby Kennedy's squad of expert political operators could not be expected to carry the ball farther without the candidate. Kennedy left his wife, who was expecting their second child, on Cape Cod. On Saturday, two days before the convention was to open, he flew into Los Angeles to find a smashing, typically well-organized reception awaiting him. The Times reported:

LOS ANGELES, July 9—Senator John F. Kennedy came to town today brimful of confidence.
The Massachusetts Democrat's forecasts fell just short of a first-ballot nomination for the Presidency, but there were signs he might be erring on the conservative side.

"I think, without any support from Pennsylvania, California, New Jersey, Iowa, Kansas and Minnesota, I will have over 600 votes on the first ballot," said the sun-tanned 43-year-old Senator at a brief news conference at the airport.

On that Saturday, it was the battle of the airports. Some 2,500 people turned out for Kennedy's arrival, including five busloads of volunteer workers, three bands and a corps of uniformed girls. Before they had cleared the runways, a host of 5,000 Stevenson greeters began to gather for another jubilant political welcome. Stevenson told the airport throng he would accept the nomination but would not campaign for it. He was flattered but not optimistic.

Kennedy's physical presence on the convention scene precipitated more gains for his cause and fresh, even more confident newspaper predictions:

LOS ANGELES, July 9—Senator John F. Kennedy of Massachusetts arrived today to find the Democratic National Convention on the verge of a stampede to his Presidential candidacy.

He arrived shortly behind Senator Stuart Symington of Missouri, whose backers were making common cause with Senator Lyndon B. Johnson of Texas in a desperate stand to stop a mass bolt to Mr. Kennedy.

In the swarming corridors and headquarters suites of the Biltmore Hotel, however, most of the breaks today were coming in Senator Kennedy's favor.

Two days before the convention opened, Johnson's strength was already ebbing. More than 50 delegates from five Southern states, led by a bloc from North Carolina, had moved over into the Kennedy camp, and others threatened to follow. New York, as expected, set aside 104 of its 114 votes for Kennedy.

The Massachusetts Senator came to a Los Angeles that already seemed to be swarming with Kennedys. In addition to his brothers Bobby and Teddy and their wives, there were his sisters—Eunice and her husband, Sargent Shriver; Patricia and her husband, Peter Lawford; and Jean and her husband, Stephen Smith, plus a sizable scattering of their children. The Senator's mother, Mrs. Joseph P. Kennedy, was on hand to preside with the sisters and sisters-in-law at a giant Kennedy reception for delegates on Sunday. The Senator's 71-year-old father was there, but strictly behind the scenes in a Beverly Hills villa he had rented from Marion Davies. The candidate himself, in search of part-time seclusion, had a secret apartment in Hollywood in addition to his official Biltmore suite.

On Sunday, caucus day for some of the key state delegations, the political spadework the Kennedy team had done outside the primary states began to prove its value. The Times reported:

GOV. BROWN FOR KENNEDY;
ILLINOIS ADDS 59½ VOTES;
CONVENTION OPENS TODAY

LOS ANGELES, July 10—Senator John F. Kennedy reaped a rich harvest of delegate votes today and virtually nailed down the Democratic Presidential nomination.

With the formal opening of the convention twenty hours away, the prospects of a first-ballot victory for the young Massachusetts Senator mounted on the strength of these developments:

Govs. Edmund G. Brown of California, Herschel C. Loveless of Iowa and George Docking of Kansas, favorite-son candidates for the Presidency, formally endorsed Senator Kennedy and promised him the overwhelming majority of the 128 votes pledged to them.

Mayor Richard J. Daley of Chicago delivered 59½ from Illinois' delegation of 69 votes to the Kennedy camp.

On Monday evening, July 11, the Democratic convention officially opened in the Memorial Sports Arena, with the result of its proceedings less and less in doubt.

Bobby Kennedy discusses strategy with Abraham Ribicoff (left) and John Bailey.

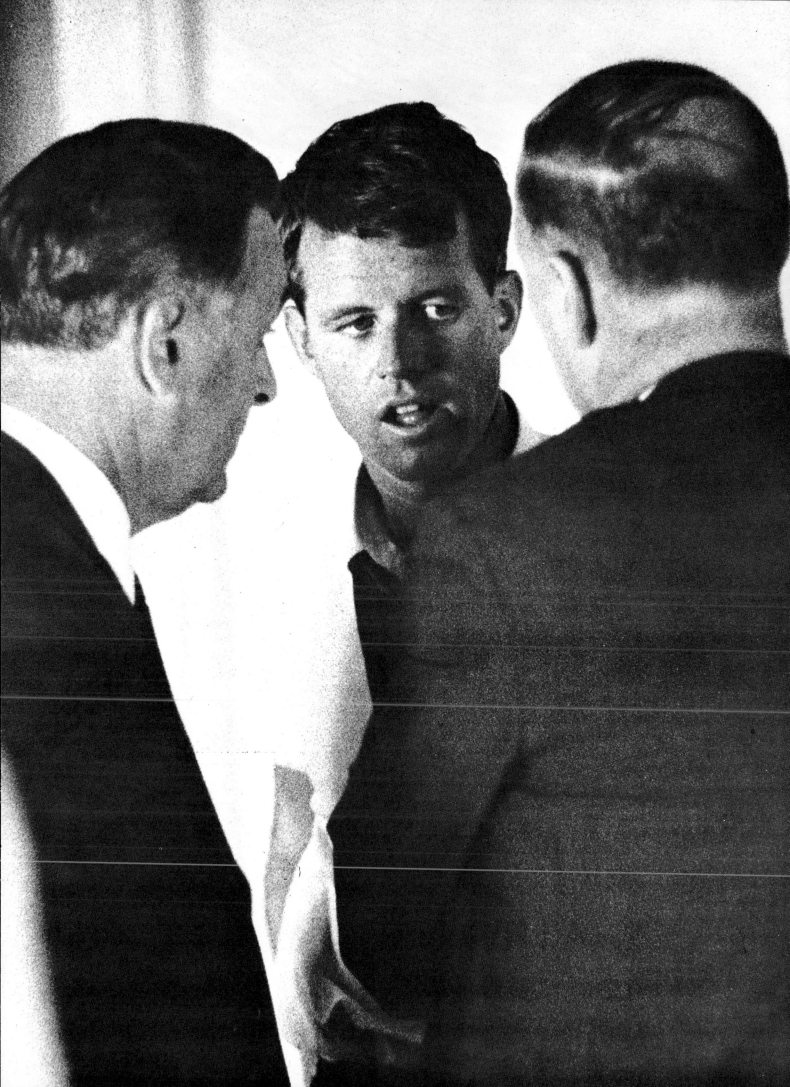

As Mrs. Eleanor Roosevelt (center) makes an unsuccessful attempt to swing the Convention's nomination to Adlai Stevenson, the Kennedy bandwagon rolls on, with help from (clockwise from upper left): John Bailey and Connecticut Congressman Chester Bowles (back to camera); delegates sporting Kennedy hats and badges; Kennedy sisters Patricia Lawford (in hat) —a delegate from California— and Eunice Shriver; Abraham Ribicoff; the Senator himself, here speaking to a state delegation; Governor Edmund G. (Pat) Brown of California; Jesse Unruh, California political power, with yawning delegate; longtime Kennedy aide Kenneth O'Donnell; a delegate from Connecticut; Tammany boss Carmine De Sapio.

KENNEDY NOMINATION SEEMS SURE; PENNSYLVANIA PLEDGES 64 VOTES; KEYNOTE SCORES ADMINISTRATION

LOS ANGELES, July 11—Senator John F. Kennedy apparently clinched the Democratic Presidential nomination today as the party's national convention opened formally on a flood of partisan oratory.

Senator Frank Church of Idaho keynoted the Democratic drive to regain the White House, striking harshly at what he termed the Eisenhower Administration's failures at home and abroad.

The talk was overshadowed by the massive pressure of the Kennedy drive, which had convinced even his opponents that the nomination of the Massachusetts Senator was now inevitable. But backers of Senators Lyndon B. Johnson of Texas and Stuart Symington of Missouri insisted their names would be placed in nomination.

Pennsylvania provided the crushing blow to the "stop Kennedy" forces when Gov. David L. Lawrence ended his long hold-out and delivered 64 of his state's 81 votes to Senator Kennedy.

Governor Lawrence, over the years one of the most loyal Stevenson supporters, had been assiduously courted by the Kennedy forces in Los Angeles. John Bailey met him at the airport and arranged a private meeting between Kennedy and the Pennsylvanian for the morning before the convention opened. The Pennsylvania decision so encouraged Kennedy that he predicted for the first time just before the convention opened that the necessary majority of 761 votes was firmly committed. He told a news conference this figure did not include any help from California, New Jersey, Minnesota or the District of Columbia, all of which remained uncertain. He conceded that his majority might have to await a second ballot.

The opening session of the convention offered some high-pitched party speech-making but no decisive politics during its three early evening hours. But on the second day of the convention, for the first time in many months, Kennedy was not the figure in the Democratic spotlight, and it seemed for a few hours that his bandwagon might have lost its momentum. In that spotlight, uncontestably, uproariously, and still a little unwillingly, was Adlai Stevenson.

LOS ANGELES, July 12—Adlai E. Stevenson won a double personal triumph at tumultuous sessions miles apart this evening.

He polled one more vote than Senator John F. Kennedy at a three-hour caucus of the California Democratic delegation in Hollywood and soon afterward received a roaring reception from the galleries when he appeared before the Democratic National Convention in the arena.

So persistent were the Stevenson delegates at the caucus, along with their allies from the camps of Senators Stuart Symington and Lyndon B. Johnson, that they forced an immediate poll of the Californians over the objections of the Kennedy strategists.

So enthusiastic were the Stevenson followers at the arena that Gov. LeRoy Collins of Florida, the convention's permanent chairman, virtually lost control.

The vote in the California caucus was Kennedy's first real defeat. Rejecting the leadership of Governor Brown, the delegation had split 31½ for Stevenson to 30½ for Kennedy, with the other 19 votes scattered. At the same time, anticipated Kennedy support from Kansas, Iowa, Minnesota and New Jersey failed to materialize, with only one more day before the balloting for the Presidential nomination was to begin.

The Stevenson demonstration had really begun the night before, as the convention was opening. All around the Sports Arena as the speeches droned on within, a band of placard-carrying supporters had marched, chanting, "We Want Stevenson!" On Tuesday evening, this insistent, angry, pleading, demanding chorus had swelled to thousands and spread up into the galleries as well. When the Democratic nominee of 1952 and 1956 took his seat with the Illinois delegation shortly after 6 P.M. that evening, pandemonium broke loose in the Sports Arena. For 17 minutes the crowd shouted uncontrollably

88

for Stevenson. When he was finally pushed, pulled and pummeled to the platform, his acknowledgment was a characteristically wry prediction: that in a convention of such unmerciful shoving, the nomination would go to "the last survivor."

The formal business of the convention on that Tuesday night was the adoption of the party platform. The Times summarized the action:

PLATFORM WINS
AFTER CLASHES
ON CIVIL RIGHTS

LOS ANGELES, July 12—The Democratic National Convention overrode Southern protests tonight to adopt a "big-budget" platform that included the strongest civil rights plank in party history.

The civil rights pledge to utilize Federal powers to end all forms of discrimination because of race, creed or color was aimed at attracting to the Democratic ticket the largest possible Northern Negro vote in November.

Although ten Southern states dissented, there was no immediate threat of a walkout, but there were warnings that the strong language might endanger Democratic victories below the Mason-Dixon line.

Despite the headlines, it was not a significant renewal of the Democrats' perennial controversy. From the reading of the planks to the delegates, by the platform chairman, Chester Bowles, through the minority reports, the debate and the voice voting, a little more than three hours elapsed—a mere moment as slow-paced conventions go. The South did not even demand a roll-call; outnumbered shouts of "No!" were enough to satisfy the sons of the Old Confederacy that night.

During the first two days of the convention, Kennedy had addressed more than two dozen caucuses —most of individual states, others of geographical blocs or nationality groups. Wednesday morning, just for a change, although his committed vote total had reached 740 of 761 he needed, the candidate spoke to a meeting of farm state delegates and caucuses of Indiana, Virginia, Colorado and Hawaii.

Then in midafternoon, Kennedy returned to his apartment hideaway in Hollywood to find reporters and television cameramen staked out on his doorstep. He went in, then sneaked over the back fence and drove to his father's rented villa for an afternoon of swimming and a quiet dinner. Back in his apartment unobserved before 10 P.M., Kennedy watched the balloting on his television set with a state-by-state sheet of personal expectations before him.

In the Sports Arena, it had taken nearly seven hours to nominate and second nine candidates, two of whom promptly withdrew in favor of Kennedy. The emotional highlight was Minnesota Senator Eugene McCarthy's nomination of Stevenson, which revived the demonstrations of the past two nights and surpassed in warmth and duration the reaction accorded any other candidate.

But the roll-call was the payoff. At 10:07 P.M., as thousands in the convention hall and millions in the television audience watched and listened, the convention clerk called the first question out over the tense mass of delegates: "Alabama, 29 votes?"

"Alabama," came the reply, "casts 20 votes for Johnson; Kennedy, 3½; Symington, 3½." The rest of the votes were scattered.

Forty-four minutes later, at 10:51 P.M., with six delegations still to be called, the Kennedy vote had reached 750, and the clerk had reached Wyoming.

"Mr. Chairman, Mr. Chairman," Tracy S. McCraken, head of the Wyoming delegation, shouted, "Wyoming's vote will make a majority for Senator Kennedy!" Over the ensuing bedlam, he appealed to Governor Collins for some semblance of order.

"Can we get the vote from Wyoming?" the convention chairman pleaded with the rising tide of cheers.

"Wyoming votes . . . we have 15 votes . . ." McCraken seemed overcome by his role. ". . . 15 votes from Wyoming for Kennedy!"

Amid mounting chaos in the Sports Arena, the moment was history. The Times recorded it as follows:

KENNEDY NOMINATED ON FIRST BALLOT, OVERWHELMS JOHNSON BY 806 VOTES TO 409

LOS ANGELES, Thursday, July 14—Senator John F. Kennedy smashed his way to a first-ballot Presidential nomination at the Democratic National Convention last night and won the right to oppose Vice President Nixon in November.

The 43-year-old Massachusetts Senator overwhelmed his opposition, piling up 806 votes to 409 ballots for his nearest rival, Senator Lyndon B. Johnson of Texas, the Senate majority leader.

July 13, 1960: Kennedy grins at front-page headlines announcing his nomination on the first ballot.

Senator Kennedy's victory came just before 11 o'clock last night (2 A.M. Thursday, New York time).

Then the convention made it unanimous on motion of Gov. James T. Blair Jr. of Missouri, who had placed Senator Stuart Symington of Missouri in nomination.

Senator Kennedy, appearing before the shouting convention early today, pledged he would carry the fight to the country in the fall "and we shall win."

It had taken Kennedy six months and 11 days from his formal declaration of candidacy to capture the highest prize his party had to offer. Now ahead of him stretched three months and 26 days of the fiercest political combat and, more immediately, the choice of a man to fight at his side during that combat.

PICKING THE VICE PRESIDENT

As soon as Wyoming had cast the last votes John F. Kennedy needed to obtain the Democratic Presidential nomination, party leaders at the convention shifted their interest to the question of a running mate for the new candidate. Even before the first ballot was completed in Los Angeles, Democratic leaders from the big states and big cities had slipped off the convention floor, one by one, to meet with Kennedy in the cottage just outside the amphitheater that had served as his convention command post. They wanted to congratulate the young candidate, of course, and promise their loyalty for the campaign. But they also wanted to talk with each other and with Kennedy about the next big decision: who could help the ticket—and the leaders—the most as the nominee for Vice President?

There was no question who was going to make the final choice. Three days before he won the nomination, the Senator from Massachusetts told a reporter he would not leave the Vice-Presidential nomination wide open, as it had been in 1956; then, Kennedy himself had been edged out for second place on the ticket by Senator Estes Kefauver in a tense floor fight. The Sunday before the 1960 convention opened, Kennedy had indicated interest in a running mate from the Middle West or West, someone fully qualified for the Presidency and familiar with farm issues. From this interview and others the following picture emerged:

SYMINGTON IS SAID TO TOP LIST FOR VICE-PRESIDENCY

LOS ANGELES, July 10—Senator Stuart Symington of Missouri was reported tonight to head a list of possible nominees for Vice President acceptable to Senator John F. Kennedy if he is chosen to head the Democratic ticket.

Senator Kennedy was said authoritatively to have made no agreements with anybody. However, sources close to him acknowledged that Senator Symington fitted the description of a running mate described by Senator Kennedy as acceptable.

Senator Hubert H. Humphrey also meets qualifications set by Senator Kennedy. However, the Minnesotan said today that he was not available and his state's delegation endorsed Gov. Orville L. Freeman for the post.

Among the leaders who met with Kennedy after his nomination just outside the convention hall were several with a common view as to the Vice-Presidential nominee: he should be one of the three men who had run closest to the winner in the Presidential balloting. This, they argued, would insure a well-known candidate and eliminate any need for a publicity build-up.

Such a strategy would have limited the field to Senator Symington, Senator Lyndon B. Johnson and Adlai E. Stevenson. Those behind the idea included Democratic politicians from New York (Carmine G. DeSapio and Michael Prendergast), Pennsylvania (Governor David L. Lawrence and Representative William L. Green Jr.), Illinois (Jacob L. Arvey and Mayor Richard J. Daley of Chicago) and California (Governor Edmund G. Brown).

These party stalwarts and others talked with Kennedy in the cottage and formed a mass escort to take him to the convention for a short speech to the cheering delegates. Then they all went back to the command post for more conversations. It was 2 A.M. before Kennedy returned to the "secret" apartment he had rented to escape the mania of convention hotels.

Those who observed Kennedy and the politicians in the cottage Wednesday night and Thursday morning, when the decision seemed to be taking shape, believed there were really only two contenders: Symington and Senator Henry M. Jackson of Washington. They could not have been more wrong.

92

Back in his apartment early Thursday morning, Kennedy found a telegram of congratulation from Senator Johnson, so warmly worded that the Presidential nominee paused over his fried eggs, toast and milk. Heretofore, generally, the New Englander had considered the Texan out of reach as a running mate for at least these reasons:

¶ Senator Johnson had said many times that he would prefer retaining the considerable power and prestige of Senate majority leader to assuming the Vice-Presidency, with its limited Constitutional responsibility and political influence.

¶ The Texan was not particularly well-regarded as a national candidate by some Democratic leaders in the party's liberal wing. His nomination could cost a Kennedy ticket as many votes in the North as it gained in the South.

¶ Particularly in the previous ten days, Johnson had been so bitterly critical of Kennedy—his tactics, his voting record, even his family—that the two men might now find an accommodation difficult, even impossible.

Once again, Kennedy weighed these questions and slept on them for a few hours. By 8 A.M. he was phoning the Johnson suite on the seventh floor of the Biltmore Hotel. Awakened by his wife, Lady Bird, Johnson talked with Kennedy and agreed to receive him in his suite about two hours later.

A little later Kennedy called the Biltmore rooms occupied by his own staff, just a floor above Johnson's, and put his brother Bobby and some other aides to work. The candidate wanted a compilation of electoral vote totals of the New England states and others in the secure Northeast, combined variously with Texas and others in the solid South. The Kennedy staff was flabbergasted by the implied proposal. Most of them had anticipated that Johnson would get a ceremonial offer of the Vice-Presidential nomination—frankly expecting a refusal. Few thought it would be a serious political proposal, as now it seemed. They remembered too clearly the Kennedy-Johnson "debate" of just two days before:

JOHNSON STRIVES
TO HALT KENNEDY

LOS ANGELES, July 12—Senator Lyndon B. Johnson seized the headlines momentarily today in what was widely regarded as a last-ditch bid to slow the bandwagon of Senator John F. Kennedy.

The Texas candidate arranged a nationally televised face-to-face "debate" with his front-running opponent from Massachusetts and sought to take him to task for Senate absenteeism and for his voting record on the farm issue and natural resources.

However, more compliments than brickbats were exchanged. And the brickbats themselves, if any struck home, failed to do any visible damage.

In that exchange, Johnson recalled the 24-hour sessions of the Senate on the civil rights bill and said: "For six days and nights I had to deliver a quorum of 61 men on a moment's notice to keep the Senate in session to get any bill at all and I'm proud to tell you that on those 50 quorum calls Lyndon Johnson answered every one of them. Although some men who would [be President] on a civil rights platform answered none." Deadly serious, Johnson continued in his slow Texas drawl, "Admittedly, I didn't have the same problem that some of my people had opposing Senators Humphrey and Morse in four primaries."

With a grin, Kennedy arose to reply. He said: "He made some general reference to shortcomings of other Presidential candidates, but as he was not specific, I assume he was talking about some other candidate and not about me. It is true that Senator Johnson made a wonderful record answering those quorum calls and I want to commend him for it. I was not present on all those occasions; I was not majority leader. As Lyndon knows, I never criticize. In fact, on every occasion I said that Senator Johnson should not enter the primaries, that his proper responsibilities were as majority leader. If he would let Hubert, Wayne and I settle this matter, we could come to a clear-cut decision."

The delegates laughed and Kennedy concluded, "So, I come here today full of admiration for Senator Johnson, full of affection for him, strongly in support of him for majority leader, and I'm confident that in that position we're all going to be able to work together."

At the Texas caucus on July 12, Lyndon Johnson (opposite and above) questions the maturity and responsibility of his young opponent for the Presidential nomination. At right, Kennedy and Bobby consider possible rejoinders to Johnson.

Two days later, on Thursday morning in Johnson's hotel suite, the talk was otherwise. As the wit-nesses recall it today, Kennedy expressed hope that Johnson might agree to be his running mate, stressing the majority leader's credentials as the best qualified successor. Johnson replied that he would prefer remaining in the Senate, but he agreed to think it over. He was clearly receptive.

Standing with Mrs. Johnson before the Texas delegation, Lyndon Johnson (left) makes the V-for-victory sign. Kennedy (right) rises to reply.

After about 20 minutes, Kennedy left Johnson and consulted in the corridor briefly with Speaker Sam Rayburn, the majority leader's closest adviser. Since his fellow Texan had lost the Presidential nomination, Rayburn had been flatly opposing his acceptance of second place. Then, Kennedy climbed up to his own ninth-floor suite, and a critical day of conferences began. At issue was whether Johnson should not be made a firm offer of the Vice-Presidential nomination.

For the second time that morning, the Kennedy staff was surprised. Their astonishment that Johnson was to be offered second place was very modest compared to their reaction when they learned

Senator Kennedy jokingly promises the Texas delegates that he will support Lyndon Johnson—for majority leader of the Senate next year.

that he was interested. All hands insist today that this was not a question of opposition to Johnson as a running mate, but disbelief that he might be willing to leave the Senate.

While newspaper, radio and television reporters choked the hall outside the Kennedy suite, a steady stream of the Democratic party's major figures came, singly and in groups, to talk with their candidate about Lyndon Johnson. Generally, these party men liked the Johnson idea; they respected and admired the Texas Senator and saw his presence on the ticket as preserving the restive South for Kennedy. Governor David Lawrence of Pennsylvania told Kennedy that if Johnson was his choice, then he, Lawrence, would support him.

But then came a delegation of major labor leaders, men nearly as influential in the Democratic party as in their own unions. They strongly opposed Johnson; they said he would lose the votes of many working men and most Negroes. They found him otherwise objectionable; only yesterday, they recalled, he had made most offensive personal attacks on Kennedy. The Times had reported:

JOHNSON'S ATTACKS ON KENNEDY RANGE FROM McCARTHY TO HITLER

LOS ANGELES, July 13—Senator Lyndon B. Johnson wound up his pre-balloting campaign for the Democratic nomination today with a series of personal thrusts at Senator John F. Kennedy and his family.

The Texan, in high spirits and predicting victory, hit obliquely at the wealth of the Kennedys, at Senator Kennedy's record on McCarthyism and at the prewar attitude of Senator Kennedy's father toward Hitlerism.

He exuberantly proclaimed the halting of the Kennedy bandwagon and predicted a "revolt" of delegates who were "hogtied," as he put it, to the front-runner from Massachusetts.

Mr. Johnson was an aggressive, self-assured candidate as he made a final round of six convention delegations in downtown hotels and held a news conference.

To some, Senator Johnson's air of confidence was convincing. To others, his tactics seemed to be those of a man desperately striving at the last minute to stave off defeat.

Throughout the discussions, Kennedy was importantly if silently influenced by his father's advice. The candidate had telephoned Joseph P. Kennedy early that day with the Johnson proposal. His father had enthusiastically approved, predicting that current criticism of the Texan as a running mate would fade as Johnson's potential contribution to the Democratic ticket became clearer.

While Kennedy listened, the subject of the debate was receiving conflicting advice himself, two floors below. Some Southerners insisted Johnson could not share the ballot with a Roman Catholic and an apostle of civil rights. Others argued that the South could not afford to refuse its traditional place on the national ticket. Still others deprecated the office of Vice President.

Upstairs in the Kennedy suite, it seemed increasingly possible that the labor opposition and its allies might stage a floor fight if Johnson were nominated. Early in the afternoon, this message was carried down to the Johnson suite by Bobby Kennedy, giving the Texan an option to withdraw if he wanted to sidestep such a controversy and become chairman of the Democratic National Committee instead. Declining the option, Johnson invited a firm offer from the candidate. "If Jack wants me, I'm willing to make a fight for it," he said.

By mid-afternoon, the decision was final. Kennedy talked to most of the other Vice-Presidential possibilities—Jackson, Brown, Symington and Freeman—and explained his choice to them. He then called Johnson, who said, "Jack, if you want me to run, I'll do it."

Kennedy drafted a news announcement and read it to Johnson for his approval. A little after 4 P.M., in the basement hall of the Biltmore, the candidate made his selection public.

"We need men of strength if we are to be strong and if we are to prevail and lead the world on the road to freedom," Kennedy declared. "Lyndon Johnson has demonstrated on many occasions his brilliant qualifications for the leadership we require today."

So surprised were newsmen by the Johnson choice that gasps greeted the announcement. Many of the reporters had believed that Kennedy's morning visit to the majority leader's suite had been merely a grace note struck by the winner for his chief defeated opponent. They were wrong.

The rest was anticlimax. No floor fight ever developed, in part because a strategy was adopted to interrupt the roll-call of the states with a motion for unanimity before any rebellious states were reached.

Johnson's nomination was presented to the convention that evening and confirmed by a shouting voice vote of acclamation:

JOHNSON IS NOMINATED FOR VICE PRESIDENT: KENNEDY PICKS HIM TO PLACATE THE SOUTH

LOS ANGELES, July 14—The Democratic National Convention selected Senator Lyndon B. Johnson of Texas tonight as its Vice-Presidential nominee.

The nomination was by acclamation.

Senator Johnson was nominated on the recommendation of Senator John F. Kennedy, the Presidential nominee. The Massachusetts Senator acted boldly in an effort to restore party unity and to strengthen the Democratic ticket in the South.

There were some protests from organized labor that the Texan's voting record would imperil the liberal image of the Kennedy candidacy on a strong New Deal type of platform.

Kennedy's decision was by no means universally popular in Los Angeles that night—as he had known it would not be. An official of Americans for Democratic Action declared hotly that Kennedy had promised to choose "a Midwestern liberal," which Johnson clearly was not.

A few state delegations had noisy and rebellious caucuses before the evening convention session that accepted Kennedy's decision, notably Wisconsin and Michigan. The delegation from Michigan, probably closer to the anti-Johnson labor element than any other, shouted "No!" in the convention voice vote but was overwhelmed.

Perhaps the reporters, the politicians and the American public should not have been quite as surprised as they were by Johnson's willingness to run for Vice President. Nine days before, while announcing his Presidential candidacy, the Texas Senator had been asked the traditional question: would he settle for second place?

"I have been prepared throughout my adult life to serve my country in any capacity where my country thought my services were essential," Johnson replied.

OVERLEAF: Thursday morning, July 14: In his private bedroom at the Biltmore, the nominee and his brother confer once more before Kennedy goes to his 10:15 meeting with Lyndon Johnson. Succeeding pages tell the story of that day.

Kennedy telephoned Johnson's suite before the majority leader was up, and arranged to meet with him two hours later. In the right foreground above is James McShane, later U. S. Chief Marshal.

After seeing Johnson, Kennedy confers with Pennsylvania Governor David Lawrence on his choice of a running mate. Looking on (center) is Matthew McCloskey, who became Ambassador to Ireland.

Getting opinions from other Democratic leaders on the Vice-Presidential choice. ABOVE: With Chester Bowles (center) and Terry Sanford of North Carolina (right); Michigan Governor G. Mennen Williams in bow tie, left foreground. BELOW: With Ohio Governor Michael DiSalle (center) and Abraham Ribicoff of Connecticut.

ABOVE: The candidate and his Vice-Presidential choice, facing the possibility of a floor fight from Liberal and labor forces opposing Johnson's nomination. BELOW: By mid-afternoon, Kennedy had told the other Vice-Presidential hopefuls of his decision. Senator Henry M. Jackson of Washington (left) shows his disappointment, as does California Governor Pat Brown (right).

ABOVE: Kennedy with Minnesota Governor Orville Freeman and two aides, discussing his selection of Johnson as a running mate. Freeman was later appointed Secretary of Agriculture. BELOW: Two other Vice-Presidential possibilities, Missouri Senator Stuart Symington (left) and Adlai Stevenson (right), leaving the Kennedy suite. Both accepted the decision quickly and offered their support.

At 4:30 P.M., after conferring again with his brother Bobby and with Lyndon Johnson, Kennedy announced his choice at a press conference.

BEFORE THE CAMPAIGN

Back in Hyannis Port, the problems were clear: it was necessary to bind up the party wounds, plan the campaign and get some rest for the weeks ahead. Kennedy sailed with Jackie and Bobby, he played with Caroline, he read the newspapers and he watched television as the Republicans nominated Richard M. Nixon to oppose him. His mood was bad. He had a slight throat infection, the Catholic issue was festering and a special session of Congress was coming up. One by one, the party leaders came to see him. First was Adlai Stevenson; after the visit the headlines said:

STEVENSON GIVES KENNEDY PLEDGE OF HELP IN RACE

Then came Lyndon Johnson, Soapy Williams, Scoop Jackson, Bob Wagner and, most important of all, former President Harry S. Truman. A party man above all else, Truman made it clear that he would support his party's candidate. The Times reported:

> HYANNIS PORT, Mass., August 2—Senator John F. Kennedy made peace today with former President Harry S. Truman. He won Mr. Truman's pledge of active support in the Presidential campaign. It was the first conversation between the two men since Mr. Truman boycotted the Democratic National Convention in Los Angeles on the ground that it was prearranged by party officials to produce Senator Kennedy's nomination.

In those days of early August, Kennedy conferred almost constantly with his brother Bobby, who was his chief campaign strategist, and with O'Donnell, O'Brien, Salinger, Bailey and Jim Rowe. He arrived at the basic campaign strategy. As his approach to Johnson at the convention indicated, he wanted to ensure the South; there were perhaps 60 to 70 votes there. But Kennedy decided that the big push would come in the populous industrial states—New York, New Jersey, Massachusetts, Pennsylvania, Michigan, Illinois and Ohio—and in Texas and California. It would be up to Johnson to carry his home state of Texas; Kennedy would campaign in California, but would depend on Stevenson and his supporters to carry that state; and Kennedy himself would devote major attention to the big seven states.

Kennedy broke his conferences for a day and flew to New York City to try to make peace with the warring Democratic factions there, but then it was back to Hyannis Port for more campaign councils. The strategists decided on a massive registration drive; O'Donnell was put in charge of scheduling trips; O'Brien was entrusted with "organization"—he had the delicate job of meshing the eager volunteers with the old pros; and an idea and speech-writing corps was set up.

On August 8, Johnson returned. The headlines reported:

KENNEDY AND JOHNSON MAP TRIP TO HAWAII AND ALASKA

The key sentence in the dispatch was: Kennedy's "post convention visit here had been concerned primarily with party unity moves, perfecting campaign organization plans and setting campaign policy on a number of vital issues."

When Kennedy flew out of Hyannis Port, it wasn't to Alaska or Hawaii, but to Washington, where Congress was in special session. The actual campaign didn't start until that session ended on September 1.

Caroline Kennedy with her parents at Hyannis Port.

OPPOSITE: Jacqueline Kennedy, pregnant with her second child, painting in an upstairs room at Hyannis Port.

RIGHT: Painting done by Jacqueline Kennedy in 1960 as a birthday present for Joseph P. Kennedy shows the Hyannis Port house, with Nurse Maude Shaw, Caroline, Jack, Jackie, and "Grandpa" himself in golf clothes in the foreground.

Riviera scene painted by Senator Kennedy in 1955, while convalescing from his back operation.

Jacqueline Kennedy's present to her husband on his return from the Los Angeles convention: the painting shows the Senator, in Napoleonic garb, landing in triumph from a boat named Victura II; on the Hyannis Port dock to welcome him are his wife and daughter, Nurse Shaw, their pets, and a brass band. The airplane with streamer is a greeting from his parents, who had flown off to France.

CAMPAIGN

The last lap of Kennedy's long race for the Presidency really began on that balmy mid-July night in the Los Angeles Coliseum when the Senator, no longer *a* Democratic candidate but *the* Democratic candidate, set his course, and the nation's if it would follow him.

KENNEDY CALLS FOR SACRIFICES IN U.S. TO HELP THE WORLD MEET CHALLENGES OF 'NEW FRONTIER'

LOS ANGELES, July 15—Senator John F. Kennedy formally opened his Democratic Presidential campaign tonight with a warning that the national road to "a New Frontier" called for more sacrifices, not more luxuries.

He slashed at his probable Republican Presidential rival, Vice President Nixon, as he joined with his surprise Vice-Presidential running mate, Senator Lyndon B. Johnson of Texas, in formally accepting nomination at the final session of the Democratic National Convention.

The 43-year-old Massachusetts Senator said that world and domestic challenges required new, positive answers to the unknown problems ahead. It is essential, he said, for Democrats to move beyond the New Deal and Fair Deal concepts.

Later, as Kennedy rested at Hyannis Port, the Republicans moved into the convention spotlight. They gathered in Chicago for formal ratification of a decision that had been made many months before: the choice of Nixon as their 1960 Presidential candidate.

Governor Rockefeller of New York had started to contest the nomination the previous October, withdrawn in December, then resumed making noises like a candidate in May. All Rockefeller finally did, however, was to wedge some of his views into the party platform. Nixon was nominated; he chose his running mate and the Republican campaign was on:

NIXON IS GIVEN NOMINATION BY ACCLAMATION AFTER GOLDWATER GETS 10 LOUISIANA VOTES; CANDIDATE PICKS LODGE FOR SECOND PLACE

But the direct Kennedy-Nixon contest was still a month or more away. For Congress, controlled by the Democrats, had merely recessed for July so that members could attend the conventions. The Democratic strategy, originally developed to serve Johnson as a nominee, was that the August Congress would write a legislative record on which the party candidate could run. Now Kennedy and his running mate, adapting that plan hopefully to their joint advantage, called on Congress for certain minimum achievements before all-out politicking became the order of the day.

Nixon took advantage of a brief lull before the session for a fast swing through Nevada, California, Hawaii and Washington, beginning to redeem his pledge to campaign in every state. He was back in the capital to preside over the Senate—and the two Democratic candidates—when Congress reconvened.

During the session both candidates made flying political trips to nearby states. In theory, these were confined to weekends, when Congress was not sitting; in practice, they were not always. Generally, these appearances were inconclusive, part of a campaign that had started and yet hadn't.

Mrs. Kennedy poses with Caroline

Most unsatisfactory of all for the Kennedy ticket was the Congressional session itself. James Reston wrote:

Washington
Democratic Plans Backfire in Senate

WASHINGTON, Aug. 16—The Democrats are far from happy about the current phase of the campaign.

Their Presidential nominee, Senator John F. Kennedy, has not only fallen behind Vice President Nixon in the first nationwide poll since the conventions—44 per cent to 50 for Nixon, with 6 per cent undecided—but has lost his voice.

Their plans for the recessed session of the Congress have run into strong opposition, not only from President Eisenhower and the Republican opposition but also from the conservative Southern Democrats.

The international situation is getting worse in both Africa and Latin America, and every crisis overseas is generally believed here to help Mr. Nixon.

Republicans continually embarrassed Kennedy and Johnson by pressing for Senate action on civil rights, a move that would have instantly paralyzed the session with a Southern filibuster. It became increasingly clear that the Democratic candidates would fail to reach four of their major legislative goals: a housing bill, a higher minimum wage, medical care for the aged and Federal aid for education.

Growing increasingly restive, Kennedy shook himself loose of his Capitol Hill duties more frequently. One weekend he flew to Missouri to accept the support of former President Truman, then on to a major farm speech in Iowa. The next week he visited Detroit for a veterans' convention. Pressing constantly on Kennedy was the growing success of his opponent's early forays into the South. In mid-August, Nixon received a warm welcome in North Carolina, despite the firm civil rights stand he took. Even more disturbing to the Democrats, in the light of the loosening grip on the South, was Nixon's late August visit to Alabama and Georgia.

200,000 WELCOME NIXON IN ATLANTA

ATLANTA, Aug. 26—Vice President Nixon was almost mobbed by well-wishers in this deep South capital today.

The enormous turnout—estimated by the police at more than 200,000 in the streets, of a population of 980,000—followed a similarly enthusiastic reception for the Republican Presidential candidate in Birmingham, Ala.

In Birmingham and later in Atlanta, the Vice President laid down this challenge to the Deep South's normally Democratic traditions:

"It is time for the Democratic candidates to quit taking the South for granted. And it is time for the Republican candidates to quit conceding the South to the Democrats."

Three days later Nixon was hospitalized with a recurrent knee injury and was immobilized for nearly two weeks. But not Kennedy. Realizing how little Congress was helping his cause, he left Washington and went campaigning in Boston, New Hampshire and Maine.

As the session in Washington fumbled to a close, Kennedy tried to salvage something by promising to push, as President, the Democratic civil rights pledges ignored in the Capitol during August. On his way to Alaska after adjournment, he opened the real campaign by trying to shift the blame for Congressional inaction onto the Republicans:

SAN FRANCISCO, Sept. 3—Senator John F. Kennedy appealed to voters today to remove the threat of Republican Presidential vetoes that he said had blocked legislation for higher minimum wages, medical care for the aged, housing and school aid.

The Democratic Presidential nominee carried his campaign to California, with its 32 electoral votes, and in midafternoon left for Alaska, the 49th state, which will cast three electoral votes for the first time in this year's election.

Fresh from the reconvened post-convention Congressional session, Senator Kennedy spoke at a rally at the International Airport here. He laid the blame for the defeat of the legislative programs he sponsored to President Eisenhower's repeated threats to veto bills of which he did not approve.

Then the big push was on. To a Democratic fund-raising dinner in Anchorage, to a Labor Day speech in Detroit, to a hedge-hopping tour of Idaho, Washington and Oregon, to an old-fashioned whistle-stop train ride down through California. Over a weekend of rest in California, Kennedy and his aides worked on what was to be one of his most important appearances of the campaign the following Monday in Texas. For the religious issue, he found already, had not been buried with the West Virginia primary. The Times reported:

KENNEDY ASSURES TEXAS MINISTERS OF INDEPENDENCE

HOUSTON, Tex., Sept. 12—Senator John F. Kennedy told Protestant ministers here tonight that he would resign as President if he could not make every decision in the national interest "without regard to outside religious pressures or dictates."

Senator Kennedy's address, before the Greater Houston Ministerial Association, was televised throughout Texas.

It constituted an affirmation of his belief in the separation of church and state. It was also his answer to critics who have sought to mobilize anti-Catholic sentiment against him by contending he would not resist church pressure on major issues.

"I do not speak for my church on public matters," Senator Kennedy declared, "and the church does not speak for me."

In Houston, Kennedy also answered Protestant ministers elsewhere who had questioned his freedom from Catholic domination in time of crisis. His speech and question period, recorded as they were televised, were shown repeatedly all over the country for the rest of the campaign. Some felt they were one of his most important defensive weapons.

Nixon, meanwhile, was out of the hospital and off to a flying start. As he moved, Nixon developed his campaign themes: the nation needed the candidate best qualified in foreign affairs, the nation was strong and solvent after eight years of Republican rule and its voters should reject criticism of their country and ignore party lines in favor of experience.

Kennedy through mid-September was swinging through the East: New York City, New Jersey, Pennsylvania, Maryland, into North Carolina. Everywhere he told the cheering crowds: "The Republicans say that we've never had it so good. I say we can do better."

As the first month of the campaign drew to a close, the major themes began to emerge. Kennedy argued that the national defense and the national economy must be strengthened; Nixon replied that this was "selling America short" and "national self-disparagement." Nixon stressed his experience in foreign affairs; Kennedy replied that the Republicans, inept in crisis, had allowed Cuba to become "a Communist satellite 90 miles off our shores." Curiously, Kennedy the intellectual seemed to be arousing more emotional reaction with his personal presence than with the logic of his speeches, while Nixon, who had relied in the past on summoning pride and fear and hate, was now trying to impress the voters with carefully reasoned arguments.

Even before the first of the television debates, the emerging public interest in Kennedy as a dynamic national figure was beginning to show. The Times reported:

CLEVELAND, Sept. 25—Senator John F. Kennedy received one of the most tumultuous ovations of his campaign today as he motored through 12 miles of Cleveland streets to a Democratic rally on the Lake Erie waterfront.

Thousands upon thousands of persons lined the streets of heavily Democratic Slovene, Italian, Slovak and Negro districts. Those in the vast throng at Euclid Beach Park trampled and crushed one another for a glimpse of the Democratic Presidential candidate.

The Cleveland turnout was probably the greatest Mr. Kennedy has yet had anywhere.

In many ways, it was reminiscent of the huge public receptions that greeted President Eisenhower throughout the 1956 campaign.

As usual, official estimates of the turnout bordered on the incredible. The Cleveland police were estimating the street crowds at more than 200,000 and the throng at the park at 120,000.

While the debates (see page 132) increased public recognition of Kennedy enormously, they seemed to give the better-known Nixon a similar boost. His crowds continued to grow remarkably—in Memphis, Charleston, West Virginia and Boston. As they did, Nixon gradually became sharper, more personal and more partisan. As October opened, Nixon plunged on through the hustings. In the South he stressed congenial themes: states rights, local autonomy in education and government economy. In the sub-urban consumer belt of New Jersey he launched one of his strongest attacks:

NIXON SAYS FOOD WILL GO UP 25% IF KENNEDY WINS

This sort of charge spurred Kennedy to the offensive, and he warned the unemployed of depression; he shackled the Republican Administration with responsibility for Fidel Castro; and he intensified his claim that the nation had declined in power and prestige during the previous eight years.

Suddenly, in the curious way of national campaigns, the voters were made aware of two tiny obscure islands off the China coast, Quemoy and Matsu. The issue: If the Chinese Communists attacked, should the United States defend these islands as it had promised to do for Nationalist Formosa? Kennedy said the islands were militarily indefensible and strategically unimportant. Nixon said such a position was an open invitation to Communist attack. The Democrat responded in a New York City speech with his strongest accusation to date:

KENNEDY CHARGES NIXON RISKS WAR

Senator John F. Kennedy charged here last night that Vice President Nixon "invites war" by an all-out commitment to defend the Chinese offshore islands of Quemoy and Matsu. He implied that Mr. Nixon would be "a trigger-happy President."

For himself, the Democratic candidate for President said, he would make one pledge to the American people above all others:

"Should I become your President, I will take whatever steps are necessary to defend our security and to maintain the cause of world freedom—but I will not risk American lives and a nuclear war by permitting any other nation to drag us into the wrong war at the wrong place at the wrong time through an unwise commitment that is unsound militarily, unnecessary to our security and unsupported by our allies."

Like many such political arguments, the issue was never settled. Kennedy insisted Nixon later retreated to his own position. Nixon said he hadn't and that Kennedy stood for "surrender" of these small pieces of the free world.

One of the most ironic exchanges of the campaign, viewed with the wisdom of hindsight, took place on the issue of encouraging an invasion of Cuba by anti-Castro exiles. Kennedy, who was to be casti-gated six months later for failure to support such a move sufficiently, called for United States aid to those who would liberate Cuba. Nixon, whose Administration was even then helping plan such an inva-sion, called this "the most shockingly reckless proposal ever made in our history by a Presidential candidate."

On the campaign trail: the strain was beginning to tell.

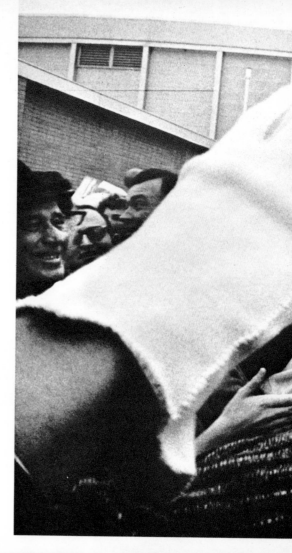

Kennedy in the Middle West: wherever he went,
hands reached out to greet him and touch him.

Kennedy addressing Connecticut voters before the
Grecian columns of the Hartford Times building.

From Anchorage to the Appalachians, women of all ages responded to the candidate's appeal.

125

Late in October, as the candidates rolled on across the land, The Times took a survey of their chances in the 50 states:

> Two weeks before the Presidential election, reports from all sections of the country indicate that Senator John F. Kennedy has made substantial gains since his nomination at the Democratic convention in Los Angeles.
>
> As yet these gains do not appear enough to assure his election. At the same time they appear to be sufficient to have wiped out the margin credited to Vice President Nixon following his nomination at the Republican convention in Chicago.

The survey showed states with 237 electoral votes going to or leaning toward Kennedy, compared to 155 electoral votes for Nixon. Not included were a number of doubtful key states, including California and Pennsylvania.

One factor in Kennedy's rise since the convention had certainly been his development as a speaker, a public personality and something of a folk hero. Two weeks before the election, Russell Baker wrote:

> The fact is that in the last month he has flowered into a magnificent campaigner with a Pied Piper magic over the street crowds, and especially the ladies, and with a considerable talent for what is ungraciously called rabble-rousing.

Sometimes it is hard to judge in the heat of a fast-moving political campaign the importance of a seemingly modest story. Such a story appeared on October 27 on page 22 of The Times, buried at the end of a 600-word dispatch from Decatur, Ga. It read:

> WASHINGTON, Oct. 26—Senator John F. Kennedy telephoned Mrs. [Martin Luther] King in Atlanta this morning to express concern over the jailing of her husband.
>
> "Senator Kennedy said he was very much concerned about both of us," Mrs. King said. "He said this must be hard on me. He wanted me to know he was thinking about us, and he would do all he could to help. I told him I appreciated it and hoped he would help," she said.
>
> In Atlanta, it was reported that Republican headquarters had asked for some kind of a statement on the King case from Vice President Nixon or from Republican campaign officials. An aide said the Vice President would have no comment.

That was all, three obscure paragraphs, but the episode had critical importance. Word of Kennedy's gesture spread rapidly through the Negro community, assisted by 2,000,000 copies of a pamphlet describing the incident that were distributed outside Negro churches the Sunday before election.

As October closed, Nixon stepped up his promises and his attacks. He met Lodge in Cincinnati for his own first campaign speech on national television. The Vice President promised, if elected, to visit the Communist satellite nations of Eastern Europe, a strong bid for votes from these nationality groups. President Eisenhower, largely ignored until now, was enlisted for a last-minute round of television speeches and rally appearances, in which he tried to counter Kennedy's charges of national decline. And bitter language began to creep in, as Nixon accused his opponent of telling "lies" about his country.

While continuing his serious themes, Kennedy was becoming more and more adept at poking fun at Nixon. He pictured the Republican as a man whose convictions changed like trends in fashion. He called him the latest in a string of Republican performing elephants that included McKinley, Taft, Harding, Coolidge and Landon. It was relaxed joking, and his crowds loved it.

A week before the election came one of those rare moments in politics, the unveiling of an idea that outlived the rash rhetoric of the campaign to take permanent, valuable shape:

KENNEDY FAVORS U.S. 'PEACE CORPS' TO WORK ABROAD

> SAN FRANCISCO, Nov. 2—Senator John F. Kennedy detailed today a proposal to create a "peace corps" of young men who would serve with technical aid missions abroad as an alternative to the military draft.

Mr. Kennedy's proposal for a "peace corps" suggested that young men of ability serve abroad for three years.

They would be qualified by rigorous examinations and trained in language, special skills and customs needed for the countries in which they would serve.

Coming down the homestretch, Kennedy talked of Nixon's inability to deal with foreign crises and of the overriding issue of peace. He swung back again to the key states of the East, to New York, New Jersey and the New England states, and his confidence rose with the remarkable crowds. While there were thousands at almost every stop, a memorable high point was Waterbury, Connecticut, at 3 o'clock on the Sunday morning before election; there were some 25,000 jamming the village green, blanketing its monuments, waiting hours for the candidate and refusing to let him go to bed.

Over the closing weekend, Nixon predicted that Kennedy as President would be a "captive" of the labor leaders. He called Democratic economic proposals "poison" for the nation. He foresaw Democratic spending producing "Kennedy inflation followed by a Kennedy depression." In a final flourish, he once more invoked Eisenhower:

LOS ANGELES, Nov. 6—Vice President Nixon said tonight that if elected President he would propose sending President Eisenhower on a mission to Eastern European countries. He said he would invite the Communist leaders of those nations to visit the United States.

The Republican Presidential nominee also suggested that former Presidents Truman and Hoover, if willing, could accompany President Eisenhower behind the Iron Curtain.

On the day before election, a final New York Times survey gave Kennedy a "substantial lead" but warned that 15 states remained so much in doubt that they could swing the result to Nixon if most of them shifted in that direction.

For Kennedy, the last day was a homecoming. He swept through all six New England states and wound up, of course, in Boston:

BOSTON, Nov. 7—Hundreds of thousands of Bostonians gave Senator John F. Kennedy an ear-splitting welcome tonight as he returned from a tour of New England and wound up his campaign.

The narrow streets of downtown Boston were solid with Kennedy fans. It took his motorcade 90 minutes to crawl two miles from his hotel to the Boston Garden, where a shrieking, jam-packed audience of 20,000 had been waiting for hours.

For 10 minutes the crowd at the Garden stood and screamed its adulation. Vast crowds blocked the streets outside.

Even after the Boston rally, Senator Kennedy continued his quest for votes. He appeared for the second time tonight on a nation-wide telecast.

And then it was done. The speeches, the handshakes, the autographs, the debates, the missed meals, the midnight plane flights, the plotting, the praying—all of it was done now. Kennedy drove to the last of a hundred indistinguishable campaign hotel suites—this one in the Boston Statler—and went to bed. Tomorrow would decide it, and tomorrow would only come at its own pace.

OVERLEAF: Speaking in Iowa before a hostile audience of farmers and conservatives, Kennedy for the first time shows a tinge of anger.

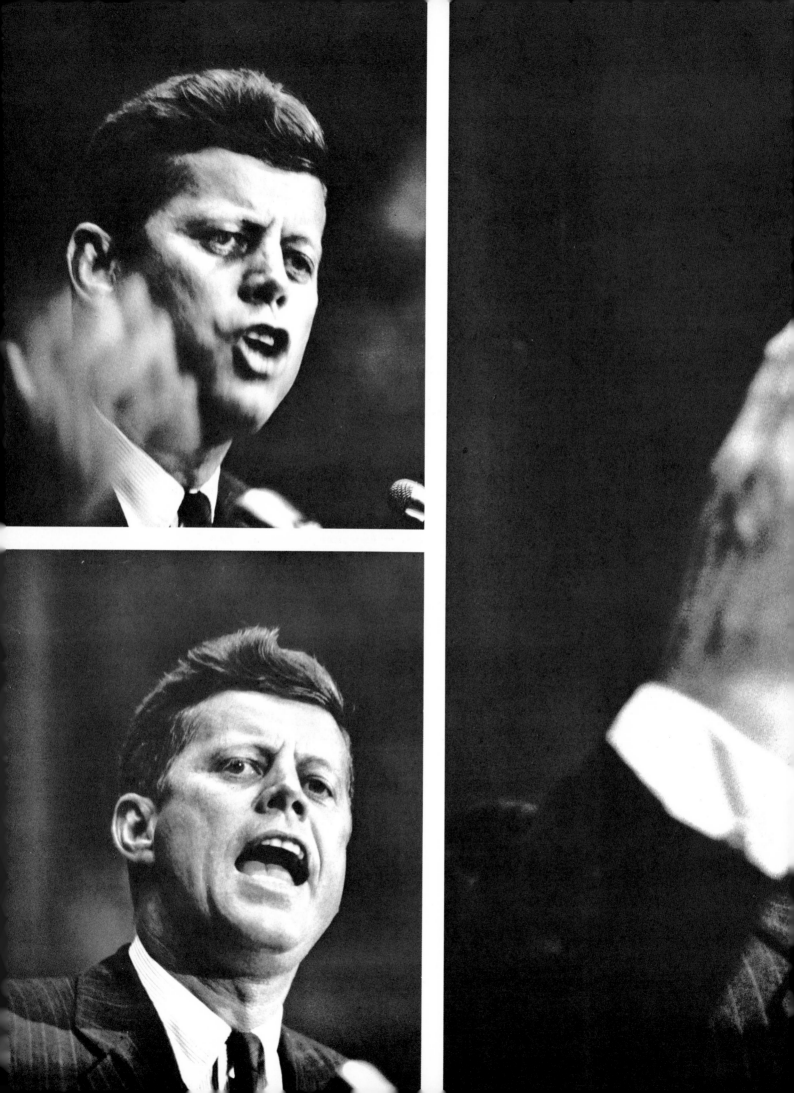

THE DEBATES

For many, the highlight of the 1960 campaign was the series of four television debates between Kennedy and Nixon. Television had been used before by candidates for the Presidency in 1952 and 1956, but always for separate appearances by one party's nominee or the other. An American tradition 100 years before, the political debate had fallen into disuse. Its revival, curiously, was brought about not by the politicians, the candidates or the voters but by the radio and television industry. The industry offered choice evening television time free to the two major party candidates if they would agree to discuss the issues face to face.

Kennedy, the underdog and challenger, wasted no time in agreeing. On the same July day that Nixon officially accepted the Republican nomination at the Chicago convention, the Democratic Senator made his announcement in New York, reported by The Times as follows:

KENNEDY ACCEPTS
NIXON TV DEBATE

A series of television debates this fall between the Republican and Democratic candidates for President became a likelihood last evening.

In Hyannis Port, Mass., Senator John F. Kennedy accepted an invitation by the National Broadcasting Company to appear on eight one-hour evening programs with his opponent.

In Chicago, Herbert G. Klein, Vice President Nixon's press secretary, said Mr. Nixon was "willing to debate a rival candidate, including Senator Kennedy, if this is the desire of the networks and the public."

Then came nearly two months of negotiations between representatives of the two candidates and the three major networks, laying out ground rules, dates, times and formats for the debates. Also, Congress had to suspend the law that would have required giving equal television time to the dozen minority party candidates for President. Finally, agreement was reached on four debates spaced between late September and late October. And on Monday, September 26, while some 70,000,000 Americans watched and listened, Kennedy and Nixon, flanking a moderator and facing four television reporters, went on the air live for an hour.

Despite a tremendous build-up of publicity before the encounter, there were no real fireworks. The sharpest moment came when Nixon charged that Kennedy's domestic program, if put into effect, would raise taxes more than $13,000,000,000. Kennedy called this "wholly untrue" and said that the expanding economy he advocated would provide most of the money. Other talk ranged politely over agriculture, inflation, Kennedy's youth, medical care and school construction. The Times reported:

PRECEDING PAGES: A wildly cheering throng greets the candidate's motorcade in the town of Pekin, Illinois.

NIXON AND KENNEDY CLASH
IN TV DEBATE ON SPENDING,
FARMS AND SOCIAL ISSUES

CHICAGO, Sept. 26—Vice President Nixon and Senator John F. Kennedy argued genteelly tonight in history's first nationally televised debate between Presidential candidates.

The two men, confronting each other in a Chicago television studio, centered their argument on which candidate and which party offered the nation the best means for spurring United States growth in an era of international peril.

The first debate paid a rapid and significant dividend for Kennedy. The following day, 10 Southern Governors telegraphed him their enthusiastic support. Lukewarm to the Bostonian's cause before, they had been won over by his television performance. Among the voters, however, the reaction was generally mixed. There seemed to be no clear winner in the public eye, although many Americans already familiar with Nixon had been able to take a long and interested look at Kennedy. Nixon, who had been a champion high school debater, spoke as if he were going to be judged as a debater; Kennedy spoke directly to the television audience. The Times television critic, Jack Gould, hailed the experiment:

Last night's discussion between Vice President Nixon and Senator John F. Kennedy was a dignified and constructive innovation in television campaigning. Undoubtedly it helped to quicken public interest in the Presidential contest.

The presence of both candidates on the same platform had an element of drama that simply could not be matched by a single nominee in the solo delivery of a speech.

The long negotiations between the radio and TV networks and the Presidential candidates proved fruitful in the finished product. There was no free for all, and the format precluded any hint of the declaration of the winner on the air.

The most common immediate response to the first debate was that Nixon had not looked good physically. His heavy beard showed through amateur make-up, he perspired uneasily, he seemed tired and hollow-eyed, all in contrast to the unsmiling but cool and apparently nerveless Kennedy. Nixon's supporters felt that the Vice President's smiling, outgoing platform personality had somehow been masked. Some Republicans, as the time for the second debate approached, even suggested that their candidate had been the victim of some television conspiracy, designed to make him look bad literally to the voters. But Nixon said no. A Times report said:

Although three make-up experts were available, Vice President Nixon's staff made a "do-it-ourselves" project of applying powder to his face prior to his television debate with Senator John F. Kennedy last Monday in Chicago.

Mr. Nixon's image was described by some viewers as "tired" and by others as "haggard." Suggestions were made that there might have been sabotage by a Democrat posing as an impartial make-up artist.

Herbert G. Klein, the Vice President's press secretary, brushed off these suggestions yesterday. He said the Republican Presidential candidate had used only a light dusting of face powder, and that such preparations did not require the services of an expert. Several staff members did the job.

For the second debate, televised from Washington, Nixon had a make-up professional on hand, although Kennedy continued to decline such assistance. For an hour in a somewhat more informal set, the two candidates gave 2½-minute answers to questions from newspapermen, reported as follows:

NIXON AND KENNEDY CLASH ON TV
OVER ISSUE OF QUEMOY'S DEFENSE;
U-2 'REGRETS' AND RIGHTS ARGUED

WASHINGTON, Oct. 7—Vice President Nixon and Senator John F. Kennedy raised the campaign temperature tonight, clashing sharply on foreign policy and civil rights on the second of their nation-wide television debates.

OPPOSITE: Jacqueline and Bobby Kennedy watch one of the debates in a specially built screening room in ABC's New York studios. ABOVE: The candidates in the first of the televised debates, Sept. 26, 1960. Howard K. Smith (center) was moderator.

The question of who won will have to await the surveys of voters, but the equally nagging question for Republicans—of how Mr. Nixon would "project" after his unhappy appearance in the first debate—was answered immediately. The Vice President did not have the thin, emaciated appearance that worried Republicans across the nation during the first debate.

One of the high points of tonight's debate was a direct conflict between the Presidential candidates over policy for dealing with the islands of Quemoy and Matsu off the Chinese mainland.

The first debate had been limited to domestic issues. In the second, open to foreign policy discussion too, the Quemoy-Matsu problem arose. It was here that Nixon first maintained these islands should be defended at any cost, while Kennedy called them practically indefensible and of little value as bases. There was also a sharp exchange over civil rights. Kennedy attacked the Eisenhower Administration's record on rolling back racial segregation, particularly in the public schools. Nixon charged that Kennedy's running mate, Johnson, was really opposed to the civil rights cause. Besides looking more like himself, Nixon was more aggressive in the Washington debate than he had been in Chicago. Kennedy continued to be serious, unsmiling and fast-talking. Mutual accusations of inaccuracy and exaggeration seemed a little more harsh, but still under restraint.

Six days later the two candidates were back at it again. This time the campaign had taken them to different cities—the Democrat to New York and the Republican to Hollywood—and a split-screen television technique was used to present them simultaneously for reporters' questions:

NIXON AND KENNEDY RENEW FIGHT OVER QUEMOY IN HEATED DEBATE; ALSO CLASH ON LABOR PROGRAMS

Senator John F. Kennedy and Vice President Nixon bitterly accused each other before a national television audience last night of advocating policies on Quemoy and Matsu that would lead to war.

While the rhetorical temperature of the third debate was torrid, the actual policy difference between the two Presidential candidates appeared to have narrowed considerably. Mr. Nixon pulled back from the strong position he took last week.

Distance and the mounting pace and pressure of the campaign had produced the most cutting debate thus far. If Nixon appeared to retreat on the Quemoy-Matsu issue, he stung Kennedy with a charge that the Senator favored compulsory arbitration on labor-management disputes. Flung back and forth across the continent electronically were accusations that one candidate was misrepresenting the other's views, along with a flat charge of untruth. When the air of the third debate had cleared, political observers were increasingly impressed with Kennedy's command of facts and his ability to push Nixon into generalization. James Reston observed:

WASHINGTON, Oct. 13—Senator John F. Kennedy is gradually switching roles with Vice President Nixon in these TV debates.

He started out, like the Pittsburgh Pirates, as the underdog who wasn't supposed to be able to stay the course with the champ, but is winding up as the character who has more specific information on the tip of his tongue than Mr. Nixon.

The third game of the political world series tonight did more to illustrate the difference in the approach and appeal of the two candidates than either of the others.

Mr. Nixon's presentation was general and often emotional; Mr. Kennedy's curt and factual. Mr. Nixon, whose campaign is based on his reputation for knowledge of the facts and experience, was outpointed on facts.

In the week left before the final debate, Republican leaders accused Kennedy of having "cribbed" in the third telecast by relying on written notes. Nixon professed to be "shocked." Kennedy said he had merely brought along a paper so he could quote Eisenhower accurately.

The Democratic candidate now began to press more pointedly for a fifth television meeting, one that would be still closer to Election Day. His advisers believed that the debates were steadily strengthening Kennedy's campaign position, and they wanted more such nationwide exposure. No agreement had been reached when the fourth confrontation took place in New York on October 21, reported as follows:

NIXON AND KENNEDY DEBATE CUBA; ALSO CLASH OVER QUEMOY ISSUE, ATOM TESTING AND U.S. PRESTIGE

Vice President Nixon and Senator John F. Kennedy clashed before a national television audience last night over United States policy toward Cuba and the Chinese off-shore islands of Quemoy and Matsu.

In one of the sharpest exchanges of their fourth debate, which seemed comparatively tepid after the last two meetings, Mr. Nixon called Senator Kennedy's proposals for dealing with Premier Fidel Castro's regime in Cuba "probably the most dangerously irresponsible that he's made in the course of this campaign."

Aside from the clash over Castro Cuba, the fourth debate was mild. Nixon wanted to resume nuclear testing; Kennedy was for "one last effort" at a test ban treaty. They differed, as of old, on the decline in American prestige and the value of a summit parley, but new controversies did not develop.

For the next week, Kennedy continued to push Nixon toward an extra television debate, taunting the Vice President for his apparent reluctance to continue. Nixon accepted conditionally, and negotiations between their television advisers resumed. But the Kennedy needle became sharper and the Nixon reaction angrier with the election only a week away. Finally this story appeared:

G.O.P. BREAKS OFF ALL NEGOTIATIONS FOR A 5th DEBATE

WASHINGTON, Oct. 29—The Republicans broke off negotiations today for a fifth nationwide television debate between Vice President Nixon and Senator John F. Kennedy.

Fred C. Scribner Jr., Under Secretary of the Treasury and Mr. Nixon's debate negotiator, halted the talks in a 400-word telegram to J. Leonard Reinsch, his Democratic counterpart. He said they could not be resumed unless Senator Kennedy apologized for charges of "bad faith" against Mr. Nixon.

A few hours later, Senator Kennedy, campaigning in Philadelphia's suburbs, replied that since Vice President Nixon would not choose to debate, "I am not going to drag him up in front of the microphone."

On this note of derisive challenge ended the first great experiment in television debating between Presidential candidates. In terms of audience, it had succeeded beyond the industry's wildest dreams. One estimate held that 120,000,000 people had seen at least one of the four debates. Never before, surely, in the other 43 Presidential campaigns had so many Americans seen and heard the two men between whom they had to choose and heard their views.

That the debates influenced the outcome of the election seems inescapable. Several public opinion polls indicated at the time that a majority of the voters felt that Kennedy had "beaten" Nixon in their joint appearances. Later another poll showed that nearly 75 per cent of those voters who had made up their minds on the basis of the debates had supported Kennedy.

OVERLEAF: The debates over, the way to victory seemed open to Kennedy and running mate Lyndon Johnson, shown here with Hubert Humphrey (far left) and Iowa Governor Herschel C. Loveless (second from left) in a crowd of supporters.

ELECTION

At 8:43 on the morning of Nov. 8, 1960, John F. Kennedy of 122 Bowdoin Street, Boston, cast his vote, one of 68,838,979 who voted before the day was out. Then John F. Kennedy, Democratic candidate for President, flew to his summer home in Hyannis Port. There was nothing more he could do.

Under the bright sun in the family compound at Hyannis Port, he played with Caroline, tossed a football with Bobby and Teddy, lunched alone with his wife and, at 3:30, tried to take a nap. He was out of bed by 5, tensely awaiting the returns, which could not come in for hours. The first fragments filtered in at 6:25. At 7:15, C.B.S., using early returns and a computer technique, flashed a prediction: Nixon would win. There was momentary gloom, but Kennedy knew that it was too early to tell. He bounced Caroline on his knee and said good night to her; he had a drink with his wife and a friend, William Walton; they had dinner; Ted Sorensen joined them later and together they watched television. The networks were now predicting Kennedy's victory.

As the votes poured in, the Kennedy popular and electoral total mounted. By midnight, in newspaper offices around the country, it seemed to be a sure Kennedy victory. But in the Kennedy compound there was an uneasy feeling. Three key states—Minnesota with 11 electoral votes, Illinois with 27 and California with 32—were close. The Kennedy electoral total mounted to 258 of the 269 he needed to win. It was clear that Nixon could not win the election, but there was a chance, because of unpledged elector slates in some Southern states, that the election could be thrown into the House of Representatives.

In the early hours of the morning, The Times said:

KENNEDY APPARENT WINNER; LEAD CUT IN TWO KEY STATES; DEMOCRATS RETAIN CONGRESS

As the night started to turn into day, Nixon appeared before his supporters in Los Angeles and on television. "If the present trend continues," he said, "Senator Kennedy is going to be the next President of the United States." But he did not concede the election. "Why should he concede?" Kennedy said to his disappointed staff. "I wouldn't." He went to bed at 4 A.M., with the results still unclear.

He didn't sleep very long that morning. He got up fairly early, had his breakfast, gave a piggy-back ride to Caroline and walked to Bobby's cottage. He noticed that during the night a squad of 16 Secret Service men had unobtrusively taken up positions in the area. In his election headquarters, he heard the news that Minnesota had definitely gone Democratic—and with that the suspense was over. Kennedy was elected.

The first thing the President-elect did was to go out by himself to find his wife, who had been walking alone on the beach. They came back for a family picture in the living room of his father's house, and then the entire family made a triumphal trip to the Hyannis armory, where the press was waiting. The Times reported as follows:

> HYANNIS PORT, Mass., Nov. 9—Senator John F. Kennedy accepted in a solemn mood his election as President today.
> He pledged all his energy to advancing "the long-range interests of the United States and the cause of freedom around the world."
> He made his pledge inside the flag-decked Hyannis armory at 1:45 P.M., an hour after Vice President Nixon, his Republican opponent, had conceded defeat.

Election Day evening: the Kennedys waiting for news at Hyannis Port. TOP LEFT: Eunice Shriver (left) and Pat Lawford. BOTTOM LEFT: Teddy and Bobby. RIGHT: Joan.

BELOW: Early next morning: Mrs. Rose Kennedy with son-in-law Peter Lawford.

CENTER: Watching the television returns in Bobby's living room at 11 A.M., the outcome still in doubt. (From left) William Walton, Pierre Salinger, a friend, Ethel and Bobby, the Senator, Bobby's secretary Angie Novello and William Haddad.

FAR RIGHT: Bobby and Teddy working off tension tossing a football outdoors.

142

OPPOSITE: Jubilant smiles as the Minnesota vote puts Kennedy over the top, and Nixon concedes.

RIGHT: Caroline greeted her father that day with "Good morning, Mr. President."

OVERLEAF: The entire family assembled in the elder Kennedys' house for a picture: (from left) back row, Ethel, Steve Smith, Jean, the President-elect, Bobby, Pat, Sargent Shriver, Joan, Peter Lawford; front row, Eunice, Mrs. Rose Kennedy, Joseph P. Kennedy, Jacqueline, Teddy.

Kennedy ended his serious statement at the Hyannis armory with a grin and this announcement: "So now my wife and I prepare for a new administration and a new baby."

The electoral vote as he spoke was 300 for Kennedy and 185 for Nixon; the final figures were to be 303 for Kennedy, 219 for Nixon, with 15 for Senator Harry F. Byrd of Virginia. The headlines said:

KENNEDY'S VICTORY WON BY CLOSE MARGIN; HE PROMISES FIGHT FOR WORLD FREEDOM; EISENHOWER OFFERS 'ORDERLY TRANSITION'

145

INAUGURATION

The eight-inch snowstorm of the night before had stopped. The winds were bitter, the temperature was sub-freezing—22 degrees. But the sun was out, looking down from a cloudless sky. This was the scene before the newly renovated East Front of the Capitol as President-elect Kennedy arrived on January 20, 1961, to be sworn in as the nation's 35th President. He appeared on the inaugural platform at 12:15 P.M., top hat in hand, and chatted with outgoing President Eisenhower, seated beside him. At 12:21, the ceremonies opened.

Thirty minutes later, after prayers, a poem, and the swearing-in of Vice President Johnson, Kennedy stood up and slipped off his coat. With one hand on the family Bible, he repeated after Earl Warren, the Chief Justice of the United States, the brief 35-word constitutional oath of office. In less than one minute, John F. Kennedy had become President of the United States.

He shook hands with the Chief Justice, then turned and took the hand of Richard Nixon, the man who had come so close himself to taking the Presidential oath that day. Then, without hat or coat, before the gathering on Capitol Hill and the millions watching on television, Kennedy began his inaugural address. He spoke slowly, with an occasional chop of his right hand for emphasis, saying, in part:

"Let the word go forth from this time and place, to friend and foe alike, that the torch has passed to a new generation of Americans, tempered by war, disciplined by a hard and bitter peace, proud of our ancient heritage, and unwilling to witness or permit the slow undoing of those human rights to which this nation has always been committed, and to which we are committed today at home and around the world. . . .

"Let us never negotiate out of fear, but let us never fear to negotiate."

It was a relatively short speech—at 1,355 words, the shortest since Franklin D. Roosevelt delivered his fourth inaugural address of just 559 words. The Times reported the story the next morning:

KENNEDY SWORN IN, ASKS 'GLOBAL ALLIANCE' AGAINST TYRANNY, WANT, DISEASE AND WAR; REPUBLICANS AND DIPLOMATS HAIL ADDRESS

WASHINGTON, Jan. 20—John Fitzgerald Kennedy assumed the Presidency today with a call for "a grand alliance" to combat tyranny, poverty, disease and war.

In his inaugural address, he served notice on the world that the United States was ready to "pay any price, bear any burden, meet any hardship, support any friend, oppose any foe to assure the survival and the success of liberty."

But the nation is also ready, he said, to resume negotiations with the Soviet Union to ease and, if possible, remove world tensions.

He also said, "In your hands, my fellow citizens, more than in mine, will rest the final success or failure of our course." Then in a passage that was to become more closely identified with him and his Administration than any sentence in any other speech he was to make as President:

"And so, my fellow Americans: ask not what your country can do for you—ask what you can do for your country."

Kennedy had worked hard on the speech. Part of it was sketched on a yellow pad three days before

Nov. 9, 1960, at the Hyannis armory: "So now my wife and I prepare for a new administration and a new baby."

The President-elect and Mrs. Kennedy (left) arriving at the inaugural gala, Jan. 19, 1961, held in Washington's National Guard Armory.

Frank Sinatra (below, center, with stars) produced the program; Juliet Prowse (above) danced; Leonard Bernstein (right) conducted.

on his flight north after a brief vacation at Palm Beach. Revisions were made up to the last minute. When he awoke in his Georgetown home that inaugural morning, he called for the final copy for still another reading. Mrs. Evelyn Lincoln, his personal secretary, who had been unable to get home the night before because of the snowstorm, brought it to him.

The President had had very little sleep. The day before the inauguration had been a long one. He had met with Eisenhower at the White House, then worked for a while at the home of family friend William Walton, and, with his wife, fought his way through falling snow to the inaugural concert at Constitution Hall and an inaugural gala at the National Guard Armory, produced by Frank Sinatra. Traffic was almost at a standstill that snowy night. Half the symphony orchestra missed the beginning of the concert. The gala began two hours late.

Mrs. Kennedy, radiant in a white gown, left the Sinatra show at the Armory early, but the President stayed until it ended at 2 A.M. Then he went to a Washington restaurant where his father was giving a party. Not until 4 A.M. did President-elect Kennedy get to sleep that morning of his inauguration. He awoke at 8 o'clock.

The Times reported his early activities on inaugural morning:

> Breakfast was Mr. Kennedy's usual menu—a large orange juice, two poached eggs, three strips of crisp bacon, coffee with cream and sugar.
> He left the house at 8:54 for church—The Holy Trinity Roman Catholic Church, just a few blocks away. A crowd of perhaps 300 on the narrow Georgetown sidewalks watched him climb into a white Lincoln Continental and drive off.
> The parish is the oldest Catholic parish in Washington—founded in 1788, when there was no Washington, only a Georgetown. Today the altar was decorated with red, white and blue carnations.

He returned home for some last moments of privacy. Then at 10:56 the bubble-top Presidential car arrived to take the President-elect and his wife to the White House. Eisenhower came out to greet Kennedy and they walked in together.

At 11:30 the two men emerged, both wearing silk top hats, and neither liking it very much. Eisenhower had chosen a Homburg for his own inaugural, and his successor had a lifelong aversion to hats of all kinds. Throughout the drive from the White House to the Capitol, Kennedy wasn't quite sure what to do with his topper. He took it off, put it on, took it off and put it on again.

They drove past a crowd that tried to keep at least a little blood circulating in the freezing weather. One man wore a surgical mask; a white-haired, 75-year-old woman wore a sleeping bag; three waiting chauffeurs gave up watching the parade and went to sleep in the front seat of the Nicaraguan Ambassador's car with the heater on.

At the Capitol Richard Cardinal Cushing of Boston had begun the invocation when he saw wisps of fine blue smoke drifting up from under the lectern in front of him. Cardinal Cushing continued his prayer as Secret Service men huddled around his knees looking for the source of the smoke. The audience wasn't sure of what was happening, but The Times reported the details:

> One guard stood by with a fire extinguisher. A technician was summoned. The trouble was finally located. There was a short circuit in a motor that powered the raising and lowering of the lectern to adjust to its user's height.
> The motor was housed behind a locked panel. It took some time to find the man with the key. But by that time, when the trouble was known, smiles were spreading through the gathering of notables. President Kennedy and ex-President Eisenhower shared in the relief and the smiles.
> With about 80,000,000 people watching on their television screens, it may have been the most widely observed mechanical failure in history.

Marian Anderson then sang "The Star-Spangled Banner" and, as Times television critic Jack Gould noticed, Kennedy was the "only man on the TV screen who seemed to know the words to the second verse." After a prayer by Archbishop Iakovos, Greek Orthodox Archbishop for North and South America, Lyndon Johnson came forward.

Limousines approaching the Capitol for the inauguration ceremony.

President Eisenhower escorts his successor to
the platform on the East Front of the Capitol.

RIGHT: Chief Justice Earl Warren administers the Oath of Office.

OVERLEAF: The inaugural party leaving the platform, as dignitaries applaud.

At the ceremony: Marian Anderson, Robert Frost, Rabbi Nelson Glueck; (below) the President's parents.

JOHNSON IS SWORN
BY FELLOW TEXAN

WASHINGTON, Jan. 20—Lyndon Baines Johnson of Texas was sworn in as Vice President at 12:41 P.M. today.

The former majority leader took the oath of office from a fellow Texan, Sam Rayburn, Speaker of the House of Representatives. It was the first time that a Speaker had administered the oath to a Vice President.

Following a prayer by the Rev. John Barclay of the Central Christian Church of Austin, Tex., Robert Frost, who had described himself as a "rather unhappy Democrat" since Grover Cleveland left the White House in 1897, rose to speak. The 86-year-old poet, who appeared at the invitation of Kennedy, had composed some new lines for the occasion, but the glaring sunlight prevented him from reading them. Instead he recited from memory an old poem of his, "The Gift Outright":

> The land was ours before we were the land's.
> She was our land more than a hundred years
> Before we were her people. She was ours
> In Massachusetts, in Virginia,
> But we were England's, still colonials,
> Possessing what we still were unpossessed by,
> Possessed by what we now no more possessed.
> Something we were withholding made us weak
> Until we found out that it was ourselves
> We were withholding from our land of living,
> And forthwith found salvation in surrender.
> Such as we were we gave ourselves outright
> (The deed of gift was many deeds of war)
> To the land vaguely realizing westward,
> But still unstoried, artless, unenhanced,
> Such as she was, such as she would become.

Kennedy then took the oath and delivered his inaugural address. Rabbi Nelson Glueck, president of the Hebrew Union College of Cincinnati, delivered the benediction. At 1:11, about a half hour behind schedule, the band again played "The Star-Spangled Banner," and again Kennedy's lips moved with the words. Then the official party walked out and the band played "Hail to the Chief" for the first time for President Kennedy.

Lunch followed in the old Supreme Court Chamber. The President ate some lobster, and at 2:15 the official party left the Capitol. In typical motherly fashion, Mrs. Rose Kennedy turned to her son and said, "I hope you won't be cold, dear."

At 3 P.M., the President walked onto the open-air reviewing stand at the north side of the White House. With the President in the front row were his mother and father, his wife, and Vice President and Mrs. Johnson. The parade began.

CAPITAL PARADERS DON OVERCOATS
TO PASS IN WHITE HOUSE REVIEW

WASHINGTON, Jan. 20—President Kennedy had warned that it wouldn't be easy on "the New Frontier" and, for 32,000 marchers in today's inauguration parade, it wasn't.

A Siberian wind knifing down Pennsylvania Avenue in the wake of last night's snowfall turned majorettes' legs blue, froze baton twirlers' fingers and drove beauty queens to flannels and overcoats.

"This," said Cathy Magda, Miss Florida from Fort Lauderdale, "is the coldest parade I can ever remember."

Under her gown, she confided, she was wearing flannel pajamas.

Venerable faces in the crowd at the inauguration ceremony. RIGHT: Speaker of the House Sam Rayburn. BELOW: Former President Harry S. Truman. OPPOSITE: Justice Felix Frankfurter.

FOLLOWING PAGES: After riding in the procession down Pennsylvania Avenue, the President watched the colors go by from the reviewing stand at the White House.

There were some 40 bands, 275 horses, 40 floats, a dog sled, 22 mules and a buffalo rider costumed like Buffalo Bill but looking, as The Times said, "like a beatnik on an avant-garde horse." The biggest hit with Kennedy seemed to be the Navy PT boat, similar to the one he commanded in World War II, that came floating down the avenue on a truckbed.

The new First Lady and her mother-in-law withdrew to the White House shortly after the parade began, but Kennedy and Johnson remained. "I'll stay if it takes all night," Kennedy said. Not until 6:15 P.M. did the last marcher go by.

But Inauguration Day was not over. The President entered the White House for the first time as the Chief Executive, not to conduct business, but to change into formal evening dress. At 8:15 he set out for a dinner party given by a friend. He returned to the White House about 9:30 and a few minutes

LEFT: Navy PT boat with crew commanded by Kennedy in World War II passes reviewing stand. ABOVE: The President and Vice President enjoying the parade. BELOW: William Walton, with Dean Rusk at right.

before 10 P.M. emerged with Mrs. Kennedy on his arm. The Presidential caravan, Secret Service cars close behind, began a round of visits to the five inaugural balls. Mrs. Kennedy lasted through the first three, but at 1 A.M. decided to return home. The President went on to the others and at one point remarked, "I don't know a better way to spend an evening—you looking at us and we looking back at you."

At 2 A.M. the day seemed ended. But instead, the President's limousine pulled up before the George-town home of Joseph Alsop, the newspaper columnist and an old friend. The President walked up the steps alone, knocked on the door, and waited more than a minute before someone let him in.

At 3:30 A.M. the President returned to the White House. The parties were over. The work was to begin.

The President in his top hat.

OVERLEAF: At the inaugural ball at the Armory.

Jan. 20, 1961: The President enters the White House for the first time as Chief Executive. He has called a staff meeting for nine the next morning.

THE PRESIDENT

$\mathbf{T}$he first official business of the new Administration was conducted in the old Supreme Court chamber in the Capitol immediately following the inaugural ceremony. Amid the red and white carnations, the white snapdragons and the light purple iris that decorated the room for the inaugural lunch, the President signed the formal nomination of his Cabinet. "To the Senate of the United States—I nominate," it began, continuing with a list of the men he had so carefully selected during those 10 weeks between election and inauguration.

The 10-week period in which he chose the men who were to help him run the new Administration and laid the groundwork for the policies they were all to carry out had been as hectic in many ways as the campaign itself. The President-elect's close aides met with him constantly, going down the list of potential Cabinet and sub-Cabinet appointments. Kennedy was about to assume control of 50 separate executive departments, employing more than 2,300,000 persons, and during the campaign he had talked about recruiting a "ministry of the best available talent."

The activity during the interregnum went on in a stucco villa in Palm Beach, in a penthouse of the Carlyle Hotel in New York and in Kennedy's red-brick Georgetown home in Washington. The President-elect set up task forces to make proposals on a variety of issues, from medical care to defense reorganization. He named Clark Clifford, a White House aide under President Truman, to act as his liaison on problems of transition with the outgoing Eisenhower Administration. And he maintained a daily schedule comparable to that of a President already in office.

But it was the selection of new aides that took much of his time. These appointments were being watched carefully. As a Times article noted, "since a man is usually as big as those he gathers around him, we shall soon have a measure of the new young chief executive."

The President-elect's first personnel announcements were that J. Edgar Hoover would remain as head of the Federal Bureau of Investigation and Allen Dulles as Director of the Central Intelligence Agency. As his special counsel in the White House, he named Ted Sorensen, and as his press secretary, Pierre Salinger.

Many of his announcements were made from the steps of his Georgetown home, Kennedy standing there in the frosty air, without hat or coat. The Times described one of these sessions on December 2:

> It was time for another installment in the capital's outdoor soap opera, "Jack Picks His Team." And all the usual extras, as well as a new supporting star, were there.
>
> To the right of the President-elect as he faced the street was a battery of television and newsreel cameras, their electric cables running into the Kennedy cellar.
>
> Close in, but two steps below him, was a crowd in Arctic gear that looked like the survivors of Admiral Peary's dash to the pole—the White House press corps.
>
> Across the street, standing on the curb behind a rope barrier or perched on porches and garden walls, were the Senator's neighbors, housewives dallying on the way to market, bobby-soxers with box cameras and a scattering of tourists.

On that particular day, the President appointed David E. Bell to be Director of the Bureau of the Budget. But the appointments came slowly. It was to take a month from the first Cabinet appointment to the last. The "manhunt" for talent obviously was an agonizing process. Sargent Shriver was a chief recruiter for the new Administration; so was Larry O'Brien, who was later named to handle White House liaison with Congress.

Word of the first Cabinet selection came on November 12. Governor Luther H. Hodges of North Carolina, who had played a key role in the Kennedy drive to carry the South, was picked to be Secretary of Commerce. Abe Ribicoff was appointed Secretary of Health, Education and Welfare. Stewart L. Udall, the Arizona Representative, was named Secretary of the Interior.

But the major Cabinet jobs were yet to be filled—State, Defense and Treasury. The President looked down his list of possibilities for Secretary of State—Senator J. William Fulbright of Arkansas, former Ambassador David K. E. Bruce, Adlai E. Stevenson and Dean Rusk, president of the Rockefeller Foundation, first recommended by former Secretary of State Dean Acheson and former Secretary of Defense Robert A. Lovett. The President-elect finally announced his decision:

RUSK SECRETARY OF STATE, BOWLES UNDER SECRETARY; STEVENSON TAKES U.N. JOB

PALM BEACH, Fla., Dec. 12—President-elect John F. Kennedy selected Dean Rusk as his Secretary of State today.

Simultaneously, he announced acceptance by Adlai E. Stevenson, the 1952 and 1956 Democratic Presidential nominee, of the appointment offered last week as United States Ambassador to the United Nations, with Cabinet status.

From the executive offices of Ford Motor Company, meanwhile, came the Secretary of Defense, a registered Republican with independent voting habits, Robert S. McNamara. He was the fifth named to the Cabinet. The others then came quickly. Two days after the McNamara appointment, The Times reported:

KENNEDY NAMES GOLDBERG AND FREEMAN TO CABINET; APPOINTS BROTHER TODAY

On that day, C. Douglas Dillon was appointed Secretary of the Treasury and Robert Kennedy, the President's brother, was named Attorney General. With the appointment on December 17 of J. Edward Day, a California insurance executive, as Postmaster General, the President-elect had completed his Cabinet. His appointees were all relatively young men, whose average age was 47 as against 56 for the first Eisenhower Cabinet. And it was bipartisan in the sense that it included two Republicans—McNamara and Dillon. Senate committees went to work quickly, conducting hearings on all those named to the Cabinet so that the Senate itself could confirm them quickly after inauguration.

During this 10-week period, the President also was preparing in other ways to take on the vast responsibilities of the Executive Branch. He traveled some 15,000 miles, held 18 news conferences, resigned his Senate seat and received more than a dozen reports on major problems from his task forces.

One day he whipped over to Key Biscayne, Florida, to see the man he had defeated for the Presidency, Richard Nixon. As another gesture, he went to see Herbert Hoover, a man elected President when John F. Kennedy was an 11-year-old student at Riverdale School in New York. He met with Congressional leaders. And he conferred on world problems with the outgoing President.

There was some personal business the President-elect had to take care of as well.

KENNEDY SELLS HIS STOCK TO AVOID INTEREST CONFLICT

PALM BEACH, Fla., Jan. 12—President-elect John F. Kennedy has divested himself of all his personally held stocks and bonds within the last sixty days. His action was designed to avoid any possible financial conflict of interest when he assumes the Presidency Jan. 20.

He has reinvested the funds from the stock sales in government bonds—Federal, state and municipal.

Mr. Kennedy, whose wealth is estimated in the millions of dollars, has decided that any additional moneys that accrue to him during the occupancy of the White House will also be put into government bonds, not into the purchase of other stocks or bonds.

President of the United States John F. Kennedy at his desk.

Choosing an official photograph the day after his inauguration; with him is his naval aide, Captain Tazewell Shepard.

The groundwork was thus laid for the new Administration. And the day after the inauguration, the work began.

KENNEDY'S CABINET IS SWORN IN; HE INCREASES FOOD AID TO NEEDY; KHRUSHCHEV CALLS IN U.S. ENVOY

WASHINGTON, Jan. 21—President Kennedy and his new Administration went to work today.

The President saw his Cabinet sworn in, ordered increased food distribution to the needy, conferred with his staff, made several appointments and spoke to the Democratic National Committee.

While this was going on at the White House, in Moscow Khrushchev was renewing his bid for a summit conference and expressing his hope for a "radical improvement in relations." The President replied that "we are ready to cooperate" with all those genuinely interested in world peace.

The President was confident that he now had the best team available to help him tackle the job ahead. He had raided the universities and counted a high number of college teachers in his entourage; many came from his own college, Harvard. The "eggheads," feeling neglected during the Eisenhower Administration, hurried to Washington to take up assignments all through the vast Government bureaucracy. It was a team bursting with energy, bearing out Kennedy's promises to install a "new generation of Americans" to man the ship of state. Of his 100 top appointees, some 70 were born in the 20th century.

Some Republicans criticized Dillon for taking the important Treasury post in a Democratic Administration. There was some criticism of the President's appointment of his brother Bobby to the Justice Department job. And the Republicans had other complaints:

G.O.P. SAYS KENNEDY APPOINTS 'RETREADS'

WASHINGTON, Feb. 10—The Republican National Committee said today that the Kennedy Administration had restored a "batch of Dean Acheson retreads" to power in foreign policy positions.

Brushing aside such gibes, the President started work on a series of messages for Congress. Aware that the electorate had given him something less than a sweeping mandate at the polls, he decided on a moderate approach to Congress, even though his party had a 65-35 edge in the Senate and a 262-174 majority in the House.

His first days were summed up by The Times' "News of the Week in Review" as follows:

"The deadline for everything is day before yesterday in the Kennedy Administration," said Secretary of Labor Arthur J. Goldberg.

In his first full week in the Presidency, Mr. Kennedy set a brisk pace. The mood was one of bustle and confidence. White House reporters found a sharp contrast with the Eisenhower Administration. Mr. Eisenhower, with his military background, had been devoted to the staff system and the delegation of authority. President Kennedy gave the impression of being in the thick of things and his eagerness seemed contagious. Throughout the Administration there was a sense of freshness of approach—and of realization that the search for solutions to the problems pressing in upon the Kennedy team would be long and hard.

The week underscored the fact that the foremost of those problems were the problem of the cold war and the problems of the national economy.

The major event of that first week was the President's initial news conference as Chief Executive. He decided to move the conferences from the ornate Indian Treaty Room in the Old State Department Building, where Eisenhower had held them, to the modernistic setting of a new auditorium in the State Department Building. And for the first time, a Presidential news conference was televised "live."

The President talked about Laos, announced some appointments, discussed Cuba, nuclear tests and

The President in his
office, Feb. 11, 1961.

the need to stimulate the economy. But the most startling announcement was his disclosure that Moscow had released the two survivors of the RB-47 reconnaissance plane shot down in the Arctic the previous July.

After the news conference, the President began work on his next major appearance—the delivery of his first State of the Union message the following week, reported as follows:

KENNEDY CHALLENGES CONGRESS TO MEET GRAVE PERILS ABROAD AND WORSENING SLUMP AT HOME

WASHINGTON, Jan. 30—President Kennedy challenged Congress and the nation today to face up to grave perils abroad and a worsening economic recession at home.

In his first State of the Union message, given before a joint session of Congress, he called for executive and legislative action to strengthen the national defense to avert big and little wars and to spur the sagging economy.

Mr. Kennedy disclosed that he already had ordered a speed-up in the building of Polaris submarines, in missile development and in defense airlift capacity to meet the threat of communist expansion.

The President summarized the nation's economic condition, noting that bankruptcies were high, unemployment had increased and that profits were below what had been predicted. "In short," he said, "the American economy is in trouble."

Among other things, the President pledged "a new alliance for progress" for a better life for the people of Latin America. And he pushed for a national Peace Corps to aid underdeveloped countries. The Times reported that he had decided to name his brother-in-law, Sargent Shriver, to head the new corps.

A Times editorial called this speech "inspiring, eloquent and straightforward." It was evident, though, that if the President was to get any of the economic and welfare legislation he was talking about, something would have to be done to get around the conservative band of Republicans and Southern Democrats who held the balance of power in the House Rules Committee, the group that clears legislation for floor consideration. The President had thrown his support behind a move by Speaker Rayburn to enlarge the committee from 12 to 15 members to put the conservatives in the minority and enhance the chances for his legislative program. The President himself had made some calls to wavering Congressmen, and the day after the State of the Union message, he won the fight. By a vote of 217 to 212, the motion to enlarge the committee carried.

Now more confident of the chances for his legislative program, the President began preparing more messages to Congress, including programs for medical care and Federal aid to education. But the economy was uppermost on his domestic agenda, and in his economic message to Congress he outlined a wide range of measures to fight the recession, stimulate the growth of the economy, bring immediate help to low-paid workers and the unemployed, provide tax incentives for business investment and expansion and restrain any resulting spread of inflation.

Before his second month had ended, he had sent Congress 29 messages and almost as many draft bills. He also made a dozen public speeches during that time and held a news conference every week but one. Traffic through the White House switchboard jumped 60 per cent.

It was indeed a fast pace the President set for himself and his team. James Reston commented:

Washington

Ah, Youth, as Eve Said, It's Wonderful

WASHINGTON, Feb. 4—There is a refreshing, young, do-something attitude about this new crowd in Washington.

When President Kennedy needed a few votes to safeguard his legislative program in the House Rules Committee he didn't hesitate to pick up the telephone and argue personally with Congressmen for their votes.

When the Cuban refugees situation began to get out of hand in Florida, Secretary Abraham Ribicoff got in a commercial plane for Miami last Monday, investigated the situation all week and had Kennedy's decision in this morning's papers.

What the new Administration has done so far is actually less significant than its manner of doing it. In fact a good case can be made for the proposition that they have merely made caution interesting.

Maybe these youthful habits won't work any better than the old methods. It may be, as Miss Eve said quite a while ago, that if you monkey around with young men you will get in trouble, but at least for the time being it's different and even fun.

It did not take long, however, for Kennedy to realize the massive responsibilities resting on his shoulders. During the campaign he remarked that the Presidency would not be an "easy task in the 1960's." After holding the job for just a brief time, he confided that while he realized the country "faced serious challenges, I could not realize—nor could any man realize who does not bear the burdens of this office—how heavy and constant would be those burdens."

Early, the President had made it clear how he wanted the White House to operate. He emphasized, just after the election, for example, that many members of his staff would have direct access to him, without going through a chief of staff like Eisenhower's Sherman Adams. In fact, he dropped the Adams job—The Assistant to the President—from the payroll.

As it developed in those first few weeks, there were different centers of responsibility for different functions, with no top staff man as such. McGeorge Bundy, Special Assistant for National Security Affairs, emerged as the President's principal staff aide on foreign policy and security matters. Sorensen worked on ideas and speeches and politics. Arthur M. Schlesinger Jr., the Harvard historian, helped on special studies of long term problems, both foreign and domestic, and there were others like O'Donnell, O'Brien and Reardon, members of the so-called "Irish Mafia" who had been with Kennedy during his days in the Senate.

Vice President Johnson was given some administrative duties, too. He did not assume any major policy-making roles, but he was named by the President to head the National Aeronautics and Space Council and the Committee on Equal Employment Opportunity and he undertook several good will missions abroad.

The President found no purpose in having regularly scheduled Cabinet and National Security Council meetings. Instead, he worked with small groups of each on specific issues. He commented that he saw no reason why the Secretary of Agriculture had to spend his time listening to the Secretary of State talk about such matters as Laos at lengthy Cabinet sessions. He also did away with the Operations Coordinating Board that had been set up to implement decisions of the Security Council, and he quickly ordered the discontinuance of 17 interdepartmental committees, finding them a hindrance to efficient government.

Other changes were in the works. The large oval Presidential office took on a Kennedy look. A rocking chair was moved in. Two naval pictures now flanked the fireplace and on the mantel there stood a model of the "Constitution." And Mrs. Kennedy went looking for a new White House cook.

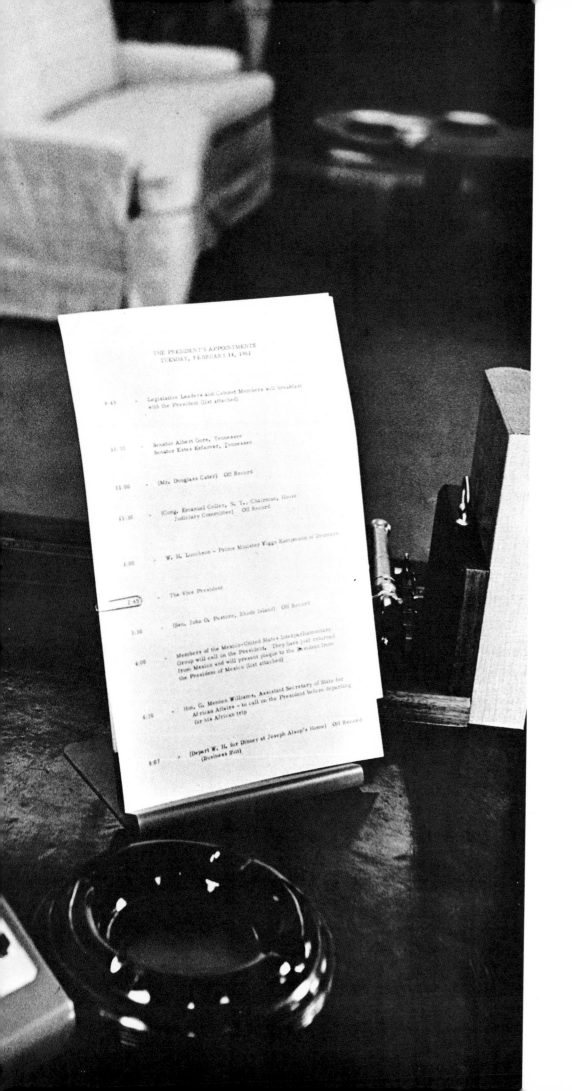

THE PRESIDENT'S APPOINTMENTS
TUESDAY, FEBRUARY 14, 1961

8:45 — Legislative Leaders and Cabinet Members will breakfast
with the President (list attached)

10:15 — Senator Albert Gore, Tennessee
Senator Estes Kefauver, Tennessee

11:00 — (Mr. Douglass Cater) Off Record

11:30 — (Cong. Emanuel Celler, N. Y., Chairman, House
Judiciary Committee) Off Record

1:00 — W. H. Luncheon – Prime Minister Viggo Kampmann of Denmark

— The Vice President

1:45

3:30 — (Sen. John O. Pastore, Rhode Island) Off Record

4:00 — Members of the Mexico-United States Interparliamentary
Group will call on the President. They have just returned
from Mexico and will present plaque to the President from
the President of Mexico (list attached)

4:30 — Hon. G. Mennen Williams, Assistant Secretary of State for
African Affairs – to call on the President before departing
for his African trip

8:07 — (Depart W. H. for Dinner at Joseph Alsop's Home) Off Record
(Business Suit)

OPPOSITE: The President's appointments for Feb. 14, 1961.
They included (above) one with the Vice President.

183

A Cabinet meeting, with Vice President Johnson in left foreground,
the President flanked by advisers Walter Heller (left) and Theodore
Sorensen, and Secretary of the Treasury Dillon at extreme right.

Lyndon Johnson with Lawrence O'Brien, Congressional liaison, following a Cabinet meeting.

The President was photographed at the instant he heard the news of Congo Premier Patrice Lumumba's assassination. The caller was U.N. Ambassador Adlai Stevenson.

LEFT: A meeting of the Joint Chiefs of Staff. (From left) Admiral Arleigh Burke; General Andrew Jackson Goodpastor, Staff Secretary to former President Eisenhower; Marine General David Shoup; Army General George H. Decker; and Chairman General Lyman Lemnitzer. BELOW: The President meets with Air Force General Thomas D. White, Admiral Burke, and Generals Decker and Lemnitzer.

The President reacts to a memo.

ABOVE: Arthur Schlesinger Jr. BELOW: Ted Sorensen. CENTER: Kenny O'Donnell.

ABOVE: McGeorge Bundy conferring with
Pierre Salinger. BELOW: Larry O'Brien.

THE WHITE HOUSE

Like new tenants in any house, the Kennedys looked around the White House and tried to decide what had to be done. The nursery for John Jr., born three weeks after the election, was painted white with a blue trim. Caroline, then three years old, found her room painted a pale pink. But windows stuck in some rooms upstairs, and the fireplaces hadn't been used in years. Mrs. Kennedy felt that the mansion lacked an authentic "sense of history." Accordingly, she decided to make plans for transforming the public areas into a truly historic showplace of furnishings of earlier Presidential eras, so that Americans would be constantly reminded of their heritage.

With the help of a curator, she formed a scouting party that rummaged through the White House looking for forgotten furnishings. Less than a month after the inauguration, The Times reported one of her earliest finds:

> WASHINGTON, Feb. 9—A desk made from the timbers of the British ship Resolute and used by many Presidents has been installed in President Kennedy's office by Mrs. Kennedy.
>
> The White House announced this today in a release headed: "Discovery of the Table Desk from H.M.S. Resolute." It said that Mrs. Kennedy, while exploring all the rooms and familiarizing herself with their contents and backgrounds, had recently made a "most interesting dscovery."
>
> In the broadcasting room, "she came upon a massive, richly carved table desk," most of it "obscured by a covering of green baize," the account continued.
>
> It added that the President was "delighted" by her discovery and the return of the desk "to a place of honor in the White House."

Mrs. Kennedy went on with her search. Later in February she appointed a Fine Arts Committee for the White House to help locate antique furniture and raise funds through donations to purchase the pieces, if necessary.

In the meantime, Mrs. Kennedy was at work on the private quarters upstairs. A family kitchen, a butler's pantry and a spacious dining room were installed there so that food would no longer have to be carried from the huge kitchens two stories below. "The Kennedys can even prepare their own eggs on two stainless steel gas ranges if they want to," a Times article noted. "And the President will have a refrigerator of 28 cubic feet handy for midnight raiding." In addition, a new French chef was found.

Mrs. Kennedy also endeavored to make her children feel comfortable in the huge mansion. A playground, complete with a tree house, was built on the south lawn. The two children and their friends frolicked in the fountains as the weather warmed. Caroline rode her pony across the grounds. John crawled under his father's desk. And a special school was set up in the third floor playroom for Caroline and a group of children her age. The children were also permitted a menagerie. There were new arrivals almost daily—a pet canary, a gray cat, a Welsh terrier, 13 ducks, two hamsters named Debbie and Billie, two ponies and Pushinka, a white puppy sent by Khrushchev.

The public developed an insatiable appetite for details of the home life of the Kennedys. Headlines in The Times reflected the interest:

KENNEDY'S SON CRAWLS
AND HAS 2 FRONT TEETH

CAROLINE VISITS SHOP

PRESIDENT'S SON GETS
A HAIRCUT AND A PART

While there was intense interest in news about the children, the 31-year-old First Lady also captured the fancy of the public. Her activities suggested those of a full-fledged member of the so-called jet set. She spent winters in Palm Beach, water skiied at Cape Cod in the summer, enjoyed weekends in the Virginia hunt country and vacationed abroad without her husband. She wore bouffant hairdos, Oleg Cassini gowns and pillbox hats. It was not long before girls all over had that "Jackie" look, and agencies in New York advertised for models who looked like her. A column on The Times editorial page commented that "everywhere young women, eagerly helped by the magazines, are copying her hairdo, dress, smile and manners." Another story said: "Jacqueline Kennedy is selling eyeglasses on Madison Avenue. Although the First Lady may be unaware of it, her name and face are starting a new fashion fad—curved sun spectacles."

The trend finally became embarrassing. The White House started to receive protests from across the country, though there was little it could do to stop such exploitation. For example, The Times late in 1962 reported the following:

> WASHINGTON, Dec. 2—Mrs. John F. Kennedy has become the favorite "cover girl" of magazines that friends say she would never dream of reading.
> With newsstands across the country plastered with movie magazines featuring pictures and stories about Mrs. Kennedy, the White House is busy answering letters of protest.

Mrs. Kennedy's plans for White House redecoration, meanwhile, were moving along. Her fine arts hunt began to yield a rich harvest of history-laden furniture, paintings and bric-a-brac. Within a few months after its appointment, the Fine Arts Committee obtained furniture that had belonged to George Washington, Abraham Lincoln, James Madison, James Monroe, Martin Van Buren and Daniel Webster. Some was discovered in obscure corners of Washington, some was obtained through gifts, loans and bequests.

It was not long before the changes became apparent to the record number of visitors—1,322,279 in 1961 alone—who flowed through the White House to see what the First Lady was up to. They saw the Green Room walls changed from emerald to soft moss-green watered silk with matching drapes; they saw furniture in the Blue Room reflecting the President Monroe period; they saw changes in the Red Room and the State Dining Room. The Treaty Room, regarded by Mrs. Kennedy as the most historic in the White House, was redecorated as a conference room with furnishings of the Ulysses S. Grant period and with framed treaties on the walls.

On Feb. 14, 1962, with the help of television, Mrs. Kennedy took the entire nation into the White House to see the interior restoration. The Times reported:

> Millions of television viewers went through the White House last night with Mrs. John F. Kennedy leading the way.
> With verve and pleasure, the President's wife undertook to explain the restoration she has made in the interior of the Executive Mansion. She was to prove a virtuoso among guides.
> In the hour-long program, recorded on tape last month, Mrs. Kennedy was a historian savoring the small facts and human story behind the evolution of White House decor. She was an art critic of subtlety and standard. She was an antiquarian relishing pursuit of the elusive treasure. She was a poised TV narrator.
> Mrs. Kennedy, wearing a wool suit of simple line and three strings of pearls, animatedly strolled through rooms on the ground, first and second floors in what was described as the most extensive public view of the White House ever shown.
> With her soft and measured voice, she ranged in comment from warm appreciation of past First Ladies and Presidents to delicate but telling dismissal of the second-rate in art.

Jacqueline Kennedy in the White House. LEFT: An upstairs drawing room redecorated for use by the Kennedy family.

Bobby Kennedy with five of his children: (from left)
Kathleen, Courtney, Bobby Jr., Michael and David.

BOBBY AND THE FAMILY

Sometime after Kennedy took office, Adlai Stevenson introduced the President's mother as "the woman who started it all, the head of the most successful employment agency in America." It was a good-natured remark, and was only slightly exaggerated. For during the Kennedy Presidency, the Kennedy family achieved a power and prominence on the national scene seldom matched in American politics. One son was President, another Attorney General, another a United States Senator. A Kennedy in-law served as director of the Peace Corps. Another Kennedy in-law became a State Department official. The entire family, including the President's sisters, who took turns traveling abroad, worked as an effective political team. Critics liked to call it all the "Kennedy dynasty," and some Republicans tried to reap some political advantage by implying that the family tentacles were reaching into too many phases of Washington life.

The first word of the role the President's relatives were to play came shortly after the election:

ROBERT KENNEDY BEING CONSIDERED FOR CABINET POST

PALM BEACH, Fla., Nov. 18—President-elect John F. Kennedy is giving serious consideration to the appointment of his younger brother, Robert, as Attorney General.

No final decision has been made, and none probably will until the two brothers have had an opportunity to talk out the matter fully.

It was difficult for many to believe that the President would in fact go ahead with the appointment. Bobby, then 35 years old, had had little legal experience. He had served as chief counsel of the Senate rackets committee under Senator John L. McClellan (his brother, then a Senator, was a member of the committee), but he had never argued a case in court. The President, using wit to counter the critics, told a dinner audience he appointed Bobby as Attorney General because he thought he ought to have some Government legal experience before going into private practice. After the appointment was announced on December 16, The Times commented editorially:

> The one appointment thus far that we find most disappointing is Mr. Kennedy's choice of his young brother Robert as Attorney General. If Robert Kennedy were one of the outstanding lawyers of the country, a pre-eminent legal philosopher, a noted prosecutor or legal officer at a Federal or state level, the situation would be different. But his experience as counsel to the McClellan committee, notably successful as he was, is surely insufficient to warrant his present appointment.

When he became Attorney General, there was widespread criticism of Bobby as calculating, narrow, intolerant, too dedicated to "winning" at any cost. During the 1960 campaign, Bobby, as his brother's campaign manager, was brilliant and abrasive. A Times report said, "This may have caused some campaign workers to nickname him 'Raul,' after Fidel Castro's rambunctious younger brother, but the campaign manager delivered the goods and, as he says himself, he did it fairly."

The first big test of the value of the intimate relationship between the President and his brother in his role as Attorney General came sooner than expected. The Times reported:

> As the Cuban adventure crumbled, he [the President] called for his brother Bob. Late in the nights that followed the ill-fated invasion, the President pondered the event

199

with his Attorney General in an intimacy denied previous inhabitants of the loneliest job. What had gone wrong? And why?

The President decided there had to be an inquiry and, as reflexively as he puffs on a cigar or rocks in his rocking chair, he also decided that his brother should play a role in the inquiry. His brother could be counted on to ask the tough questions and prod the painful places.

Within three months after the Robert Kennedy appointment, the President picked another member of his family for a high Government post. He nominated his brother-in-law, Sargent Shriver, to head the newly established Peace Corps. Shriver, who had helped the President recruit men for Government posts during the early days of the Administration, had been assistant general manager of the Chicago Merchandise Mart, owned by the President's father. Shriver took the Peace Corps job for a dollar a year. Despite criticism of his appointment on family grounds, he was an effective administrator. Much of the success of the corps in its early months was attributed to his leadership.

Early in 1961, another brother-in-law, Stephen Smith, was named a consultant to the Development Loan Fund to study various aspects of the agency's private enterprise operations. He then moved over to the State Department as deputy director of its now defunct "crisis" center. Later he resigned, to devote more time to the Kennedy family's financial affairs. He came back to Washington in 1963, however, to take an office in the Democratic National Committee and to become his brother-in-law's political agent in New York, Pennsylvania, Ohio and Michigan. A still more important task had been earmarked for him, as reported by The Times in the spring of 1963:

STEPHEN SMITH IS LIKELY TO DIRECT KENNEDY'S RE-ELECTION CAMPAIGN

WASHINGTON, April 30—The White House is approaching the 1964 Presidential campaign with only one major change in prospect for the team that managed John F. Kennedy's narrow victory in 1960.

That change would put Stephen Smith, Mr. Kennedy's brother-in-law, in over-all direction of the President's re-election effort. Robert F. Kennedy, now the Attorney General, filled this role in 1960.

While one brother and two brothers-in-law thus went to work for the Administration, the youngest brother, Edward M. (Ted) Kennedy, made his own plans to join the clan in Washington. Less than a month after the inauguration came word that Teddy would launch his political career by becoming an assistant district attorney in Boston. A year later he made his big move:

EDWARD KENNEDY IS IN SENATE RACE

BOSTON, March 14—Edward M. Kennedy officially began today his campaign for the Senate seat once held by his brother, the President.

The youngest of the three Kennedy brothers said he had made his decision to run "in full knowledge of the obstacles I will face, the charges that will be made."

Mr. Kennedy's announcement started a campaign that will first pit him against Edward J. McCormack Jr., Massachusetts Attorney General, who is a nephew of House Speaker John W. McCormack.

As the 30-year-old Kennedy predicted, there were complaints, most of them stemming from his own decision to use as a campaign slogan "He can do more for Massachusetts." Many saw in that a clear insinuation that he would receive favored treatment in Washington. As The Times noted in an editorial, it was a "none-too-subtle reminder that he has one brother who is President and another who is Attorney General."

"Teddy" beat "Eddie" in the Democratic primary and then went on to defeat Republican George Cabot

The Attorney General in his office at the Justice Department.

Lodge for the Senate seat. One result of the campaign of the youngest Kennedy was to inspire new criticism of the "Kennedy dynasty." For example, James Reston wrote:

> If the President himself had come to office defending the old familiar rules of political patronage and influence, Washington might have taken Teddy with a cynical shrug. But the President didn't do that.
>
> He came proclaiming a new pragmatism for a new age. Ability was to be the test in all things. . . . The point is that the Kennedys have applied the principle of the best man available for the job to almost everybody but themselves. Teddy's victorious headlines are resented here partly because he is demanding too much too soon on the basis of too little. . . .
>
> There is now so much discussion of the Kennedy family here that many people seem to have little time left over for the Kennedy program. What is particularly surprising about all this is that the Kennedys do not see this line of criticism at all, and in fact, deeply resent it. They have invoked the new pragmatism, but cannot see that, where the family was concerned, they applied the old nepotism.

Meanwhile, comedians were having a field day with the success of Teddy at the polls. Jack Gould, The Times' television critic, noted that the profusion of Kennedys "obviously constitutes a major bonanza for gag writers." Once upon a time, Red Skelton told his audience, the slogan in politics was "a chicken in every pot," but now it was "a Kennedy in every office." The comedian also said that when Ted Kennedy was elected and joined Robert Kennedy in Washington, the President ran over to his father and complained, "Ted and Bob are playing with my country."

The President's mother campaigned for Teddy in Massachusetts, just as she had campaigned for the President. But the President's father remained as before in the background. He was photographed with the family in his home at Hyannis Port after Nixon conceded. But this was the first time since the start of the Kennedy campaign the year before that the patriarch of the clan had permitted himself any

A working day, stretching into the night, in the Attorney General's office.   OVERLEAF: With the President.

public association with his son the candidate. As the Times' story noted, it was "no secret that Kennedy campaigners regarded his father as a political embarrassment."

Before the first year of his son's Administration had been completed, the elder Kennedy fell ill.

> WEST PALM BEACH, Fla., Dec. 19—Joseph P. Kennedy, President Kennedy's father, suffered a stroke at his home in Palm Beach today. The President flew from Washington to go to his father's bedside.
>
> Medical sources said there had been some paralysis but they did not know whether this was serious until diagnostic tests were completed.

The older Kennedy, who was 73 years old, survived, but he was confined to a wheel chair and could speak only a few words.

Kennedy's three married sisters were quite active in the public eye after he took office. Jean and her husband, Stephen Smith, accompanied Johnson in May 1961 on an around-the-world trip. Later that year Jean and Eunice Shriver went to Europe. In October 1961, Eunice was appointed a non-paid consultant to the President's Panel on Mental Retardation. Eunice and Jean also traveled in the Presidential parties to Europe in early 1963, and Jean and Pat Lawford traveled in East Europe later that year.

Of all the members of the family, however, the President leaned most on his brother Bobby in running the affairs of state. Bobby became far more than the Attorney General with all the responsibilities that alone entailed. He was the President's alter ego, confidant, counselor and trouble-shooter, expected to "talk back" with opinions others might withhold in the President's presence. Never before had an Attorney General ranged so far afield with such a large role in intelligence and national security policy.

His varied and pervasive role in the Government made him inevitably a center of controversy. There were businessmen, labor leaders and politicians who mouthed the words "Bobby Kennedy" as an oath. There were some, like James R. Hoffa, the president of the International Brotherhood of Teamsters, who believed they were the target of a Bobby Kennedy vendetta.

A Times article summed up his activities this way in 1962:

> Certainly there has never been an Attorney General like him. In the last 15 months, in addition to presiding over the regular business of the Justice Department, Robert Kennedy has debated with Japanese Communists, helped to settle the Dutch-Indonesian dispute over West New Guinea, played a vital role in the great tests of his brother's Presidency over steel prices, the University of Mississippi and Soviet missiles in Cuba, made a flying trip to Brazil to discuss her economic crisis with President Joao Goulart, took a critical part behind the scenes in the Cuban prisoner ransom and—most recently—directed the Administration's planning on youth employment and delinquency, culminating in the proposal for a domestic Peace Corps.

Some Times headlines told of his far-reaching activities:

ROBERT KENNEDY
ASSURES SUKARNO

BERLIN SALUTES
ROBERT KENNEDY;
HE VOWS SUPPORT

ROBERT KENNEDY
ASSURES VIETNAM

But a measure of the miscalculation about Bobby—or of his growth—is told in a Times article that described his comments in those somber hours when the President and chief aides talked about what they could do in the face of the Soviet missile build-up in Cuba:

Sargent Shriver (center) with Peace Corps aides Richard N. Goodwin (left) and Bill D. Moyers (right).

During the Cuban missile crisis, when the choice lay between a sudden strike on the Soviet bases and a blockade, it was the Attorney General who made the most eloquent and persuasive argument to the war council against the strike—what one participant called "a Fourth of July speech"—saying that America would never be the same if it made a Pearl Harbor-like attack.

Bobby attended National Security Council meetings, though he was not a statutory member. Among other things, besides helping to investigate the government's intelligence structure after the failure of the Cuban exile invasion, he helped with the plans for coping with the Russian missile build-up in Cuba, and undertook missions overseas with a zeal that reflected an intense interest in foreign affairs. He worked closely with the C.I.A. and on the program of training in counter-insurgency techniques. It soon became a Washington cliché to say that Bobby Kennedy was the second most powerful man in the Government. There was talk that he would run for the White House himself in 1968 after his brother served two terms.

Even the youngest Kennedys share the family passion for football. ABOVE, OPPOSITE: Ethel and Bobby scrimmaging with their children at their home in McLean, Va. OVERLEAF: Bobby runs for a touchdown, with Ethel racing him to the goal line.

The Edward Kennedys at home in Boston.
ABOVE: Joan sees her husband off for the
day. RIGHT: Teddy with daughter Cara. FAR
RIGHT: With Max Fishelson, a Boston florist.

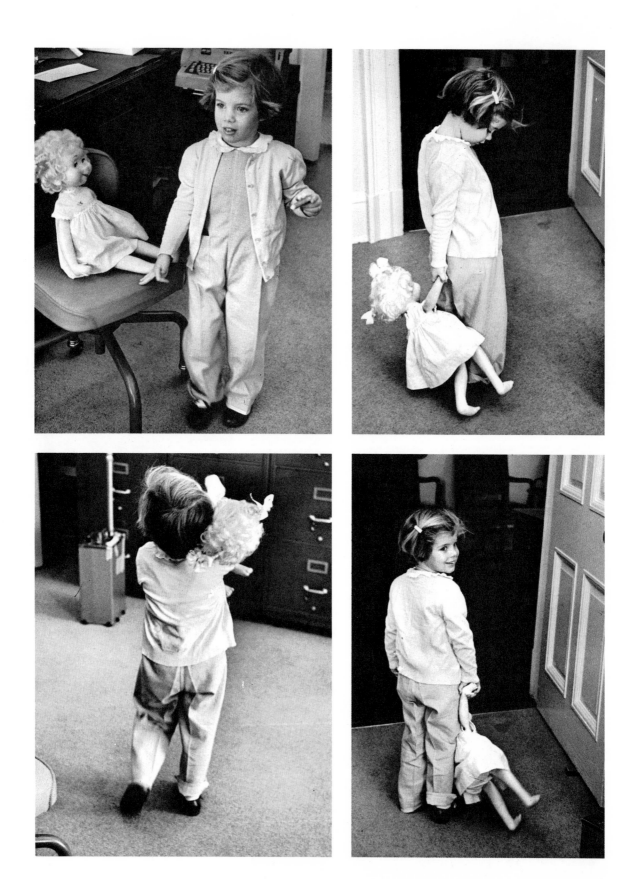

Caroline Kennedy playing in the White House.

214

STYLE

The nation became familiar with Kennedy's pronunciations of "Cuber" and "vigah"; with the chopping motion of his right arm as he emphasized points in his press conferences; with the young man in a hurry, hatless, coatless, vigorous. In the White House, a new generation of Americans had indeed taken the torch of government, as he had said in his inaugural speech, and things were different in Washington. People began to talk and write of "the Kennedy style," which was an amalgam of many things.

In his speeches, some of the flavor of the Kennedy style came through:

"In the long history of the world only a few generations have been granted the role of defending freedom in its hour of maximum danger. I do not shrink from this responsibility. I welcome it. I do not believe that any of us would exchange places with any other people or any other generation. The energy, the faith, the devotion which we bring to this endeavor will light our country and all who serve it, and the glow from that fire can truly light the world."

—Inaugural address, Jan. 20, 1961

"Life in 1961 will not be easy. Wishing it, predicting it, even asking for it, will not make it so. There will be further setbacks before the tide is turned. But turn it we must. The hopes of all mankind rest upon us; not simply upon those of us in this chamber, but upon the peasant in Laos, the fisherman in Nigeria, the exile from Cuba, the spirit that moved every man and nation who shares our hopes for freedom and the future. And in the final analysis, they rest most of all upon the pride and perseverance of our fellow citizens of the great Republic."

—First State of the Union message, Jan. 29, 1961

"The message of Cuba, of Laos, of the rising din of Communist voices in Asia and Latin America—these messages are all the same. The complacent, the self-indulgent, the soft societies are about to be swept away with the debris of history. Only the strong, only the industrious, only the determined, only the courageous, only the visionary who can determine the real nature of our struggle can possibly survive."

—Speech to American Society of Newspaper Editors, April 20, 1961

"When I ran for the Presidency of the United States, I knew that this country faced serious challenges, but I could not realize, nor could any man realize who does not bear the burden of this office, how heavy and constant would be those burdens.

"Three times in my lifetime our country and Europe have been involved in major wars. In each case, serious misjudgments were made on both sides of the intentions of others, which brought about great devastation.

"Now, in the thermonuclear age, any misjudgment on either side about the intentions of others could rain more devastation in several hours than has been wrought in all the wars of human history."

—Speech to the nation on the Berlin crisis, July 25, 1961

"These various elements in our foreign policy lead, as I have said, to a single goal— the goal of a peaceful world of free and independent states. This is our guide for the present and our vision for the future: a free community of nations, independent but interdependent, uniting north and south, east and west in one great family of man, outgrowing and transcending the hates and fears that rend our age.

"We will not reach that goal today, or tomorrow. We may not reach it in our own lifetime. But the quest is the greatest adventure of our century. We sometimes chafe at the

The President scanning a newspaper as his White House day begins.

Delivering the State of the Union address to the Congress, Jan. 11, 1962.

burden of our obligations, the complexity of our decisions, the agony of our choices. But there is no comfort or security for us in evasion, no solution in abdication, no relief in irresponsibility.

"A year ago, in assuming the tasks of the Presidency, I said that few generations in all history had been granted the role of being the great defender of freedom in its hour of maximum danger. This is our good fortune and I welcome it now as I did a year ago. For it is the fate of this generation—of you in Congress and of me as President—to live with a struggle we did not start, in a world we did not make. But the pressures of life are not always distributed by choice. And while no nation has ever faced such a challenge, no nation has ever been so ready to seize the burden and the glory of freedom."

—Second State of the Union message, Jan. 11, 1962

"According to the ancient Chinese proverb, 'A journey of a thousand miles must begin with a single step.'

"My fellow Americans, let us take that first step. Let us, if we can, get back from the shadows of war and seek out the way of peace. And if that journey is one thousand miles, or even more, let history record that we, in this land, at this time took the first step."

—Speech announcing the nuclear test ban, July 26, 1963

"Therefore, while maintaining our readiness for war, let us exhaust every avenue for peace. Let us always make clear our willingness to talk, if talk will help, and our readiness to fight, if fight we must. Let us resolve to be the masters, not the victims of our history, controlling our own destiny without giving way to blind suspicion and emotion."

—Speech at signing of test ban treaty, Oct. 7, 1963

"We set sail on this new sea because there is new knowledge to be gained, and new rights to be won, and they must be won and used for the progress of all people. For space science, like nuclear science and all technology, has no conscience of its own. Whether it will be a force for good or ill depends on man, and only if the United States occupies a position of pre-eminence can we help to decide whether this new ocean will be a sea of peace or a new terrifying theater of war. I do not say that we should or will go unprotected against the hostile misuse of space any more than we go unprotected against the hostile use of land or sea, but I do say that space can be explored and mastered without feeding the fires of war, without repeating the mistakes that man has made in extending his will around this globe of ours."

—Speech at Rice University, Sept. 12, 1962

Recognizing a questioner at a press conference.

The man who could outline the national purpose in those literate, balanced sentences could also laugh at himself, his family and the state of the world. When Robert Kennedy was being considered for appointment as Attorney General, the President remarked that his brother might get a little legal experience before having to practice law. At a Boston dinner he said, "My last campaign may be coming up shortly, but Teddy is around and, therefore, these dinners can go on indefinitely." In Paris, he introduced himself as the man who accompanied Jackie to Europe. On another occasion, just after Teddy won the nomination as Democratic candidate for the Senate in Massachusetts, he said: "I will introduce myself. I am Teddy Kennedy's brother."

At a $100 a plate party dinner, he told the audience, "I could say I am deeply touched, but not as deeply touched as you have been in coming." At another party occasion, he said: "We observe tonight

221

The camera catches Kennedy's restless energy in a sequence of pictures, taken within ninety seconds.

He is talking with Walt W. Rostow and Douglas Dillon (left), George W. Ball (right) and others.

not a celebration of freedom but a victory of party, for we have sworn to pay off the same party debt our forebears ran up nearly a year and three months ago. Our debt will not be paid off in the next hundred days nor will it be paid in the first one thousand days, nor in the life of this Administration. Nor, perhaps, even in our lifetime on this planet. But let us begin by remembering that generosity is not a sign of weakness and that Ambassadors are always subject to Senate confirmation. For if the Democratic party cannot be helped by the many who are poor, it cannot be saved by the few who are rich. So let us begin."

At one press conference shortly after a Vaughn Meader record parodying his speeches became a hit, the following colloquy took place:

QUESTION: Mr. President, it has been a long time since a President and his family have been subjected to such a heavy barrage of teasing and fun-poking and satire. There has been a book on "Backstairs at the White House" and cartoon books with clever sayings, and photo albums with balloons and the rest, and now there is a smash hit record. Can you tell us whether you read and listen to these things and whether they produce annoyment or enjoyment?

ANSWER: Annoyment. Yes, I have read them and listened to them and actually I listened to Mr. Meader's record, but I thought it sounded more like Teddy than it did me, so he's annoyed.

At another press conference, he was asked, "I wonder if you could tell us if you had to do it all over again, would you work for the Presidency and whether you can recommend the job to others?"

"Well, the answer to the first is yes and the second is no," he replied. "I don't recommend it, at least for a while."

Just before he had assumed the Presidency, Kennedy had said: "Sure it's a big job. But I don't know anybody who can do it better than I can. I'm going to be in it four years. It isn't going to be so bad. You've got time to think—and besides, the pay is good."

Kennedy was to find out, in the Cuban invasion crisis, that there wasn't always time to think, that events crept up and were upon you before you knew it. He was also to find out that it was more complicated than he thought to be President; that it was easier to criticize than to perform; that it could be a mistake to follow the advice of his most respected assistants. He came in time to know about the limitations of Presidential power, but despite these, he relished the office and its power.

In the early part of his Administration, he set a furious pace. As James Reston pointed out:

Mr. Kennedy has been something more than the principal administrator of the Government. He has been trying to be the President of the United States, leader of the Allied coalition, Secretary of State, Chief Democratic Whip, official host and greeter, principal negotiator overseas, Chairman of the Democratic National Committee, father, husband, son and brother.

On top of this he has been trying to be nice to his old pals in the House, the Senate and the press, while performing as Commander in Chief, commencement speaker, number one television star and genial host to the graduating class of Tomah High School of Tomah, Wisc.

But at the end of Kennedy's first two years in office, Tom Wicker found:

The President is willing, these days, to spend more time at his desk reading, sparing himself some of the frenetic drives of earlier days. He enjoys visitors, official and otherwise; relaxes with books, movies, in the swimming pool, with friends who date back to school and college days—particularly those who exhibit little interest in politics, policy and inside dope.

In a television interview in December 1962, when he reviewed his first two years in office, Kennedy himself said: "There is a limitation upon the ability of the United States to solve these problems . . . there is a limitation, in other words, upon the power of the United States to bring about solutions. The

Dictating in the White House, late at night.

ABOVE: Caroline, in her mother's shoes, steals the show at a press conference with her father and Senator Fulbright (right). BELOW: The President claps as Caroline and John John dance.

ABOVE: A sleighing party on the White House lawn. BELOW: Home to Hyannis Port, to be greeted by Caroline and a larger-than-life-size doll.

responsibilities placed upon the United States are greater than I imagined them to be and there are greater limitations upon our ability to bring about a favorable result than I had imagined them to be. . . . It is much easier to make the speeches than to make the judgments."

Kennedy believed in the Democratic party and the New Deal; he was convinced of the need for social change and economic progress. But his convictions were cerebral and coolly derived, leavened by humor and a sense of proportion. At ease with Ivy League intellectuals, he was ill at ease among the ward politicians of his native Boston. At home with a cigar at a baseball game, he was equally at home with Pulitzer Prize winners, of whom he was one himself.

Kennedy was, as one of the "Irish Mafia" put it, "a total political animal." He wasn't as partisan as Harry Truman or as spellbinding as Franklin D. Roosevelt, but he was a relentless and persuasive pursuer of votes, a realistic bargainer who didn't expect anything for nothing. But his record with Congress

At a diplomatic reception.

was not extraordinary; after the honeymoon of his first few months was over, Congress was back to its usual slow approach to, if not retreat from, many of the Kennedy proposals, such as medical care for the aged and the civil rights bill.

From the end of the war on, he spent most of his life thinking and playing politics. During his years in the House of Representatives, his time was spent in the usual chores for his district; in the Senate, he began to think of the country as a whole and of our relations with other nations; as President, he spoke, and thought, not only as the chief executive of his own country, but as the leader of the Western alliance. All the time, he was thinking of the next election, as well.

Politician though he was, there was one tradition of the politician that Kennedy would have no part of—wearing fancy hats and headdresses. During the 1960 campaign, he declined to put on an Indian feathered headdress for pictures; during the inauguration he was uneasy with the traditional top hat. On Nov. 22, 1963, in Fort Worth, he was presented with a cowboy hat, a Texas ritual, but he refused to put it on. "Come to Washington Monday and I'll put it on for you in the White House," he joked.

Jacqueline Kennedy and her sister Lee Radziwill (left) in a howdah, in the courtyard of the fortress palace at Amber, Jaipur, India.

Foreign visitors at the White House:
(clockwise from lower left) President
Sukarno of Indonesia; Prime Minister
Menzies of Australia; Tanganyika
President Julius Nyerere arriving by

helicopter; Prime Minister Macmillan of England; the Nigerian Economic Mission; President Tito of Yugoslavia; Prime Minister Nehru of India, with Vice President Johnson at left.

BAY OF PIGS

They liked to say around the White House in those early days of the new Administration that John Kennedy had never really tasted defeat. It was an ebullient crowd, self-confident, sure that the New Frontier would come through the coming months with record untarnished. But their euphoria was short-lived. The shock came at the Bay of Pigs.

Kennedy had made Cuba an important issue during the campaign, repeatedly suggesting that more could and should be done about the island thorn just 90 miles away. He often linked Nixon with the "glaring failure" in foreign policy that permitted Fidel Castro's rise to power. "We must attempt to strengthen the non-Batista democratic anti-Castro forces in exile and in Cuba itself who offer eventual hope of overthrowing Castro," he said on October 20. What Kennedy did not know during the long campaign was that the Eisenhower Administration had already made plans for training an army of Cuban refugees to liberate the island and that a civilian political group in exile had been set up to help run it.

It was 10 days after the election, on November 18, in the library and beside the pool of his Palm Beach house, that Kennedy first learned of what was going on. The word came at a meeting between the President-elect and Allen Dulles, head of the Central Intelligence Agency, and Richard Bissell Jr., a Dulles deputy. Less than two months later, The Times reported from Guatemala that the United States was helping to train an anti-Castro force at a secret Guatemalan air and ground base. The story, published on January 10, said the United States was assisting the effort not only in personnel but in "matériel and the construction of ground and air facilities."

After the inauguration, Kennedy heard more about an invasion. The C.I.A. argued that if the invasion was to come at all, it ought to be soon. Castro military strength was building; more weapons and planes from Iron Curtain countries were on their way to aid Castro. Several meetings were held on the Cuban plans and the President turned to the Joint Chiefs of Staff for their opinion. The word came back that, in the military view, the invasion could succeed. If there were those in the Pentagon who had their doubts, the President never heard them. Nevertheless, Kennedy himself apparently had lingering doubts and made clear that he might still call it off at any time. In any event, he emphasized during these meetings that he did not want any United States forces used directly in the landings. Some old B-26 planes would be made available to the rebel brigade, however.

In the meantime, the Administration began preparing the American people for what was to come. On April 3, the State Department issued a 36-page pamphlet written in the White House under the close direction of Kennedy. The Times reported as follows:

U.S. URGES CASTRO TO CUT
HIS TIES WITH COMMUNISM;
WOULD AID A FREE REGIME

WASHINGTON, April 3—The United States called on the regime of Premier Fidel Castro tonight "to sever its links with the international Communist movement and to restore the dignity" of the original Cuban revolution. . . .

"It is the considered judgment of the Government of the United States of America that the Castro regime in Cuba offers a clear and present danger to the authentic and autonomous revolution of the Americas—to the whole concept of spreading political liberty, economic development, and social progress through all the republics of the hemisphere . . ." [the pamphlet said].

Premier Castro, the publication charges, has instituted a "repressive dictatorship" in Cuba, delivered his country "to the Sino-Soviet bloc" and is mounting an attack on the whole inter-American system.

It was clear that the Cuban crisis was entering a new phase. One of the objectives of the pamphlet was obviously to give hope to the anti-Castro forces inside and outside Cuba that the United States would support any genuinely democratic government that might succeed Castro. Quickly there came signs that the United States was keeping in close touch with the leadership of the Cuban exile groups seeking the overthrow of Castro. Two days after the pamphlet came out, Dr. José Miró Cardona, president of the Revolutionary Council in exile, met at the State Department with Adolph A. Berle Jr., United States coordinator of Latin-American policies, and Philip W. Bonsal, former Ambassador to Cuba. The State Department, when it was asked about the purpose of the visit, officially said only that Berle and Bonsal "are both old friends of his."

The day after the visit of Miró Cardona, and 11 days before the invasion, The Times ran another story on the training of the exiles:

ANTI-CASTRO UNITS
TRAINED TO FIGHT
AT FLORIDA BASES

MIAMI, Fla., April 6—For nearly nine months Cuban exile military forces dedicated to the overthrow of Premier Fidel Castro have been training in the United States as well as in Central America.

An army of 5,000 to 6,000 men constitutes the external fighting arm of the anti-Castro Revolutionary Council, which was formed in the United States last month. Its purpose is the liberation of Cuba from what it describes as the Communist rule of the Castro regime.

Within Cuba, the Revolutionary Council counts on an ever-growing underground network engaged in organizing guerrillas, carrying out sabotage and gathering intelligence. . . .

Most of the instruction given to the anti-Castro forces was reported to have been centered in the Guatemalan camps where infantry and artillery units are being trained by United States experts.

But special instruction has been available in small camps in Florida. Reports said that some of the air and paratroop units are in the Louisiana camps.

If Castro had any lingering doubts about what was about to happen—there is no question that he had long been aware of the training of these forces—they were now dispelled. For in Miami, bulging with refugees and revolutionaries, the preparations were an open secret. They were discussed in cafes, and local papers openly referred to incidents in the camps. There was obviously a ring of truth when, a day after the detailed Times story on the training, Miró Cardona said that a general revolt against the Castro regime was now "imminent." The next day he issued a call to arms to all Cubans. It said: "To arms, Cubans! We must conquer or we shall die choked by slavery. Cubans! To Victory! For democracy! For the Constitution! For social justice! For liberty!"

The meetings among the highest Administration officials continued in Washington. Kennedy debated within himself whether to let the invasion proceed. It would, after all, be quite a coup if it proved successful. To call it off now, to call off a well-publicized plan devised by the Eisenhower Administration, might well prove a major Administration embarrassment. Besides, the exiles were eager and ready to go, and it was conceivable they would act on their own even if "no" came from Washington.

The President ordered that there be no direct help from American armed forces. The Cubans were to control the air using the old B-26's and their own pilots. An American Navy task force would escort the landing party, but jet aircraft would not be used in the battle. And Kennedy would allow only two blows by the B-26's at Castro's planes on the ground, one two days before the landing and the other on the morning of the invasion.

What was perhaps the major pre-invasion meeting took place on April 4 in a State Department conference room. Besides the President, those attending included Secretary of State Rusk, Secretary of Defense McNamara, Secretary of the Treasury Dillon, General Lyman L. Lemnitzer, chairman of the Joint Chiefs, Dulles and Bissell of the C.I.A., White House aides Arthur Schlesinger and Richard Goodwin, and Senator Fulbright, chairman of the Senate Foreign Relations Committee. Bissell outlined the plan once again. The exiles, organized as Brigade 2506, would land 100 miles west of Trinidad at the

Bahia de Cochinos, the Bay of Pigs. The Revolutionary Council would call for internal support. The invasion date: April 17. Everyone there apparently was for it; no one expressed any opposition. The Kennedy Administration was now well on its way to its biggest blunder.

Five days before the target day, the President held a news conference. The Times report said:

PRESIDENT BARS USING U.S. FORCE TO OUST CASTRO

WASHINGTON, April 12—President Kennedy gave a firm pledge today that the United States armed forces would not intervene in Cuba "under any conditions" to help bring about the downfall of Premier Fidel Castro.

Furthermore, the President said at his news conference that the Government would do everything possible "to make sure that there are no Americans involved in any [anti-Castro] actions inside Cuba."

The President was equally positive when asked whether the United States would oppose any attempt by Cuban exiles "to mount an offensive against Castro from this country."

The President did not say whether the Government would take action to prevent the departure from the United States of small landing forces of Cuban exiles bent on overthrowing Premier Castro and setting up a democratic government.

Fidel Castro

Not that it would have made any difference, but those close to the developing situation thought the President may have been too firm in publicly ruling out United States involvement, thereby eliminating an important element of suspense. And some of the Cuban exiles said that the news conference was the first clear word they had had about Administration limits on the use of United States forces.

Early Saturday morning, the B-26's, now carrying the markings of Castro's air force, began their attacks as scheduled on Cuban bases. The invasion barges began loading, and Castro, certain the time had come, began complaining to the world. The B-26 attacks proved largely ineffective in damaging Castro's air force. Later that morning two of the B-26's, both bullet-ridden, landed in Florida, one at Key West Naval Air Station, the other at the Miami International Airport. Castro charged that the bombers had come from foreign bases. The Revolutionary Council in New York said the planes were flown out of Cuba by defecting fliers who had bombed the fields as they fled. Immigration service officials, who had taken the pilot who landed at Miami into custody, backed that story.

In Washington, Kennedy's press secretary, Pierre Salinger, denied any knowledge of the aerial bombings. He said the United States was trying to get all the information it could on the attacks. The United States was attempting to cover its tracks, but it was heading into trouble anyway, as this Times story showed:

U.S. AVOIDING QUESTIONS ON CUBA BOMBING DETAILS

WASHINGTON, April 16—Government officials were avoiding probing questions today on the point of origin of the B-26 planes that bombed three Cuban military air bases yesterday.

The questions were prompted by some puzzling circumstances attending the attack and the statement made by one of the pilots who landed his damaged bomber at Miami International Airport.

One of the unanswered questions was how the president of the Cuban Revolutionary Council in New York, Dr. José Miró Cardona, could have had advance knowledge of the mission if the pilots were all members of the Cuban Air Force and if the decision to make the attacks was made suddenly only last Thursday, as the B-26 flier said in Miami.

Another question that got no satisfactory answer here is why immigration authorities withheld the name of the pilot who landed in Miami even though pictures were taken and published that clearly showed his features and the number of the plane.

A high-level meeting to discuss the Cuban situation. (From left) General Clifton, White House military aide; Defense Secretary McNamara; Assistant Defense Secretary Paul Nitze; General Lemnitzer; Allen Dulles; Richard Bissell Jr.; Walt W. Rostow in right foreground.

At the United Nations, United States chief delegate Adlai Stevenson denied Cuban charges that the attacks meant the beginning of an American invasion. Unaware of how much the United States knew about the bombings, he said "these pilots and certain other crew members have apparently defected from Castro's tyranny." Castro challenged Kennedy to present before the United Nations the fliers who allegedly were defectors. Miró Cardona now said "spectacular things have begun to happen."

That weekend, Kennedy went to join his family at their leased estate, Glen Ora, in the Virginia hunt country. The White House communications network kept him informed of the developments. Because of the furor over the first attack, the second air strike was ordered canceled, much to the dismay of the C.I.A.

On Sunday, April 16, the Revolutionary Council members in New York were told that important events were forthcoming and that they ought to pack their bags. Without being told where they were going, the members were secretly flown to Opa Locka, just outside Miami. As reported by The Times 10 days later, the council members were kept incommunicado in an old house there. Invasion communiqués were to be issued in the council's name. Enraged, several of them threatened to leave even if it meant being shot.

At midnight Sunday, as the council members turned in for the night, the invasion boats moved closer to the Bay of Pigs. The Times reported the next day:

ANTI-CASTRO UNITS LAND IN CUBA; REPORT FIGHTING AT BEACHHEAD; RUSK SAYS U.S. WON'T INTERFERE

MIAMI, April 17—Rebel troops opposed to Premier Fidel Castro landed before dawn today on the swampy southern coast of Cuba in Las Villas Province.

The attack, which was supported from the air, was announced by the rebels and confirmed by the Cuban government.

In a communiqué issued tonight, the Revolutionary Council, the top command of the rebel forces, said merely that military supplies and equipment were landed successfully on the marshy beachhead. The communiqué added that "some armed resistance" by supporters of Premier Castro had been overcome.

There were no indications of how the assault was progressing.

Today as the word of the attack spread in Miami, additional hundreds of volunteers began appearing at the recruiting offices of several of the movements that make up the Revolutionary Council.

Kennedy was awakened at Glen Ora early Monday morning and told the news. He returned to Washington. Moscow charged that the United States was responsible for the landing by what it described as "American hirelings." A Times story said an "atmosphere of tension gripped the Soviet capital after the announcement" of the invasion. Secretary of State Rusk called a news conference that morning to express the sympathy of the American people for those who struck against Castroism in Cuba. He said "There is not and will not be any intervention there by United States forces." The Times story added:

> What disturbs many observers here is that the United States may now find itself in a situation where it is blamed for giving aid to the refugees but not enough aid to bring Premier Castro down.

That very first day, a cloud of gloom fell over the White House. Failure was in the air. Even so, the second air strike was reinstated, only to be prevented by bad weather. The next day, Tuesday, the news was not good:

> MIAMI, April 18—The forces of Premier Fidel Castro appeared tonight to have mounted a major, tank-led offensive designed to dislodge rebel fighters from their narrow beachhead on the marshy southern coast of Cuba.
>
> An announcement over Cuban television said that "news of victory" would be broadcast within a few hours. . . .
>
> Deep concern was developing here over the immediate and long-range political repercussions of a possible failure of the rebel landing operation in southern Cuba.

The 1,500 men in the brigade fought bravely. But they quickly ran short of ammunition and food. Castro's men were upon them, and his T-33 jet trainers roamed the sky, untouched by early missions of the rebel B-26's. It was not disclosed until later that four American advisers, employed by the C.I.A., lost their lives flying relief missions for the rebels.

That night, Tuesday, the White House prepared for the annual Congressional reception. Beginning at 10 P.M., Kennedy played host. Shortly before midnight, he and Mrs. Kennedy left the party, but the President returned to his office for midnight meetings with McNamara, Rusk, Bissell, Dulles, Lemnitzer and most of the White House staff. Finally, at 4 A.M., the talks ended, and a weary and saddened President walked toward his bedroom. The next day, the invaders began surrendering.

Wednesday was the darkest of the 90 days the President had been in office. From noon until after 7 P.M., officials gathered for talks. There was some discussion of sending the Marines to conquer the country; other proposals were heard as the President moved from room to room listening to the ideas and reports from the disaster scene. The six leaders of the Cuban Revolutionary Council were quietly flown from their temporary confinement in Florida to meet with the President. He told them, among other things, that he would do all in his power to save the men. But he turned down their suggestions that the United States intervene directly.

Kennedy now decided to turn his speech the next day before the American Society of Newspaper Editors into a discussion of Cuba. Two years before, ironically, Castro had spoken to the same audience from the same rostrum in the same hotel. The President talked in general terms, saying that United States restraint was "not inexhaustible" and that it did not intend to abandon Cuba to Communism.

Assessments of the failure began at once. The day after Kennedy addressed the editors, The Times reported from Washington:

> Tonight, after four days of uncertainty, it is clear that the expedition has involved the United States in a disastrous loss of prestige and respect. Among high Administration officials there is recognition that a serious miscalculation was made.
>
> The effects of the resulting setback were being appraised here in this way:
>
> ¶ The regime of Premier Fidel Castro has presumably been strengthened. Dr. Castro himself could boast to his people that he had survived an invasion that had United States support. . . .
>
> ¶ The reviving confidence of United States allies in its qualities of leadership has been shaken. In allied embassies here there was a feeling of shock at what had happened.
>
> ¶ The momentum President Kennedy was gaining in foreign policy has been checked.
>
> ¶ In short, the feeling here is that the repercussions could hardly have been worse if President Kennedy had sent the Marines into Cuba.

Kennedy publicly took full responsibility for the failure, telling a news conference, "there is an old saying that victory has 100 fathers and defeat is an orphan." But he learned some lessons. He had accepted bad advice from men who should have known better. He himself should have been more wary, asking more questions, prodding more after opinions were given. The White House organization needed a new hard look. And so did the entire national security and intelligence machinery.

On April 22, Kennedy named General Maxwell D. Taylor, then retired, to review United States capabilities in intelligence and paramilitary and guerrilla warfare. To help him, Kennedy later named his brother Robert, Allen Dulles and Admiral Arleigh Burke, Chief of Naval Operations. Taylor, who subsequently moved into the White House as Kennedy's full-time military adviser, was to find that the invasion plan from the start had too many basic faults and that victory was never really possible.

The day of the Taylor appointment, Kennedy also moved to try to build national unity on the issue. He asked former President Eisenhower to meet him at Camp David in the Catoctin Mountains. "I'm all in favor of the United States supporting the man who has to carry the responsibility for our foreign affairs," Eisenhower said after the meeting. Within a week, however, Republicans in Congress began hammering at Kennedy for what they called "disastrous" miscalculations in the Cuban invasion.

In the aftermath of it all, there was one major piece of unfinished business—getting the invaders out of Castro's jails. The beginning of what developed into 18 months of negotiations came almost unnoticed. Precisely one month after the invasion, a small story inside The Times reported the following:

> KEY WEST, Fla., May 17—Premier Fidel Castro said today he would exchange his prisoners of the April 17 invasion of Cuba for 500 bulldozers from the United States—or else the prisoners would be put to hard work. . . .
>
> "If President Kennedy says they are his friends and he loves them so much, let him send 500 bulldozers and we will send them back," he reiterated, referring to the invaders.
>
> "The invaders have to pay for the damage they have done."

A week later, the President said the Government could not be a party to the negotiations, but added it would not interfere with the "humanitarian efforts" by others. The Government was to become involved later, but its full role would not be disclosed until the prisoners had returned. Backed by Kennedy's statement, a group of prominent Americans tried to negotiate with Castro on his offer to exchange the prisoners

for 500 agricultural tractors. No agreement was reached. The contributions from Americans to buy tractors were returned. A group of Cubans, mostly parents and wives of the prisoners, then formed the Cuban Families Committee, which tried to raise $28 million, the value of the tractors Castro demanded. By the following April, prospects of getting the prisoners back had dimmed. Castro had the men brought to trial, and they were swiftly sentenced to up to 30 years hard labor or given fines of up to $500,000. However, 60 ailing prisoners were released by Castro on "credit" against a subsequent cash payment of $2,900,000.

In August some of the prisoners and representatives of the Cuban Families Committee came to see Robert Kennedy about their stymied efforts to free the remaining 1,113 captives. He suggested they get help from an outside lawyer not emotionally involved in the situation and proposed James B. Donovan of New York. Donovan began negotiations with Castro. A rough agreement was reached: $53,000,000 in food and drugs for the prisoners. The Castro regime got up an enormous catalogue of the items it wanted. Finally, the release was arranged and The Times reported:

CUBA PRISONERS
LAND IN FLORIDA;
RANSOM IS PAID

MIAMI, Fla., Dec. 23—The first Cuban war prisoners liberated from Fidel Castro's jails in exchange for medicine and food reached United States soil today.

Two days later The Times told the full story of how the exchange was arranged:

GROUP RAISED 3 MILLION IN CASH
IN 24 HOURS TO RANSOM CUBANS

WASHINGTON, Dec. 25—General Lucius D. Clay, Attorney General Robert F. Kennedy and others raised almost $3,000,000 in cash this week to make possible completion of the Cuban prisoners' release.

The money was raised in 24 hours ending yesterday afternoon. At 3 P.M., a $2,900,000 check drawn on the Royal Bank of Canada was in the hands of Premier Fidel Castro, who had been promised this sum and demanded its payment as evidence of good faith.

This remarkable money-raising effort climaxed a wholly extraordinary three-week campaign to meet Premier Castro's price for freeing the prisoners. Details of the enterprise were learned today from officials and others involved.

Perhaps the most notable aspect of the effort was the collaboration between Government and private citizens. The work was done by an informal committee of officials and private lawyers who volunteered their services.

The story told how the committee in three weeks obtained pledges of $53,000,000 in food and drugs from American companies—the ransom price. It also arranged for free transportation of the goods by airlines, railroads and trucks from all over the country. And it worked out a complicated financial assurance to Castro that he would be paid if all the material failed to arrive.

The President confers with Dean Rusk (left) and Richard Bissell.

Bissell (left), McGeorge Bundy and Secretary of State Rusk.

One week after the prisoners flew to the States, Kennedy went to Miami to address the freed brigade and about 40,000 Cuban refugees, gathered in the sun-baked Orange Bowl Stadium. The President accepted the battle flag of the surviving troops and pledged it would be returned to them "on Cuban soil." He and his wife, who spoke in flawless Spanish, praised the courage of the invasion force. Many of the troops were near tears; others smiled broadly. There seemed to be a note of personal expiation in the President's speech. He undoubtedly felt responsible for what they had been through. As Robert Kennedy had put it earlier in the month: "My brother made a mistake. These men fought well; the disaster was no fault of theirs. They are our responsibility."

President Kennedy clearly had had his first taste of defeat.

PARIS—VIENNA—LONDON

On April 3, 1961, in Palm Beach, the President announced that he would fly to Paris for three days of talks with General de Gaulle, followed by a brief visit to Britain. Soon after, there were unofficial reports that Kennedy also would meet Khrushchev in Vienna; on May 16 Washington sources confirmed the reports. Even before Kennedy's inauguration, Khrushchev had sought a meeting. His aim had seemed apparent: to size up the new American President and to impress him with his toughness, to mount a great propaganda drive and to persuade Kennedy that the world balance of power had indeed swung to Communism. To many the spring of 1961 seemed an even less propitious time for a summit meeting than had the fall of 1960. But as The Times' foreign affairs columnist, C. L. Sulzberger, noted:

> PARIS, May 21—The obvious implication of the Vienna meeting is that our President is determined to erase from Khrushchev's mind any impression that, because of recent diplomatic defeats, the United States is less resolved to protect its widespread interests.
> During the past month the Soviet Union has had remarkable good luck. Gagarin was orbited around the earth; the Cuban intervention was smashed; our clients in Laos were defeated; the French Army was dislocated by the recent generals' putsch; and the ultimate meaning of the South Korean coup isn't clear.

And although some welcomed the summit—the British, notably, believing Winston Churchill's dictum that "Jaw, jaw is better than war, war"—there was criticism on Capitol Hill. The Republican leaders of Congress, for example, wished Kennedy success but were frankly pessimistic about his prospects. They also took pains to remind the President that as a Senator he had called for a completely worked out agenda as a "minimal requirement" for a summit meeting, and that this requirement had not been met.

Kennedy spent the weekend before his departure at Hyannis Port. On Sunday he heard a prayer for divine guidance; on Monday, his 44th birthday, he addressed 5,000 Democrats at a party dinner in Boston. As he was driven through the city he passed the familiar statue of William Lloyd Garrison, the 19th century abolitionist. When he reached his destination he sent a motorcycle patrolman back to copy the words from the base of the statue. The Times reported the speech that night this way:

> BOSTON, May 29 —President Kennedy said tonight that he would meet Premier Khrushchev in the spirit of no equivocation and no retreat.
> He goes to Vienna for that meeting next Saturday, the President said, "as leader of the greatest revolutionary country on earth."

Then he quoted the words from the base of the statue: " 'I am in earnest. I will not equivocate. I will not excuse. I will not retreat a single inch. I will be heard.' "

The next day Air Force jet No. 1 left New York International Airport for Paris, carrying a Presidential party of 31 and a crew of 13. Two items were to dominate the Paris talks: Western defense and Berlin. Kennedy knew that total rapport between himself and de Gaulle was improbable, and that rapprochement with Khrushchev was impossible. But he was experimental, and the meetings represented

Jacqueline Kennedy in Paris, June 1961.

OVERLEAF: Entering the Palais de Chaillot; the Eiffel Tower in the rear.

Marching up the Champs Elysées with General de Gaulle to
the Arc de Triomphe, where (right) both sign the register.

OVERLEAF: At dinner in the Hall of Mirrors, Versaille

at least an opportunity. Europeans, however, were not confident about the trip. James Reston wrote:

LONDON, May 29—Europe is not very optimistic about President Kennedy's quick trip of the Continent. The general feeling in the Western capitals seems to be that he has taken on too much in too short a time.

This reaction, however, may be based on a misconception about why President Kennedy is coming to Paris, Vienna and London in the next few days. He is not expecting to transform the Soviet, French and British policies so much as to get a personal impression about how to modify his own policies.

In time it was to be recognized that Kennedy stood for the gradual erosion of national sovereignty—for the political and philosophical unity of the Western world. And on this, his first major venture into personal diplomacy, he largely sought to determine if the Soviet Union and the Western Allies would accept greater international control of world affairs and disputes, or if they would insist on national control of international problems.

After the first day in Paris, The Times headline read:

KENNEDY AND DE GAULLE
AGREE TO DEFEND BERLIN;
DISCUSS ASIA AND AFRICA

Kennedy and de Gaulle had conferred twice that day. After a 37-minute discussion before lunch, they proclaimed their "complete identity" of view on defending West Berlin. In the afternoon they spoke of Asia and Africa, and in the evening there was a formal state dinner in the Elysée Palace, with 150 guests and a receiving line of 1,500. Outside the palace, Paris writhed in a traffic jam caused by official cars and swarms of sightseers; inside the palace, the General in full military dress, Kennedy in white tie and tails and Mrs. Kennedy in a sophisticated sheath moved gracefully through the mirrored elegance of the salons.

At the dinner, Kennedy spoke of the interdependence of France and the United States. He pledged that "American forces will remain in Europe as long as they are required, ready to meet any threat with whatsoever response is needed." In a sense, the pledge was a prelude to Vienna; despite the West's stoic acceptance of defeats in Cuba and Laos, Kennedy was committing any American army to go all the way, including, apparently, nuclear war, in defense of Berlin.

The next day, June 1, was for the most part impressive, glittering and solemn with grandeur. It was apparent that Kennedy was beginning to enjoy Paris and that Paris, finding him "sympathique," was enjoying Kennedy. At noon he spoke at the Hotel de Ville, Paris's City Hall, where he noted that Washington had been designed by a Frenchman, Major Pierre l'Enfant, who billed Congress $90,000. Congress, in an economizing fervor "for which it is justifiably famous," Kennedy said, granted only $3,000. Some believed, he added, that Paris dress designers had been collecting the bill ever since.

In the evening, de Gaulle was host at a dinner and a ballet performance at Versailles. During the day there had been two conferences cloaked in official silence. The Times story began:

PARIS, June 1—President Kennedy and President de Gaulle approached the heart of the matter today—their divergent views on the Atlantic alliance and defense generally—and decreed total silence on the substance of their talks.

After three hours and twenty minutes of private meetings between the two leaders, in the morning and afternoon, the White House spokesman, Pierre Salinger, was permitted to list only the topics discussed and French spokesmen did not do even that.

Despite the promise of further conversations, neither Kennedy nor de Gaulle had any real hope of

Mrs. Kennedy leaving the Elysée Palace.

resolving their differences. Rather, the meeting was one of exploration. In his column, Reston said:

> PARIS, June 1—Every three-day conference between allied leaders tends to follow a common pattern. On the first day, the great men proclaim their perpetual love and unity. On the second they try to prove it and fail. And on the third, they write a communiqué saying that they love each other anyway.
> This was the second day of the Kennedy–de Gaulle conference, halfway between aspiration and realization, and when it was over they had nothing to say.
> Accordingly, the 1,000 reporters present, who assume that these meetings are held solely for their benefit, were outraged, but the silence of the two Presidents indicates that while they did not resolve their differences, at least they faced them.

Meanwhile, a small phenomenon was sweeping Paris; Jackie, a Sorbonne student in 1950, was back in town. The phenomenon had begun inconspicuously: a ride into Paris in a closed Citroen; a visit that afternoon to a child-care center; then, official receptions, Versailles, state dinners, a hurriedly arranged trip to the Jeu de Paume Museum with André Malraux, where Jackie particularly admired a Manet nude; then more visits and more receptions, all bathed in the hot glare of publicity.

On June 2, Kennedy was a guest at a press luncheon. He began his talk this way: "I do not think it altogether inappropriate to introduce myself. I am the man who accompanied Jacqueline Kennedy to Paris, and I have enjoyed it."

The two Presidents met for the final time at the Elysée Palace, where they held a two-hour conversation. Though there were still divisive issues, it was by now apparent that the three-day meeting had been a success. Of that last talk, The Times headline read:

KENNEDY FINDS DE GAULLE IN ACCORD ON MOST ISSUES; MEETS KHRUSHCHEV TODAY

The Paris talks had brought together two disparate men: a young, pragmatic New Frontiersman and an aging, traditionalist, European aristocrat. Further, each man had been trapped in contradictions. Kennedy chose to speak of France as the "full and equal" partner in the Great Alliance, which it was not, say, in the sharing of atomic information. De Gaulle, in turn, chose to speak for all Europe, even on non-European affairs, which the other NATO nations could scarcely countenance.

The Paris talks hardly solidified Atlantic unity; indeed, de Gaulle was to block the entry of Britain into the Common Market, oppose the nuclear test ban treaty and interfere with American policy in southeast Asia. But Kennedy found that more things joined him and de Gaulle than separated them. The two Presidents parted in firm agreement on the defense of Berlin, better informed of their distinctive viewpoints on other matters and—strikingly—with great mutual esteem. Further, the talks bore unexpected fruit: they helped to restore Kennedy's confidence, sense of history and sense of humor. Kennedy, whose Administration had been oppressed by Castro's Cuba, was ready to think again in terms of generations and of long-range policies.

The next morning, Kennedy's jet left Paris for Schwechat Airport outside Vienna, 20 miles from the borders of Hungary. In the context of world affairs the forthcoming confrontation was of obvious importance. A Times article said:

> VIENNA, June 2—Premier Khrushchev has staked much of his prestige in the Communist world on obtaining profitable results from his meetings with President Kennedy here this weekend.
> There are risks in the Vienna talks for Mr. Khrushchev's personal position in much the same way that an unfavorable outcome would detract from the reputation of the President. These impressions were gained in Moscow and Geneva in conversations with Communist and Western officials while preparations were being made for the first encounter between the two men.

The stakes for East and West were high. Khrushchev wanted a peace treaty for Germany that would recognize the present borders of the country; Kennedy would insist on reunification through free elections. Khrushchev wanted to end Western military occupation of West Berlin and neutralize the sector; Kennedy would insist that the Soviet Union abide by World War II agreements. Khrushchev wanted key international organizations to be governed by the unanimous consent of Communist, Western and neutral members; Kennedy would insist on majority rule.

On the eve of the summit an ominous portent was heard, and reported this way:

> VIENNA, Saturday, June 3—Soviet officials denounced last night the talks in Paris between President Kennedy and President de Gaulle as "poor preparation" for Mr. Kennedy's meeting here today with Premier Khrushchev.
>
> The comments were made after Mr. Khrushchev had arrived from Czechoslovakia for the summit conference.
>
> In what appeared to be resentment against the emphasis in the Paris talks on Western determination to defend West Berlin, a responsible member of the Khrushchev delegation said:
>
> "It was a militaristic exercise and poor preparation for the meeting here."

The first conference was held in the United States Embassy residence, a gray stucco structure of severe modern lines. Thick firs and weeping willows dripped rain that day and screened a small graveled courtyard in front of the residence. In the garden, flowering with red, white and lavender rhododendron, Austrian policemen prowled with chained and muzzled German sheep dogs.

The atmosphere of the conversations was more cordial than had been expected after the rising controversies of the preceding months, but no agreements were reached. Indeed, Laos, the only subject discussed at length, was to plague Kennedy throughout his Administration.

The first meeting was held in two parts. The first involved Kennedy, Khrushchev and their aides; the second, at Kennedy's suggestion, was limited to the two leaders and their interpreters. Kennedy was concerned by Moscow's insistence that it had the right to intervene in disputes that it deemed just, whereas the United States and the United Nations should stay out of controversies that involved national or even ideological interests of the Soviet Union. Further, Kennedy sought clarification of Khrushchev's statement that "wars of national liberation" were not only permissible but necessary and would have the support of the Communist peoples.

The second and final confrontation took place in the Soviet Embassy. It began, typically, with a handshake and a proverb by Khrushchev, who awaited the President's arrival at the entrance to the Embassy. When Kennedy's car drew up, the Premier emerged with a broad grin and thrust out his hand. "I greet you on a small piece of Soviet territory," he said. Then came the proverb. "Sometimes," Mr. Khrushchev said, "we drink out of a small glass, but we speak with great feelings."

Khrushchev led Kennedy to a small sofa in a second floor conference room that was draped in red damask. American and Soviet officials sat down in a circle around a table. Reporting on the talk, The Times headline said:

KENNEDY AND KHRUSHCHEV FIND LIMITED LAOS ACCORD BUT SPLIT ON BERLIN AND KEY ARMS ISSUES

Beneath the bland official communiqué, there lay hard controversy and a sharp three-hour disagreement on all questions concerning Germany, Berlin and the Soviet demands for a veto over international control of nuclear testing and other disputes. Kennedy argued the whole legal and moral question on Berlin—a point-for-point rebuttal of the Soviet position—and reminded Khrushchev that the United States had twice gone to war to prevent Western Europe from being overwhelmed. He also noted that he considered the freedom of West Germany essential to the freedom of Western Europe.

Great international turning points are seldom clearly illuminated. The talks with Khrushchev did not go particularly well for Kennedy; the Russian sought to bully the American and misread his determination. But if the results of the conference were less than conclusive, one clear fact had emerged: "Jahkee" was a hit in Vienna, too. In the splendor of a state dinner at the Schoenbrunn Palace on the Kennedys' first night in Vienna, a photographer had asked Khrushchev if he would pose shaking hands with

At a reception in Vienna, the Kennedys converse, via interpreters, with Premier and Mrs. Khrushchev. Khrushchev was frankly admiring of the American First Lady.

the President. Grinning, the Premier glanced at Jacqueline Kennedy, stately and beautiful in a long white gown, and replied, "I'd like to shake her hand first."

The next day, Mrs. Kennedy lunched with Mrs. Khrushchev at Pallavicini Palace. About a thousand persons squeezed themselves into the cobbled square in front of the palace. There were cheers and applause when Jacqueline Kennedy arrived, and a great sigh of "ah's" when she stepped from her car. When she was inside the palace, the crowd began bellowing, "Jah-kee." When Mrs. Kennedy and Mrs. Khrushchev came to the window, the Premier's wife took Mrs. Kennedy's hand and held it aloft; she, too, had joined the salute.

The Kennedys left Vienna for London at noon on June 4. The Times described their arrival this way:

> LONDON, June 4—This old and stately city gave a young President a regal welcome tonight.
> President Kennedy, with Prime Minister Macmillan at his side, drove through lanes of cheering Londoners to begin a 28-hour visit whose international aspects are becoming increasingly important. Theoretically, the visit is a private one.
> West Berlin, Laos and Cuba were forgotten by about 250,000 persons—men in their shirt sleeves and women in their summer dresses—to catch a glimpse of the cheerful young man and the already legendary "Jackie."

During the ride, Kennedy was constantly reminded that many Britons did not agree with his policies; groups of youngsters from nuclear disarmament organizations waved banners and signs. But fundamentally it was a good-natured crowd that cried out, "You're all right, Jack."

That night the Kennedys stayed at the London home of Mrs. Kennedy's sister, Lee, and her husband, Prince Stanislaus Radziwill. The next day the President had the most fruitful meeting of his trip. The Times headline said:

KENNEDY AND MACMILLAN SEE LAOS AS SOVIET TEST; DIFFER ON BERLIN TACTICS

Kennedy arrived for the meeting at Admiralty House a half hour early and then stayed 20 minutes longer than had been expected. The only disagreement was over Berlin. Macmillan clung to the British view that the West should issue only a statement of principles on its position in West Berlin. Kennedy, however, favored a statement that would in effect draw a line that the Russians could cross only at the risk of Western counteraction.

Still, the man who was the grandson of a Boston-Irish politician and the son of an Ambassador who wrote the British off in 1940 made a distinctly favorable impression at Whitehall. Kennedy warmed Macmillan with what one British leader called his "informed reasonableness"; he argued his policy but listened, too, to the British view.

After a ceremony at Westminster Cathedral in which the Radziwills' daughter was christened, the President and his wife dined at Buckingham Palace. That day a cartoon by Vicky appeared in The London Evening Standard. It showed the Statue of Liberty with Jacqueline Kennedy's face; one hand held the torch of freedom, the other a copy of Vogue.

On his arrival home, the President made a television report to the nation; it had a somber tone. He said that he saw some hope of resolving the conflict in Laos, but he conceded that in general "the gap between us was not, in such a short period, materially reduced." Grimly he told the nation that his hopes for a nuclear test ban and for slowing the arms race "suffered a serious blow" at Vienna. But the "most somber" subjects in the meeting with Khrushchev, he said, were Germany and Berlin.

Kennedy appeared immensely satisfied by his meetings with the Allied leaders, and he said that Khrushchev, too, recognized the value of a cease-fire in Laos. But of Berlin he said:

"I made it clear to Mr. Khrushchev that the security of Western Europe, and therefore our own security, are deeply involved in our presence and our access rights to West Berlin, that those rights are based on law and not on sufferance, and that we are determined to maintain those rights at any risk, and thus meet our obligation to the people of West Berlin and their right to choose their own future."

Summing up his experiences with Khrushchev, he said: "No spectacular progress was either achieved or pretended. No advantage or concession was either gained or given." Nevertheless, he went on, he found the talks "immensely useful" because the channels of communication were now clearer. And no matter how difficult it might seem to give an affirmative answer to the question of living in peace with an antagonistic philosophy, he said, "I think we owe it to all mankind to make the effort."

At Buckingham Palace with the Queen and the Duke of Edinburgh.

255

The President was godfather at the christening of his niece, Princess Radziwill's daughter Anna Christina, at Westminster Cathedral.

Prime Minister Macmillan (top, center) was among the guests at a reception following the Radziwill christening. The President poses at left with his godchild, as Mrs. Kennedy and her sister Lee (left foreground, above) show themselves to the London crowds.

STEEL CRISIS

"You have Mr. Blough at a quarter to six."

Those nine words, spoken to President Kennedy by his personal secretary Evelyn Lincoln on the quiet Tuesday afternoon of April 10, 1962, were to serve as the White House preface to the "Great Steel Crisis of 1962." Roger M. Blough, chairman of the board of the United States Steel Corporation, had called the White House to ask for an appointment that evening because he had something "important" to say. A few minutes after 5:45 the President received him in his oval office. Blough sat on a sofa to the right of the President, who was in his rocking chair. Then Blough handed the President a press release about to be sent to newspapers in Pittsburgh and New York.

UNITED STATES STEEL CORPORATION
PUBLIC RELATIONS DEPARTMENT
71 BROADWAY, NEW YORK 6, N. Y.

TELEPHONE
DI 4-9000

NIGHT TELEPHONE
DI 4-9054

FOR A.M. PAPERS
WEDNESDAY, APRIL 11, 1962

Pittsburgh, Pa., April 10 - For the first time in nearly four years, United States Steel today announced an increase in the general level of its steel prices. This "catch-up" adjustment, effective at 12:01 a.m. tomorrow, will raise the price of the company's steel products by an average of about 3.5 per cent -- or three-tenths of a cent per pound.

The President scanned the announcement, and immediately summoned Arthur J. Goldberg, then Secretary of Labor. Goldberg was there in minutes. He glanced at the announcement, and proceeded to lecture Blough with some heat. He said it could be viewed only as a double-cross because the company had given no hint of its intentions while the Administration was urging the United Steelworkers of America to soften its wage demands in the recent contract negotiations. The President listened to the discussion without losing his temper. Blough defended himself and left. As The Times reported later:

> When he [Blough] had gone President Kennedy called for the three members of his Council of Economic Advisers. Dr. Walter W. Heller, the chairman, a lean and scholarly-looking man, came running from his office across the street. Dr. Kermit Gordon followed in three minutes. James Tobin, the third member, came to the office later in the evening.
>
> Into the President's office came Theodore C. Sorensen, the White House special counsel, Mr. [Kenneth] O'Donnell and Andrew T. Hatcher, acting press secretary in the absence of Pierre Salinger, who was on vacation.
>
> Now the President, who usually keeps his temper under rein, let go. He felt he had been double-crossed—deliberately. The office of the President had been affronted. The national interest had been flouted.
>
> It was clear that the Administration would fight. No one knew exactly what could be done, but from that moment the awesome power of the Federal Government began to move.

The President decided to deliver his first counter-attack the next day at his scheduled news conference. He asked his aides to develop material for his statement. And he asked for some statistics to help show the price increases unjustified.

The news had surprised the President and confronted him with a major challenge. In the next 72 hours, he was to use all the powers and prestige at his command to overturn the decision. His young Administration—just 15 months old—had placed great emphasis on economic stability and had watched closely as steel management and labor negotiated a contract it regarded as noninflationary. Now the President saw betrayal. The Kennedy Administration had asked union negotiators to moderate their demands at the bargaining table. And the President felt that a stable price line was implicit in the steel contract, signed just four days before. He saw in jeopardy his whole grand design for holding the line against inflation and for stable prices and wages. He undoubtedly saw his political fortunes damaged. He made the decision to fight.

And as James Reston wrote in his column:

> The Kennedys do not like to lose. They do not like to be double-crossed. And when they think they have been double-crossed, brother, hand me down my steel shillelagh!

The Washington story in The Times reported the events of that Tuesday as follows:

U. S. STEEL RAISES PRICE $6 A TON; KENNEDY ANGERED, SEES AFFRONT; TWO INVESTIGATIONS ARE ORDERED

WASHINGTON, April 10—President Kennedy was infuriated by tonight's news that the United States Steel Corporation was raising its prices.

The word from White House intimates was that he regarded the move as an unjustified and deliberate affront to his Administration. There was some feeling here that tonight's unexpected development would have a profound effect on the President's attitude toward the business community and possibly on his economic policies in general.

There was no immediate on-the-record comment from the White House on the increase. However, a spokesman for the Department of Justice said:

"Because of past price behavior in the steel industry the Department of Justice will take an immediate and close look at the current situation and any future developments."

Another story that same day reported:

> PITTSBURGH, April 10—The United States Steel Corporation announced tonight price increases averaging $6 a ton, effective at midnight.
>
> The other members of the "Big 11" steel companies were expected to announce increases soon.
>
> United States Steel, the nation's No. 1 producer, termed the increase a "catch-up" adjustment amounting to about three-tenths of a cent a pound. It was the first rise by the company since 1958.
>
> United States Steel said the increase would affect all its principal products, as well as those of its three operating divisions—American Steel and Wire, National Tube and Tennessee Coal and Iron.

But there was no direct word that Tuesday evening from the President. The Justice Department and Senator Estes Kefauver, Democrat of Tennessee, chairman of the Senate Anti-Trust and Monopoly Subcommittee, both indicated investigations. Behind the mention of Senator Kefauver's inquiry in the news report was a phone call by the President to the Senator. Kefauver, at his home, was getting ready to go out for the evening. The phone rang. Would the Senator publicly register "dismay" at the price increase, the President asked. And would the Senator consider an investigation? The Senator said he would. So did the Justice Department.

The wheels were now in motion. Officials were called downtown for night work in Heller's office in the old State Department Building across the street from the White House. The President, his mind on the steel dispute, changed to a black tie. The annual Congressional reception was set for 9:45, just four hours after the Blough meeting. The President recalled that the news of the Cuban disaster in the Bay of Pigs had also arrived during his reception, in 1961.

"I'll never hold another Congressional reception," he remarked.

He lapsed into small talk with the guests, slipped out occasionally to talk about steel and stayed until 12:08 A.M. Then he went to bed. But the lights continued to burn in the offices across the street.

The news conference came at 3:30 P.M. the next day. The Times reported the President's reaction:

PRESIDENT ASSAILS STEEL
FOR 'IRRESPONSIBLE' RISE
AND 'CONTEMPT' OF NATION

WASHINGTON, April 11—President Kennedy accused the major steel corporations today of "irresponsible defiance" of the public interest and "ruthless disregard" of their duty to the nation in raising steel prices by $6 a ton.

Arriving at his news conference a minute late, the President strode quickly to the lectern and in a tone of cold anger read a long indictment of the steel companies' action.

At a time of grave crisis in Berlin and Southeast Asia, the President began, when reservists were being asked to leave their families and servicemen to risk their lives, he found it hard "to accept a situation in which a tiny handful of steel executives" could show "such utter contempt for the interest of 185,000,000 Americans."

After reciting the probable effects of the action on the nation's economy, the President ended:

"Some time ago I asked each American to consider what he would do for his country, and I asked the steel companies. In the last twenty-four hours we had their answer."

The President's anger and disappointment were all the greater because the Administration had been working for almost a year to get the steel industry and the United Steelworkers Union to exercise restraint on prices and wages. The Administration had congratulated itself that this effort had paid off in the "noninflationary" work contract concluded last week.

The President made clear today in response to questions that the Administration had "never at any time asked for a commitment" from either side in the negotiations. Nevertheless, he charged the steel industry, in effect, with bad faith. The whole purpose and effect of the Administration's role, he declared, "was to achieve an agreement which would make unnecessary any increase in prices," and both parties understood this.

Also on the front page that morning was this news story:

PITTSBURGH, April 11—Five big steel producers increased their prices today in line with a $6-a-ton increase announced yesterday by the United States Steel Corporation.

They were the Bethlehem Steel Corporation, the Republic Steel Corporation, the Jones & Laughlin Steel Corporation, the Youngstown Sheet and Tube Company and the Wheeling Steel Corporation.

At the same time, other steel concerns said that they planned to study the situation. At least one hinted broadly that it would follow suit.

The steel price rise, coming after a labor settlement that was labeled as noninflationary, set off a wave of protests in the nation's capital. The labor contracts provided new fringe benefits estimated to be worth 10 cents an hour.

Tucked at the end of this story was one sentence: "The Inland Steel Company took no immediate action on prices." The mention of Inland went virtually unnoticed by the public. It looked as if all the big companies were about to leap. But Inland was to figure prominently in the outcome.

The President's strategy that Wednesday was beginning to take some shape. He met for breakfast with his top advisers. Later, he called Secretary of Commerce Luther Hodges, who spent most of the day calling businessmen across the country.

A Times recapitulation later told of the developing counter moves:

In his conference statement the President had seemed to hold out no hope that the price increases could be rolled back. If the increases held, what imminent comfort could there be in possible antitrust decrees that would take three years to come from the courts?

Actually, the possibility of making United States Steel retract the increase had been considered early in the consultation.

Drs. Heller and Gordon, and possibly some of the other economists, had argued that the principal thrust of the Administration's effort should be to convince one or two significant producers to hold out. In a market such as steel, they said, the high-priced sellers would have to come down if the others did not go up.

This suggested a line of strategy that probably proved decisive . . .

Everything pointed to Inland as the key to the situation.

Inland Steel Corporation, with headquarters in Chicago, is a highly efficient producer. It could make a profit at lower prices than those of some of the bigger companies. And any company that sold in the Midwest, such as United States Steel, would feel Inland's price competition.

That same day, Arthur Krock, "In the Nation" columnist of The Times, wrote:

> If one of the important segments of the steel industry that has not yet joined what the President called the "parade" of almost identical price-raising should keep out of the procession awhile, the pressure of competition on the paraders conceivably could force them to break ranks.

The Administration began approaches to Inland and other companies still holding out. Edward Gudeman, then Under Secretary of Commerce, put in a call to his former schoolmate, Philip D. Block Jr., vice chairman of Inland. Another call was made by Henry H. Fowler, Under Secretary of the Treasury and Acting Secretary in Dillon's absence, to John F. Smith Jr., Inland's president. And Secretary Goldberg called Leigh B. Block, vice president of Inland for purchasing. (Joseph Leopold Block, Inland's chairman, was in Japan at the time.) Details of all the calls were not made known at the time, but The Times reported later as follows:

> Though no concrete assurance was asked or volunteered in these conversations, the Administration gathered assurance that Inland would hold the line for at least another day or two.
>
> Next came Armco, sixth largest in the nation. Walter Heller had a line into that company. So did others. Calls were made. And through these channels the Administration learned that Armco was holding off for the time being, but there would be no public announcement one way or the other.
>
> Meanwhile, Mr. Gudeman had called a friend in the upper reaches of the Kaiser company. Secretary McNamara had called a number of friends, one of them at Allegheny-Ludlum, a large manufacturer of stainless.
>
> How many calls were made by President Kennedy himself cannot be told. But some time during all the activity he talked to Edgar Kaiser, chairman of Kaiser Steel, in California.
>
> According to one official who was deeply involved in all this effort, the over-all objective was to line up companies representing 18 per cent of the nation's capacity. If this could be done, according to friendly sources in the steel industry, these companies with their lower prices soon would be doing 25 per cent of the business. Then Big Steel would have to yield.

The pressures were building up to divide the industry, but the President moved on other fronts, too. A day later, The Times said:

STEEL RISE INVESTIGATION BY GRAND JURY ORDERED; BLOUGH DEFENDS PRICING

WASHINGTON, April 12—Attorney General Robert F. Kennedy announced tonight he had ordered a grand jury investigation of the price increases announced by leading steel makers.

Evidence will be presented to one of the grand juries now sitting in New York.

This move under the Sherman Antitrust Act was one of several decisions that apparently came out of an all-day series of intensive conferences at the White House.

The Justice Department made the following announcement a few hours after the news conference held in New York by Roger M. Blough, chairman of the United States Steel Corporation:

"In response to questions about a statement made by Mr. Blough in his press conference that U. S. Steel Corporation documents had been subpoenaed, the Attorney General said tonight that he had authorized a grand jury investigation of the steel price increases."

The Justice Department subpoenaed records of the company, but it went further and laid itself open to sharp criticism later. The story went on to say:

Special agents of the Federal Bureau of Investigation awakened several newspaper reporters early this morning to question them about a statement opposing a price increase attributed to an officer of the Bethlehem Steel Corporation. The corporation announced an increase the next day. It said the quotation had been incorrect.

The announcement by the Justice Department came a few hours after Blough held a televised news conference at corporation headquarters, reported as follows:

U. S. STEEL SAYS INCREASE WILL STRENGTHEN ECONOMY

Roger M. Blough, board chairman of the United States Steel Corporation, defended his company's new price increase yesterday as a move to strengthen the nation's industrial assets. He also asserted the right of an individual company to make its own pricing decisions.

Mr. Blough said further that the 3½ per cent increase initiated by United States Steel on Wednesday had had no "political motivation." The action increased the composite price of steel mill products by $6 a ton, to $176.

What the stories did not report, however, was that two of the most secret moves of the entire 72-hour period had been set in motion Thursday, the day of the Blough news conference and the Justice Department antitrust announcement. One involved a newspaperman, Charles L. Bartlett, then the Washington correspondent of the Chattanooga Times. "I helped two friends get in touch with each other again," Bartlett said. One of the friends was President Kennedy. The other was an officer of United States Steel. His identity, The Times said, had not been definitely established but "Mr. Bartlett knows Mr. Blough."

The other move involved Clark M. Clifford, a Washington lawyer who had served as White House counsel for President Truman. The President called him and asked him to join Secretary Goldberg in speaking to United States Steel. Clifford agreed, flew to New York and met Blough. He presented himself as a friend of the disputants, but he made clear that he was in one-hundred-per-cent agreement with the President. His purpose, he said, was to see if a tragic mistake could be rectified. The mistake, he left no doubt, was on the company's side. For 14 months, he continued, President Kennedy and Goldberg had worked for healthy conditions in the steel industry. They had tried to create an atmosphere of cooperation in the hope of protecting the national interest. Now all this was gone. The President, he went on, believed there had been a dozen or more occasions when the company's leaders could easily have told him that despite all he had done they might have to raise prices. But they never had told him. The President, to put it bluntly, felt double-crossed.

What Blough said in reply could not be learned. But he indicated at the end that he would welcome further talks and he hoped Clifford would participate in them. Clifford returned to Washington the same day. At his news conference later, Blough said among other things that if Armco Steel Corporation, the sixth largest in the industry, and Inland, the eighth largest, continued to stand pat, "I don't know how long we could maintain our position." Justice Department attorneys continued to serve subpoenas that evening. And President and Mrs. Kennedy prepared for another state dinner, the second in a row, with the Shah and Empress of Iran.

The climax came the next day, Friday the 13th. Early in the day there was some important news from Kyoto, Japan. Joseph Block, Inland's chairman, had been reached by a reporter. He said, "We do not feel that an advance in steel prices at this time would be in the national interest."

A meeting of the President's Advisory Committee on Labor Management Relations—held shortly before United States Steel announced its price rise—at which Kennedy emphasized the need for a stable price line.

At 10:08 A.M. Washington heard the official word from Inland in Chicago. Hopeful of eventual victory, the Administration decided to press on with the war. Secretary McNamara held a news conference at 11:45 A.M. saying the Pentagon had ordered defense contractors to shift steel purchases to companies that had not raised prices. Just before he left for Norfolk to go on the trial run of the first nuclear submarine, the President called another meeting of his advisers, during which word came of Kaiser's announcement to hold the line. Absent from this meeting was Goldberg, who with Clark Clifford had returned to New York for another session with Blough.

While the talk was going on, Blough was called to the phone. Bethlehem Steel, at about 3:30 P.M., had rescinded its price increase. Then, as The Times reconstructed it:

> The big capitulation came at 5:28. Mrs. Barbara Gamarekian, a secretary in the White House press office, was checking the Associated Press news ticker. And there was the announcement—United States Steel had pulled back the price increase.
> Mrs. Gamarekian tore it off and ran into the office of Mr. Sorensen, who was on the phone to acting press secretary Mr. Hatcher, in Norfolk.

"Well," Mr. Sorensen was saying, "I guess there isn't anything new."

Mrs. Gamarekian put the news bulletin under his eye.

"Wait a minute!" shouted Mr. Sorensen.

Mr. Hatcher gave the news to the President as he came off the nuclear submarine Thomas A. Edison in Norfolk.

The next day, The Times reported:

STEEL GIVES IN, RESCINDS RISES
UNDER PRESSURE BY PRESIDENT;
HE SAYS DECISION SERVES NATION

WASHINGTON, April 13—President Kennedy triumphed today over the titans of the steel industry.

Almost precisely 72 hours after the United States Steel Corporation's abrupt announcement of a price increase, the corporation backed down and rescinded the increase late this afternoon.

But the victory wasn't that simple. Ever after, the Kennedy administration was tagged as "anti-business" by business elements in the country.

During the labor-management meeting: (clockwise from bottom left) Henry Ford II, head of the Ford Motor Company; David Dubinsky of the International Ladies' Garment Workers union; the President with the then Secretary of Labor, Arthur J. Goldberg (center), and George Meany, president of AFL-CIO; George

Meany making notes on the discussion; Joseph L. Block, chairman of Inland Steel, one of the companies that later held the line against the price rise; Walter Reuther, president of the United Auto Workers; Luther Hodges, Secretary of Commerce, with Thomas Watson, chairman of IBM (center), and President Kennedy.

MISSILE CRISIS

The Cuban missile crisis burst upon the nation on the night of October 22, 1962. It brought the world to what Kennedy called the "abyss of destruction" and Washington to a time when it measured possibilities in terms of nuclear catastrophe. On that Monday night, in a speech to the nation of extraordinary gravity, Kennedy ordered a "quarantine" on the shipment of offensive military arms to Cuba—missiles that threatened the United States. Further, he extended a direct challenge to the Soviet leaders, accusing them of deliberate "false statements about their intentions in Cuba." The United States, Kennedy said, would not stop short of military action to end the "clandestine, reckless and provocative threat to world peace," and, if necessary, would do it alone. In what were perhaps the gravest lines in that speech, he said:

"It shall be the policy of this Administration to regard any nuclear missile launched from Cuba against any nation in the Western Hemisphere as an attack by the Soviet Union on the United States requiring a full retaliatory response on the Soviet Union."

The President concluded:

"Let no one doubt that this is a difficult and dangerous effort on which we have set out. No one can foresee precisely what course it will take or what costs or casualties will be incurred.

"The path we have chosen for the present is full of hazards—as all paths are—but it is the one most consistent with our character and courage as a nation and our commitments around the world.

"The cost of freedom is always high—but Americans have always paid it. And one path we shall never choose is the path of surrender or submission.

"Our goal is not the victory of might but the vindication of right—not peace at the expense of freedom, but both peace and freedom, here in this hemisphere, and, we hope, around the world. God willing, that goal will be achieved."

The crisis had begun to develop toward the end of July and throughout August, when American intelligence sources reported the beginning of an arms build-up in Cuba. However, secret photographic reconnaissance, which had been under way for some time, noted no major offensive weapons. "Were it to be otherwise," Kennedy said on September 4, "the gravest issues would arise."

Soon after, because of reports from Cuban émigrés and of concern within intelligence agencies, Kennedy ordered the entire island of Cuba photographed from the air. Some Republicans, notably Senator Kenneth B. Keating of New York, kept insisting in this period that Castro and the Russians were installing missile bases in Cuba, but Administration sources just as insistently said there was no evidence of this. However, by the beginning of October, intelligence agents were convinced that something suspicious was taking shape near San Cristobal. And on October 14, after Hurricane Ella had swept by and cloud formations had lifted, the cameras in the U-2 planes provided confirmation—missile bases were under construction.

Photo interpreters analyzed the pictures throughout the next day, and the following morning McGeorge Bundy, Kennedy's special adviser on national security affairs, visited the White House, where he found the President in his bedroom, wearing pajamas and a robe, reading the papers. It was clear to them that these missile bases posed a direct threat to the mainland of the United States.

Bundy left to summon officials to a meeting at the White House. Kennedy, meanwhile, kept a 9:30 appointment with Lieutenant Commander Walter M. Schirra Jr., the astronaut, and his wife and two children. At 11:45, Kennedy walked into the Cabinet Room to preside over a meeting of what was to be known as the executive committee of the National Security Council. The group, made up of intelligence, Defense and State Department officials, also included Vice President Johnson, Attorney General Robert Kennedy, Secretary of the Treasury Douglas Dillon and Ted Sorensen.

These men sifted the possibilities. If the United States did nothing, they concluded, the credibility of its pledges would be undermined and Moscow would make an enormous military gain. Further, as one official recalled: "Latin American affairs would never have been the same. To the Latins Mr. Khrushchev might look like a winner."

If on the other hand the United States bombed or invaded Cuba, the neutral nations would protest violently, the North Atlantic Treaty Organization would be thrown into disarray, and Khrushchev would be furnished with an excuse for counteraction in Berlin or elsewhere. Moreover, bombing would tarnish the moral position of the United States—an argument that Robert Kennedy was to press forcefully—and it would kill Russians as well as Cubans.

The third possibility was a blockade, and the dangers in this were implicit. It, too, might give Moscow an excuse for pressure on Berlin; it might not get at the missiles already in Cuba; and, as Johnson had noted as recently as October 6, "stopping a Russian ship is an act of war."

At this first meeting of the committee, Kennedy and his advisers were uncertain on objectives—whether the main goal was to get Castro or the missiles out—but two decisions were made: to increase aerial surveillance of Cuba and to make the disclosure of the missiles and the United States response to them simultaneous.

Time and secrecy were important—time so the Pentagon could work out enormous problems of logistics, secrecy so the Kremlin would not anticipate and counter the moves in Washington. Kennedy decided that he would in no way change his schedule and thus arouse suspicions. Accordingly, the next day, Wednesday, October 17, he flew to Connecticut to campaign for Democrats in Stratford, New Haven and Waterbury. He returned at midnight. New U-2 photographs made during the day showed that besides medium range missiles, sites for intermediate range missiles were under construction in the Guanajay area between San Cristobal and Havana. These missiles, Kennedy was to tell the nation in a few days, could obliterate "most of the major cities in the Western Hemisphere."

On Thursday, October 18, Kennedy met twice with his Cuban advisers—some of whom now called their group the "Think Tank" or the "War Council"—and kept an appointment with Soviet Foreign Minister Andrei A. Gromyko. Gromyko told Kennedy that he would speak frankly because he knew the President appreciated frankness. Soviet aid to Cuba, he said, was only for defensive purposes. Kennedy, in turn, recalled his earlier statement that any change in this would have grave consequences.

Two things kept Kennedy from confronting Gromyko with what he knew of the Soviet missiles in Cuba: He had not decided on what course the United States would take, and he feared that, in the face of a warning, the Russians would not back off but would take evasive action and blunt the American response.

Throughout that week, while the War Council met and pondered, Kennedy frequently stayed away from the meetings so the planners could speak out more freely in his absence. But, while the planning and deliberations were unfettered, there was no doubt that Kennedy gave the orders. "He held everyone under tight control," one official said. "He issued orders like a military commander expecting to be obeyed immediately and to be challenged only on the grounds of overriding disagreement."

On Friday, October 19, Kennedy spoke in Cleveland, stopped at Springfield, Illinois, to lay flowers on the tomb of Lincoln and then flew on to Chicago. When he entered the Sheraton Blackstone Hotel a man flashed a placard about Cuba: "Less profile—More courage." Before he left the capital, Kennedy had approved the trend in thinking toward a blockade. That night he checked his War Council by telephone and that night, too, Justice Department officials began drafting a blockade proclamation.

On Saturday, October 20, Robert Kennedy left a planning meeting to call the President in Chicago; time was growing short, tension in the White House was becoming apparent and secrecy might soon crumble. Shortly afterward, Pierre Salinger announced that the President had a cold and was flying home.

LEFT: The President meets (top) with the executive committee of the National Security Council, to discuss the threat of Cuban missile bases; (bottom) he confers with Defense Secretary McNamara outside in the Rose Garden. ABOVE: On October 22, when he was sure of the facts, and the alternatives, Kennedy made a televised report to the nation.

Kennedy arrived at the White House at 1:37 P.M. and read the first draft of the speech that Sorensen had prepared for a proposed television address. That afternoon, in the Oval Room of the White House, Kennedy all but certified the blockade. One official said later: "This was not a Solomonic decision by the President. He was not choosing between sharply conflicting views. He was approving a view that his advisers had reached after exhaustive exploration of every possibility. The process was not a series of conflicts but an exchange of ideas developing a rolling consensus."

At 11 A.M. on Sunday, October 21, Kennedy met with key officials in the White House. He pressed them with specific questions and at noon he made his final decision—the blockade was on.

Sunday and Monday were days of intense diplomatic orchestration. The State Department drafted letters for embassies concerning the speech. Dean Acheson, a former Secretary of State, was dispatched to Europe to tell de Gaulle and the NATO Council of the impending events. On Monday, October 22, the day the world was to be told, Kennedy summoned 20 Congressional leaders of both parties back to Washington. At 4 P.M. he met with the Prime Minister of Uganda, Milton Obote. When Kennedy escorted Obote through a swarm of reporters in the White House news room 45 minutes later, he said expressionlessly, "It has been a very interesting day."

At 5 P.M., two hours before the speech, Kennedy laid the aerial photographs before the Congressional leaders. "We have decided to take action," he said, telling them about the impending blockade. Senator Richard B. Russell of Georgia, the chairman of the Armed Services Committee, disagreed. Invasion was the only acceptable solution, he said; a blockade was too slow, too risky. Senator J. W. Fulbright agreed with him. Kennedy said mildly that it was easy to hold those opinions if you did not have the responsibility of action.

Two hours later Kennedy spoke to the nation. Swiftly he drew the issue with the Soviet Union:

"This secret, swift and extraordinary buildup of Communist missiles in an area well known to have a special and historical relationship to the United States and the nations of the Western Hemisphere is a deliberately provocative and unjustified change in the status quo, which cannot be accepted in this country if our courage and our commitments are ever again to be trusted by either friend or foe."

Thirteen hours later, on Tuesday afternoon in Moscow, Ambassador Foy D. Kohler was handed a letter from Khrushchev to Kennedy and a long Government statement. The statement was at once a diatribe and a panegyric—an accusation of provocation and a paean to peace. But it contained no ultimatum, no challenge to war. Moscow, it was apparent, had been thrown into confusion.

The headlines said:

SOVIET CHALLENGES U.S. RIGHT TO BLOCKADE; INTERCEPTION OF 25 RUSSIAN SHIPS ORDERED; CUBA QUARANTINE BACKED BY UNITED O.A.S.

In his column, James Reston wrote:

> WASHINGTON, Oct. 23—It is now fairly obvious that Nikita Khrushchev, in planning Soviet policy on Cuba, misjudged the spirit of America and the character of President Kennedy.
>
> This is a common European habit, reaching from George III of Great Britain to Adolf Hitler, and in Khrushchev's case it is easy to explain.
>
> He never understood the President's policy on the invasion of the Bay of Pigs in Cuba in April 1961. As he has said in numerous private conversations, he would have understood a hands-off policy at that time or an effective strike that would have brought Castro down— as Moscow moved on Hungary or the Baltic states—but he could not understand how the United States could get involved in that exercise without seeing it through to a successful conclusion.
>
> Accordingly, he has been acting on the assumption ever since that President Kennedy is weak.

Still, though it was unprepared diplomatically, the Kremlin took decisive military steps. The Defense Ministry deferred discharges for personnel in the rocket, antiaircraft and submarine fleets. And the

Warsaw Treaty forces—Russia, Czechoslovakia, East Germany, Hungary, Poland and Rumania—were ordered "to raise the military preparedness of the troops and fleets."

Throughout Tuesday, its allies rallied to the United States. Prime Minister Macmillan of Britain, in the first of what were to be daily trans-Atlantic calls, pledged his full support to Kennedy. The other NATO nations quickly joined him. That evening, in the greatest display of solidarity in the Western Hemisphere since World War II, the Organization of American States voted, 19-0, to authorize "the use of armed force" to carry out the quarantine of Cuba.

The American blockade proclamation was sent in uncoded transmission to the world capitals. Ambassadors were called in to the State Department to receive copies, and the Voice of America broadcast it on all channels. It declared that missiles and bombers were contraband and it authorized the Navy to stop and search any ship it suspected of carrying these items, to take her into custody if she refused to sail to another port—and to use force if necessary.

The blockade was to become effective at 10 o'clock on Wednesday morning, October 24. The night before, McNamara had said that 24 Soviet ships were heading for Cuba, their courses unchanged in the last 25 hours. It had been expected that the first Russian ship would enter the blockade zone at nightfall on Wednesday. However, late in the afternoon some of the vessels altered their course. Washington surmised that Moscow was still undecided on what to do and that it had held back the ships with military cargoes. The Times reported:

SOME SOVIET SHIPS SAID TO VEER FROM CUBA; KHRUSHCHEV SUGGESTS A SUMMIT MEETING; THANT BIDS U.S. AND SOVIET DESIST 2 WEEKS

The next day, Thursday, October 25, the Navy intercepted the first ship. She was not boarded, but allowed to proceed after identifying herself. Despite this, the grimness in the White House mounted as the day wore on. It was confirmed that the 12 Soviet ships that had veered from Cuba the day before had indeed swung around in an opposite direction. As a reciprocal gesture, when the first Russian ship, the oil tanker *Bucharest*, was intercepted, the Navy did not board her but only satisfied itself that her cargo was petroleum and allowed her to continue.

Although this seemed to be a hopeful sign, the first rumors of a Cuban invasion swept the capital by midafternoon. The Defense Department refused to comment on reports that a mounting military build-up in Florida was a prelude either to an invasion or to bombing sorties. And in a statement to his Louisiana constituents, Representative Hale Boggs said, "Believe me, if these missiles are not dismantled, the United States has the power to destroy them, and I assure you this will be done." In the United Nations that night Adlai E. Stevenson dramatically confronted Valerian A. Zorin, the Soviet Ambassador, and challenged him to admit that the Soviet Union had planted missile sites in Cuba. When Zorin refused to answer, Stevenson said, "I am prepared to wait until hell freezes over for your answer."

This was entertaining, but the significant action was taking place in the White House, where Kennedy met with his advisers. The President elected to maintain a tough line. While he agreed to discussions with U Thant, the Acting Secretary General of the United Nations, about his previous day's proposal for a moratorium, Kennedy said that "the existing threat was created by the secret introduction of offensive weapons into Cuba, and the answer lies in the removal of such weapons."

It was apparent that the next move was Moscow's, and on Friday, October 26, Washington intensified its pressure. The Times said:

U.S. FINDS CUBA SPEEDING BUILD-UP OF BASES; WARNS OF FURTHER ACTION; U.N. TALKS OPEN; SOVIET AGREES TO SHUN BLOCKADE ZONE

That morning, two destroyers put search parties aboard a Lebanese freighter that had been chartered by the Russians. When no contraband was found, the ship was allowed to proceed. A few hours later, the State Department called reporters' attention to a line in the speech in which Kennedy had disclosed the

Cuban missiles. If offensive preparations were not halted, the President had said, "further action will be justified." Shortly after this, the White House disclosed that construction on the missile sites was still under way and that the Russians were obviously seeking "full operational capability as soon as possible."

Moscow and Washington were now, as an official put it later, "eyeball to eyeball."

The first indication of a break came in an unusual way. The chief Soviet intelligence agent in Washington called a newspaperman, John Scalli, diplomatic correspondent of the American Broadcasting Company, and indicated that Moscow was amenable under certain conditions to eliminating the threat of nuclear war over Cuba. Mr. Scalli immediately relayed the message to the State Department and thereafter became an unofficial channel of messages between Washington and Moscow.

At about 9 o'clock that night, another apparent break in the crisis arrived—a new message from Khrushchev. It reached the State Department bit by bit as it was translated by the embassy in Moscow. It rambled, but it seemed to be conciliatory. Implicit was an offer to withdraw the missiles under the

U.S. destroyer inspects a Soviet freighter outward bound from Cuba, in November 1962, after missile bases had been dismantled.

supervision of the United Nations if the United States would lift the blockade and promise not to invade Cuba. Kennedy was told of the message at 11 P.M. He heard it with relief, confident that some sort of détente had been reached, and decided that a reply would be sent to the Kremlin in the morning.

But on Saturday morning, October 27, there arose one of the most perplexing mysteries of the cold war. As the War Council convened to draft the message to Moscow, a second letter from Khrushchev arrived in the State Department. It was distinctly different in tone and style from the earlier message and it proposed a trade: Cuban missiles for NATO bases in Turkey. The first message was a secret letter from Khrushchev to Kennedy, the second a diplomatic communication. Which was genuine? Had the Premier been overruled or was he following arcane diplomacy? The bases in Turkey were not of great military importance, but to barter them away might do irreparable harm to the Western alliance. Kennedy took personal command of the problem. The White House issued a brief statement saying there were conflicting Soviet proposals and that no negotiations could even commence until work on the missile bases was stopped.

When the Council convened again at the State Department the situation had worsened. A U-2 was missing over Cuba and presumed to be lost. Another plane had been fired on. Castro was spewing defiance and promising to shoot down all Yankee aircraft. Clearly, a new factor had been introduced. That afternoon Kennedy weighed the evidence. Reconnaissance had to continue, perhaps with fighter escorts. If the antiaircraft batteries were attacked, Russians would probably be killed. Kennedy decided to stall for time. Khrushchev might order Castro to stop firing; Castro himself might decide there was nothing to be gained in a shooting war. Accordingly, the Pentagon only warned that it would resist interference with the surveillance flights. It called up more than 14,000 air reservists to reinforce the warning.

Still to be answered was the Soviet offer on Turkey, and here the War Council elected to gamble. It sent a letter to Moscow that virtually ignored the offer. The letter said that, if the President understood Khrushchev correctly, he would remove the offensive weapons from Cuba in return for a lifting of the blockade and a promise not to invade Cuba. This, the letter said, was acceptable to the United States. The letter was given to the Kremlin at 7 on Saturday night. That same night the council sat in the White House, conscious, as one person said, that they "were coming right down to the wire of another decision—probably more than the public realized." If the offer were rejected, the United States might have to expand the blockade, possibly by declaring Soviet petroleum contraband. Then, too, there was a growing possibility that United States planes might be forced to destroy Cuban antiaircraft batteries and that the situation might become uncontrollable. Kennedy said grimly that night that it seemed to be touch and go, that now it could go "either way."

Sunday morning brought immense relief to Washington—relief that was to be tempered in the next 10 days by Castro's recalcitrance. The Times headline said:

U.S. AND SOVIET REACH ACCORD ON CUBA; KENNEDY ACCEPTS KHRUSHCHEV PLEDGE TO REMOVE MISSILES UNDER U.N. WATCH

The Moscow radio broadcast Khrushchev's reply to Kennedy's letter of the night before—the missile bases would be dismantled and the missiles crated and returned to the Soviet Union. Representatives of the United Nations, Khrushchev promised, would "verify the dismantling." The Premier said he trusted Kennedy's assurance that there would be no attack on Cuba. And then, going beyond the President's pledge, he added, "not only on the part of the United States but also on the part of other nations of the Western Hemisphere." Kennedy replied that he welcomed Khrushchev's "statesmanlike decision" as a "welcome and constructive contribution to peace."

Between that day, October 28, and November 8, when Kennedy declared that the last missile site had been dismantled, the patience of both sides was tested. Castro refused to allow U.N. inspection teams on his island but the dismantling was verified by aerial photographs, intelligence reports and the inspection of outbound Russian freighters. In the end it was a victory for Kennedy, perhaps the most formidable one of his Administration. Some critics said the crisis was perfectly timed to help the Democrats in the November elections; others said it was Kennedy's finest hour.

CIVIL RIGHTS

The year 1960 began badly for Negroes. A grand jury in Biloxi, Mississippi, refused to indict suspects in the killing of Mack Charles Parker, a Negro who had been lynched while awaiting trial. Tuskegee Institute said somberly that little had been done in 1959 to improve the life of American Negroes. School desegregation had slowed almost to a halt. The Eisenhower Administration had sent troops to Little Rock to enforce the desegregation decree of a Federal Court, but Eisenhower himself had consistently refused to lend moral support to the school desegregation ruling laid down by the Supreme Court in May 1954. His position, stated often, was, "I don't believe you can change the hearts of men with laws or decisions."

During the Presidential campaign of 1960, however, Kennedy sounded a different call. In time it could be questioned whether he led or was led by the racial revolution, but that fall he was emphatic on the role of the President.

In Los Angeles on September 9, he said:

"He must exert the great moral and educational force of his office to help bring about equal access to public facilities—from churches to lunch counters—and to support the right of every American to stand up for his rights—even if that means sitting down for them. For only the President, the representative of all interests and sections, can create the understanding and the tolerance which is necessary if we are to make an orderly transition to a completely free society. If the President does not himself wage the struggle for equal rights—if he stands above the battle—then the battle will inevitably be lost."

Even before he was elected, Kennedy made it clear that he would lend the moral and educational force of the Presidency to the cause of equal rights. Indeed, it may have been this publicly expressed position that won him the Presidency. At the height of the campaign, Dr. Martin Luther King Jr., the Negro leader, was jailed in Georgia, ostensibly for violating probation on a traffic charge. Kennedy called Mrs. King in Atlanta and expressed his sympathy. Vice President Nixon did nothing, and in the final week of the campaign Kennedy supporters printed 2 million copies of a pamphlet called " 'No Comment' Nixon Versus a Candidate with a Heart, Senator Kennedy." Whether it was because of this or for wider reasons, Kennedy, who won the election by only 118,550 votes, mustered a far greater percentage of the Negro vote than did Adlai Stevenson in 1956.

With Kennedy as President, Federal involvement in the civil rights struggle intensified. Kennedy named Andrew Hatcher as associate White House press secretary—his first appointment of a Negro to high office. On Inauguration Day, he noticed that there were no Negro cadets marching with the Coast Guard Academy contingent; that very afternoon steps were taken to see that Negroes were admitted to the academy. He named many Negroes to government jobs, including Robert L. Weaver, who became administrator of the Housing and Home Finance Agency, and the highest ranking Negro in the Administration.

Kennedy's first major move on civil rights was a simple use of Presidential power. The Times reported it this way:

KENNEDY ORDERS
EQUAL JOB RIGHTS
IN FEDERAL WORK

WASHINGTON, March 6—President Kennedy, in his first major civil rights move, created a new committee today to fight racial discrimination in hiring by the Government and its contractors.

In a sweeping Executive order he armed the group with a broad range of powers to enforce the policy against discrimination. And he designated the Labor Department as its chief investigative arm.

The new group will be called the President's Committee on Equal Employment Opportunity. . . .

The Executive order, which takes effect 30 days from today, will have a direct impact on thousands and perhaps millions of individuals, companies and groups—quite apart from the members of racial minorities.

In the early days of the Administration, Robert Kennedy began a largely unpublicized task among Southern politicians and lawyers—attempting to raise the voices of moderation. And in May of that first year of the Administration, the President was to rely largely on Bobby in resolving the problems of law and custom raised by the Freedom Riders.

The Freedom Rider phase of the civil rights movement was short-lived; it involved no more than 1,000 persons directly. Yet it provided the Kennedy Administration with its first dramatic issue in the rights battle. Freedom Riders met with violence when they sought to desegregate bus terminals in Anniston, Birmingham and Montgomery. State officials initially failed to provide protection. Federal marshals headed by Byron R. White, the Deputy Attorney General, intervened and prevented bloodshed. Robert Kennedy then asked the Interstate Commerce Commission for an order banning railroad and bus segregation—an order that was issued four months later.

Voting suits provided another dramatic instance of Federal involvement. In the first three years of the 1957 Civil Rights Act, under the Eisenhower Administration, 10 voting suits were filed; in the next three years there were 43. For the first time the Justice Department filed suit in Mississippi including one in Sunflower County, the home of James O. Eastland, chairman of the Senate Judiciary Committee.

During the Presidential campaign, Kennedy had insisted that racial discrimination could be prohibited in Federally assisted housing by a stroke of the Presidential pen on an Executive order. After the election, however, he delayed action, largely because of fear that Southern Congressmen would retaliate. On November 6, 1962, an Executive order on housing was prepared, but Kennedy decided to put off signing it until after the election. When he did The Times reported it this way:

WASHINGTON, Nov. 20—By a long-promised "stroke of the pen," President Kennedy prohibited today racial and religious discrimination in housing built or purchased by Federal aid.

In an Executive order, he directed Federal agencies to "take all necessary and appropriate" action to that end.

Administration officials said that the order would apply principally to housing projects and apartments. When the regulations are drawn, they said, sales of private homes by individual owners will probably be exempt.

The order, which had seemed so daring a few years before, was now criticized as too timid by militant rights leaders. Indeed, it did fall short of the campaign promises. But King was still able to call it "not only constitutionally sound but . . . also morally right," while Senator Allen Ellender of Louisiana could brand it "an audacious usurpation of power by the Executive branch."

Perhaps the most inflammable issue during the Kennedy years was school integration. Almost immediately the Administration rejected the position that it could enter litigation only at a judge's invitation. Two months after taking office Robert Kennedy brought the Justice Department into a school case that attacked new state statutes in Louisiana. He also sought to enter a suit in Prince Edward County, Virginia, where public schools had been closed since 1959 to avoid integration. The judge in the case refused to admit the Justice Department, but the department was able to join in the suit when it reached the Court of Appeals and the Supreme Court.

Battered helmet of a U.S. marshal, worn on the University of Mississippi campus

After a gradual decline since 1955 in the number of school districts that were desegregated, there was a sharp increase in 1961. In 1963, more than 150 new districts were integrated, the most since the years immediately after the Supreme Court decree. The influence of Washington in this was undeniable. School boards and Federal judges are sensitive to the mood in the capital, and in the 1960's the mood was one of progress.

The climactic school case, of course, was the enrollment of James H. Meredith at the University of Mississippi in the fall of 1962. During the campaign, Kennedy had said that the coming decade would demand that the President "place himself in the very thick of the fight" for equality; Mississippi gave him the opportunity.

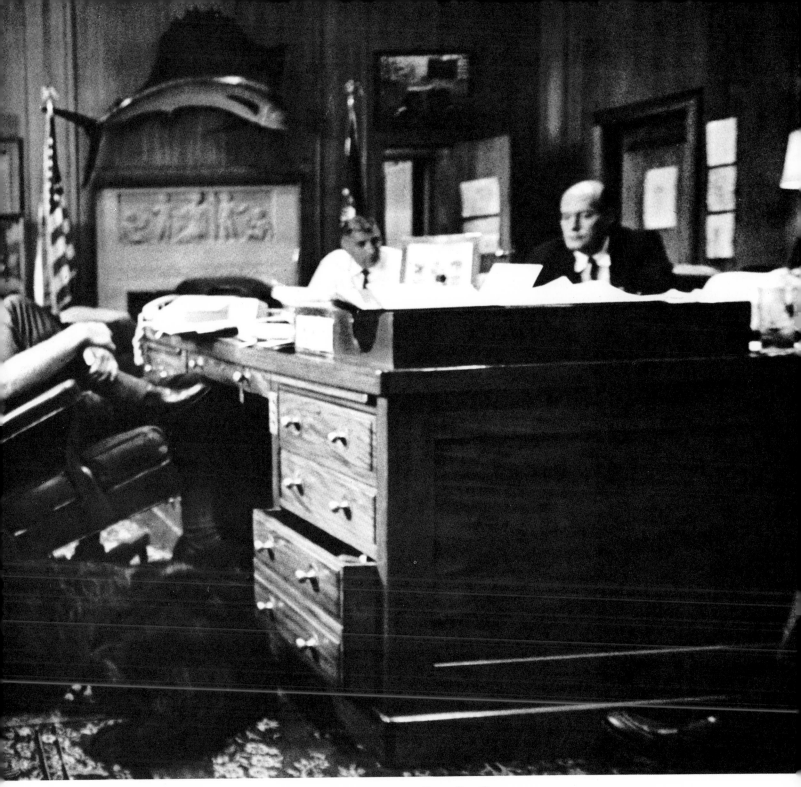

during 1962 riots, is given a prominent place in the Attorney General's office.

Shortly before the campus riots, the Justice Department entered the suit to place Meredith in the university. Both the President and Robert Kennedy called Governor Ross R. Barnett to ask for compliance. The President was determined to avoid a repetition of Eisenhower's action at Little Rock—minimal action in the early stages, followed by intervention with troops. He made an elaborate attempt in the short time yet available to seek a peaceful settlement. He pleaded for compliance with the law, he federalized the Mississippi National Guard to get it out of the way, and publicized the might of the Federal Government. On the night of September 30, 1962, when Meredith entered the university, Kennedy spoke to the people of Mississippi in a television address. "The eyes of the nation and all the world are upon you and upon all of us," he said, "and the honor of your university and your state are in the balance."

But, tragically, the plea was not heeded. The next day The Times headline said:

NEGRO AT MISSISSIPPI U. AS BARNETT YIELDS; 3 DEAD IN CAMPUS RIOT, 6 MARSHALS SHOT; GUARDSMEN MOVE IN; KENNEDY MAKES PLEA

The rioting, which lasted 15 hours, was put down by 3,000 troops and guardsmen and 400 marshals. It took the lives of two men and left one marshal critically wounded. Scores were injured and 25 marshals required medical aid. Oxford, Mississippi, the home of the university, became virtually an occupied town in the weeks after the rioting, and resentment turned into animosity and animosity into hatred. On November 21, 1962, the Mississippi Senate approved a resolution expressing defiance and "utter contempt for the Kennedy Administration." It blamed the "ruthless and corrupted Administration in Washington headed by the Kennedy clan" for the rioting and asked the separate states to join Mississippi "in ridding this once great nation of ours of the Kennedy family dynasty and accompanying evils" and to defy "all who would destroy our freedoms, heritages and constitutional rights."

Despite the bitter abuse of Kennedy, many observers believed that it was Robert Kennedy, rather than his brother, who felt the deeper emotional commitment to the cause of equal rights. Though the President spoke and acted for justice, he sometimes had an air of detachment. But in 1963, Kennedy's emotions seemed to be enlisted in the fight too.

In February 1963, Kennedy asked for a mild bill to insure voting rights and to provide Federal aid for school districts that began desegregation. But the measure was soon dropped as being inadequate; the racial revolution was moving too fast. The intensified sit-in campaign was opening up many places of public accommodation to the Negro in the South, and often the cost was high. The most notable example was the outbreak of violence in May, when pictures of police dogs attacking Negroes focused the attention of the world on Birmingham. Burke Marshall, Kennedy's chief civil rights assistant, flew to Birmingham, persuaded the whites at least to listen to the Negro complaints, and then arranged a truce that led to some desegregation. Talking with Negro leaders at that time, the President surprised them by remarking that the civil rights movement owed a great debt of gratitude to Eugene (Bull) Connor, the police chief of Birmingham, who was responsible for the use of police dogs to control demonstrating Negroes. He explained that it was the use of these dogs and the pictures of their attacks that had awakened the consciences of Americans all over the country and made it possible for the civil rights program to move ahead.

By midsummer of 1963, Federal involvement—and Kennedy's involvement—in civil rights was deeper than ever before. A critical test was in Tuscaloosa, where Governor George C. Wallace, in a carefully arranged gesture of defiance, sought to bar physically the admission of two Negro students to the University of Alabama. The Times headline said:

ALABAMA ADMITS NEGRO STUDENTS; WALLACE BOWS TO FEDERAL FORCE; KENNEDY SEES 'MORAL CRISIS' IN U.S.

After the confrontation in Tuscaloosa, Kennedy spoke to the nation. There was no criticism that night that his words were too abstract, that his mood was impersonal. He said:

"We are confronted primarily with a moral issue. It is as old as the Scriptures and it is as clear as the American Constitution. The heart of the question is whether all Americans are to be afforded equal rights and equal opportunities; whether we are going to treat our fellow Americans as we want to be treated.

"If an American, because his skin is dark, cannot eat lunch in a restaurant open to the public; if he cannot send his children to the best school available; if he cannot vote for the public officials who represent him; if, in short, he cannot enjoy the full and free life which all of us want, then who among us would be content to have the color of his skin changed and stand in his place?

"Who among us would then be content with the counsels of patience and delay? One hundred years have passed since President Lincoln freed the slaves, yet their heirs, their grandsons, are not fully free.

They are not yet freed from the bonds of injustice; they are not yet freed from social and economic oppression.

"And this nation, for all its hopes and all its boasts, will not be fully free until all its citizens are free."

Eight days later the President asked Congress for a civil rights bill. In a somber 5,500-word message, he said that the time had come "for the Congress of the United States to join with the executive and judicial branches in making it clear to all that race has no place in American life and law." The Times reported:

KENNEDY ASKS BROAD RIGHTS BILL AS 'REASONABLE' COURSE IN CRISIS; CALLS FOR RESTRAINT BY NEGROES

The legislation sought to forbid the exclusion of Negroes from hotels, restaurants and other places of public accommodation, to allow the Attorney General to start school desegregation suits, to wipe out discrimination in jobs or activities that are assisted wholly or partly by Federal funds, and to erase racial barriers in businesses and unions.

Kennedy did not live to see his bill passed; it was his successor, a Southern President, who was to prod Congress into its passage. Introduction of the legislation marked the height of Federal involvement in the cause of equal rights. It was criticized by some militants as being too little and too late. The criticism sprang in part from old resentments, in part from the civil rights battlefield. The most sinister and grisly episode took place on September 15 in Birmingham, in a church where a Sunday school teacher had just finished her lesson on "The Love That Forgives." The Times headline the next day said:

BIRMINGHAM BOMB KILLS 4 NEGRO GIRLS IN CHURCH; RIOTS FLARE; 2 BOYS SLAIN

The bomb exploded in the 16th Street Baptist Church, which was a staging point for Negro demonstrators in the five-week campaign led by King. Kennedy issued a statement expressing a "deep sense of outrage and grief" and implied that Governor Wallace's "public disparagement of law and order" had encouraged violence that fell upon the innocent.

Perhaps the summing up of this phase of the racial revolution came on August 28, 1963, when the Times reported:

200,000 MARCH FOR CIVIL RIGHTS IN ORDERLY WASHINGTON RALLY; PRESIDENT SEES GAIN FOR NEGRO

The participants in the March on Washington neither threatened nor begged; they presented a simple demand for passage of the civil rights bill. Kennedy said the cause of 20 million Negroes had been advanced by the march, but even more significant, he said, was "the contribution to all mankind." And a headline on Page 1 of The Times said:

"I HAVE A DREAM . . ."

Peroration by Dr. King Sums Up
A Day the Capital Will Remember

Three Presidents — Harry S. Truman, Dwight D. Eisenhower, and John F. Kennedy — at the burial of Speaker of the House Sam Rayburn at Bonham, Tex., Nov. 18, 1961.

BERLIN—IRELAND—ROME

In the summer of 1963, John Kennedy went barnstorming in Europe. A Presidential visit to Europe at any time stirs discussion; a visit when governments are changing, when a new Pope is being crowned, when the Atlantic Community is in disorder, provokes a controversy. A story in The Times said:

> WASHINGTON, June 22—President Kennedy is off to Europe this weekend for 10 days that will not shake this or any other world. But the greeting in Europe is certain to be warmer than the farewell here, and that about sums up the diplomatic and political consequences of the journey.
>
> The trip has been the subject of lively debate here for weeks. Some contend that popular demonstrations of affection and respect for the President will be an important asset in the contest over the shape of the Western alliance. Others contend that Mr. Kennedy will accomplish nothing and will be neglecting some pressing domestic matters to boot.

The Presidential plane touched down at Wahn Airport—midway between Bonn and Cologne—on the morning of June 23. In his welcoming address, Adenauer chose to interpret an earlier speech by Kennedy as a commitment not to make any deals with the Soviet Union at the expense of the Western allies. Actually, the speech had been an appeal to Moscow to lessen the tensions of the cold war. The lesson was apparent; there was a gulf between the President and Adenauer on Western policy.

From the airport, Kennedy was driven to the great Cathedral of Cologne, where he attended mass. Outside the cathedral, crowds of Germans stood shoulder to shoulder, waiting for a glimpse of the American President. In Bonn the next day the crowds that turned out for Kennedy were larger by far than the crowds that had cheered Eisenhower in 1959 or de Gaulle the previous fall. Kennedy responded to the cheering Rhinelanders in his customary manner—a football player's straight-arm gesture when he wanted to wave, a frequent smile and an occasional handshake. He had scored an impressive diplomatic gain. A Times story said:

> BONN, June 25—President Kennedy was reported today to have restored the intimate relationship between the United States and West German governments that has been lacking for the last three years.
>
> West German sources said that this achievement, enthusiastically welcomed in Bonn, was the most significant political accomplishment of the President's crowded two days in the West German capital.

After Bonn, Kennedy visited Hanau, Frankfurt and Wiesbaden. In Frankfurt the crush was so great that 240 persons fainted. Factory workers displayed signs saying, "Welcome, Johnnie," and toasted the President with mugs of beer. In telling a crowd in Frankfurt how much he appreciated the reception, Kennedy essayed his first German words: "Danke schoen." At the historic Paulskirche in Frankfurt, the President renewed his appeal for interdependence between the United States and what he said must become a fully cohesive Europe. Only then, he said, "can we have a full give-and-take between equals, an equal sharing of responsibilities and an equal level of sacrifice."

With West Berlin Mayor Brandt (center) and Chancellor Adenauer (right), June 26, 1963. OVERLEAF: Speaking at the Schöneberg Rathaus, West Berlin.

The reception in Frankfurt had been triumphant; in the divided city of Berlin it was overwhelming. Describing it, The Times said:

> BERLIN, June 26—President Kennedy saw the miracle and tragedy of West Berlin today as the city turned out to greet him and applaud his country.
>
> The reception was one of the largest and most emotional Mr. Kennedy has ever received.
>
> The West Berliners leaped and screamed along the curbs, waved their handkerchiefs and a variety of flags, threw flowers and broke through police barriers to run beside Mr. Kennedy's car. Some succeeded in shaking his hand. Twice he caught bouquets.

Kennedy had been scheduled to gaze over the wall through the Brandenburg Gate into East Berlin. But the five arches of the gate were covered by huge red banners—hung the night before—that blocked the view. On that emotionally charged day, Kennedy called the wall an "offense against humanity." He said:

"Freedom is indivisible and when one man is enslaved, who are free? When all are free, then we can look forward to that day when this city will be joined as one and this great country and this great continent of Europe in a peaceful and hopeful globe.

"When that day finally comes, as it will, the people of West Berlin can take sober satisfaction in the fact that they were in the front lines for almost two decades.

"All free men, wherever they may live, are citizens of Berlin. And therefore, as a free man, I take pride in the words 'Ich bin ein Berliner.' "

After the speech, Kennedy flew to Dublin, where the citizens stood four deep along the streets to cheer him. The Times headline said:

DUBLIN ACCLAIMS KENNEDY AS ONE RETURNING HOME

In his welcoming speech to Kennedy, Ireland's President Eamon de Valera said: "Cead mile failte" —a hundred thousand welcomes. Ubiquitous posters repeated the sentiment. Ireland was recognizing a local boy—three generations removed—who had made good. The next four days were an agreeable mixture of blarney, sentiment and ceremony. A headline in the Daily Irish Press of Dublin said simply, "A Big Family Picnic." At Dunganstown, the President's second cousin kissed him on the cheek and welcomed him to the birthplace of his great-grandfather. At New Ross, Kennedy sang "Kelly, the Boy From Killane" with some serenading school children.

In contrast, the atmosphere at Kennedy's next stop, Britain, was of almost startling privacy. The President stayed only 24 hours, almost all of which were spent in the seclusion of Prime Minister Macmillan's country estate. The British Government was weathering a sex and security scandal; general elections were on the horizon. It was not a time for ceremony and joint communiqués.

The next stop was Rome. In his airport speech, Kennedy said:

"I come to this ancient country, but I come on the most modern business and that is how the United States and Italy can continue in the important changing years of the sixties to maintain the intimate association, the intimate alliance which has marked our affairs for the last 15 years. Through NATO we are allies. Through necessity we are joined together. Through friendship we find that union to be harmonious."

That evening Kennedy conferred with Italy's President, Antonio Segni, as well as Pietro Nenni, leader of the Socialists, and Aldo Moro, head of the Christian Democrats. The next day Kennedy had a private audience with the newly crowned Pope Paul VI, who recalled that they first met 25 years before when Kennedy had accompanied his parents to Rome for the coronation of Pius XII. Later the Pope said that he and the President had discussed the "peace of the world." Paul also offered this message to Kennedy: "We are ever mindful in our prayers of the efforts to insure to all your citizens the equal benefits of citizenship, which have as their foundation the equality of all men because of their dignity as persons and children of God."

After the audience, the President flew to Naples. The Times story said:

NAPLES, July 2—President Kennedy ended his 10-day tour of four European countries tonight and flew back to Washington.

His last appearance, in Naples, like his first, a week ago in Cologne, Germany, was a smashing success. This hot and humid Mediterranean city gave the President one of the wildest receptions of his tour and provided a fitting climax to it.

As Mr. Kennedy took off from Capodichino Airport, he carried with him some unexpected satisfaction in an Italian visit that had turned out better than expected and a European swing that was viewed as having proved almost entirely successful.

LEFT: Drinking tea with his Irish cousins at Dunganstown, County Wexford. RIGHT: At his audience with newly crowned Pope Paul VI.

FOREIGN POLICY

As President-elect, Kennedy had expressed to Moscow his hope that "in the coming months relations between our two great countries will be marked by good will and a common desire for peace." In his inaugural address he said the nation was ready to resume negotiations with the Soviet Union to ease and perhaps remove world tensions. "Let us begin anew," he declared. "Let us never negotiate out of fear— but let us never fear to negotiate." A few days later a Times story noted:

> WASHINGTON, Jan. 25—President Kennedy indicated tonight that a conscious effort was being made by his Administration to improve United States–Soviet relations.
>
> His demeanor and his tone in his first White House press conference was that of a man who was cautiously but nevertheless definitely trying to defrost the cold war a little. Once or twice President Kennedy reverted to the usual dialogue of the world struggle by referring to the Communists as "the enemy," but his manner was conciliatory, as if he wanted to begin his responsibilities with safe but friendly gestures.

That day Kennedy announced that Moscow had freed two RB-47 fliers who had been shot down over the White Sea the previous summer. He also said that surveillance flights over the Soviet Union would not be resumed. The gestures and words were the start of a rickety East-West détente—a détente that first had to overcome ugly crises in Berlin, Cuba and a dozen lesser spots around the world.

On April 17, 1961, the United States suffered the almost incredible Bay of Pigs humiliation in Cuba. Two months later, against the background of the limping disarmament conference at Geneva, Khrushchev said he was determined to sign a separate peace treaty with East Germany and to relinquish Soviet rights in East Berlin. If the West sought to interfere, he said, he would mobilize Russia. Further, he said that negotiations must recognize the permanent division of Germany. Kennedy called the situation "grave" and insisted that Moscow abide by the World War II pledge to abandon Berlin only when it was the capital of a unified Germany. For weeks Moscow thundered its resolve. When Kennedy went before the nation to answer the challenge, The Times reported it this way:

KENNEDY CALLS FOR 217,000 MEN AND 3.4 BILLION FUND TO MEET 'WORLD-WIDE' THREAT BY SOVIET

> WASHINGTON, July 25—President Kennedy asked tonight for an over-all increase in the nation's military preparedness to meet a Soviet threat he described as "world-wide."
>
> The President proposed adding 217,000 men to the armed forces and increasing expenditures by $3,457,000,000, including $207,000,000 for civil defense.
>
> Mr. Kennedy said that $1,800,000,000 would be earmarked for non-nuclear weapons and ammunition and equipment. . . .
>
> He held out an offer to negotiate on Berlin, however, and declared that if the Russians "seek genuine understanding—not concessions—we shall meet with them."

In his speech that night, Kennedy said, "Everything essential to the cause of freedom will be done; and if that should require more men, taxes, controls or other new powers, I shall not hesitate to request them." This was the beginning of the Berlin crisis, when the President was to rely on a massive show of strength and resolution. The Pentagon placed thousands of reservists on active duty; new units were sent to West Germany to bolster the allied forces. Ultimately, it swayed Khrushchev from a separate peace treaty. It did not, however, prevent the building of what was to become a symbol of totalitarianism—the Berlin wall.

The construction of the wall—28 miles of barbed wire, concrete and steel girders—began August 13. In the next few years dozens of East Germans died while trying to climb the wall or to flee through the mine fields and barbed wire barriers of the 830-mile border dividing Germany. On the first day Berlin was physically divided, The Times said:

SOVIET TROOPS ENCIRCLE BERLIN TO BACK UP SEALING OF BORDER; U.S. DRAFTING VIGOROUS PROTEST

BERLIN, Aug. 14—Two battle-ready Soviet Army divisions were reported today to have ringed Berlin yesterday in support of East Germany's sudden and dramatic closing of the border between East and West Germany.

The Soviet divisions were said to have armor and artillery with them. Other Soviet Army divisions among the estimated total of twenty in East Germany were reported on the move throughout the restive country.

The new Communist measures shut off West Berlin to East Berliners and East Germans. They did not affect the movement from West Berlin into the Communist-controlled eastern sector of the city or the vital communications linking West Berlin to West Germany.

The wall remained, implacable and ugly, but in a sense it represented a stand-off for East and West. Kennedy protested vigorously and portrayed it as a dramatic confession of Communist failure; Khrushchev called it a barrier against Western provocation. The West retained its access rights to Berlin, but throughout the Kennedy Administration the cold war could be measured by intermittent Soviet pressure in the divided city.

In that first year of his Presidency there were few triumphs for either Kennedy or the Western alliance. Basically, he followed a policy laid down by Eisenhower, but with more willingness to spend, to innovate, to intervene, to plan and to experiment. Whereas Eisenhower's White House staff left the foreign policy questions almost wholly to John Foster Dulles, Kennedy and his assistants showed a predilection for making decisions. In the process the State Department declined in authority and Kennedy was accused of administering a disorderly government. His Administration answered that creativity was disorderly and asked that it be judged not by orderliness of procedure but by creativity of results. One White House aide said, "Creative government will always be out of channels."

One indication of this and of Kennedy's growing reliance on economic warfare and international cooperation was the Alliance for Progress.

PRESIDENT GIVES 10-YEAR AID PLAN TO LATIN AMERICA

WASHINGTON, March 13—President Kennedy set forth tonight a ten-point, ten-year economic and social development program for Latin America to meet the challenge of a "future full of peril but bright with hope."

The President outlined his program in an unusual White House ceremony that combined a diplomatic reception with a major speech.

Mr. Kennedy told 250 persons, including diplomats from Latin America and leaders of Congress and their wives, that the United States was prepared to give financial aid "if the countries of Latin America are prepared to do their part." His plan sought to help "all."

Kennedy told the diplomats, "Our motto is what it has always been—Progress, yes! Tyranny, no!; Progresso, si!, Tirania, no!" He proposed economic integration and asked that each nation outline long-range programs for itself. He promised United States cooperation for a "case by case examination of commodity market problems" and said that he would ask Congress for $500 million in aid to start the Alliance. The reaction was immediate. A few days later The Times reported:

> LIMA, Peru, March 18—President Kennedy's Alianza para Progreso—Alliance for Progress—policy for Latin America, launched this week with a White House speech followed by a message to Congress requesting funds for the initial aid programs, has been hopefully hailed throughout most of the Hemisphere.
>
> Although doubts, questions and even suspicions persist as to how the sweet music of Mr. Kennedy's words will be ultimately transmuted into actual measures designed to ease Latin America's distortions and backwardness into a rational development, the consensus, even among cynics, is that the President has opened a new chapter in the relationship of North and South America.

With Soviet Ambassador Andrei Gromyko and aides, in a conference at the White House, Oct. 11, 1963.

The Alliance was signed into law by Kennedy on May 27, 1961. The first projects—for Panama, Guatemala and Argentina—were approved on July 2. Actual progress under the Alliance in the next few years was sporadic. Although many projects were undertaken, the job was virtually overwhelming. Brazil was challenged by leftist-led peasants and was unable to cope with debilitating inflation; Argentina found no political combination for overcoming economic stagnation; Bolivia simmered with unrest; Paraguay and Haiti were manipulated by tyrants; Venezuela's democratic government was battered from both right and left. In the climate of disorder and economic lethargy the seeds of the Alliance were unable to take firm root. Capital fled and commodity prices fell even faster than United States aid arrived.

Latin America's problems of want, of disorder, of erratic government were repeated and intensified in Southeast Asia. There was an additional challenge, too—that of Communist guerrillas, particularly in that Balkanized cluster of nations that had been French Indochina. Laos, for example, was a combination of jungles, mountains and river valleys that had been ravaged by years of intermittent warfare. Its roads were poor, its people illiterate. Many Laotians simply did not care which side won the civil war there. Russia had airlifted supplies, including tanks, to the Pathet Lao. Washington, in turn, was aiding the right-wing government of Prince Boun Oum. When Kennedy took office the Pathet Lao seemed to be in the ascendency and the right wing headed for almost certain defeat. The President first intended to intervene directly; the debacle at the Bay of Pigs changed his mind. Ultimately he settled on a combination of increased military aid and diplomatic negotiation.

Laos reached a shaky peace in July 1962, when 14 nations met in Geneva to sign an agreement guaranteeing its neutrality. A coalition made up of rightist, leftist and neutral elements was to govern the torn nation, while a control commission made up of Canada, Poland and India would oversee the peace. The solution was not entirely successful. Though Laos was saved from immediate Communist domination, sporadic warfare threatened to submerge the pro-Western elements.

Kennedy regarded South Vietnam as perhaps the key to the control of other non-Communist nations in Southeast Asia. Yet the situation there steadily deteriorated as the war effort became entangled in Saigon politics. In the beginning South Vietnam seemed to be winning its war against the Communist Vietcong. President Ngo Dinh Diem appeared to command support from the people, and massive quantities of United States aid gave the country the semblance of an economy. Early in his Administration, however, Kennedy deepened the United States commitment in South Vietnam. The Times reported:

Defense Secretary McNamara and General Maxwell Taylor report to the President on Vietnam.

U.S. WILL GIVE MORE ARMS
AND MONEY TO VIETNAMESE

MANILA, May 13—South Vietnam and the United States have agreed on an eight-point program for increased American military and economic assistance. Long-range measures to meet the Communist guerrilla threat and to improve social conditions in South Vietnam were announced in a communiqué issued following Vice President Johnson's visit to Saigon.

The agreement was made public after Mr. Johnson had arrived in Manila today from Saigon on the second leg of his Southeast Asian tour on behalf of President Kennedy.

The agreement provided for an increase in the Vietnamese armed forces, with the United States widening its military assistance program to support the extra troops. Five days after the agreement was announced, a Times report from Bangkok noted that the United States had "agreed to increase its military assistance to Thailand in the face of intensified Communist pressure from the direction of Laos." Ultimately Kennedy sent Marines to Thailand while the United States fleet patrolled the Gulf of Siam.

The steadily worsening crisis in Vietnam, however, could not be met by a show of force. The regime of the Roman Catholic Diem family provoked the wrath both of its own people and of Washington by a political repression of Buddhists. Buddhist priests committed suicide on the streets of Saigon in protest. The Vietcong, meanwhile, steadily encroached on the countryside as the Diem regime failed to win the support of the village peasants. Relations with Washington grew acrimonious, and Kennedy found himself unable to sway the recalcitrant Diem. The Times reported a Presidential warning to Saigon this way:

> WASHINGTON, Sept. 12—President Kennedy placed the Saigon Government on notice today that the United States was not in Vietnam "to see the war lost."
>
> In a series of carefully phrased answers at his news conference, the President made it clear that the United States would continue to press the South Vietnamese regime to adopt internal policies likely to bring victory over the Communist guerrillas.
>
> But the President said that no "useful purpose" would be served by discussing publicly now the steps the Administration planned to take in the complex Vietnam crisis.

One step became known a few days later. It was reported that the Administration had decided to reduce its aid to South Vietnam unless the Diem regime drastically revised its policy. Washington was convinced that the war against the Communist guerrillas could not be won under the existing conditions. In early October, a story from Saigon noted that the United States had quietly suspended aid that had been given in the form of commercial exports. Further cuts, it said, were being considered. By November 1, the question had become moot. The headline said:

REBELS IN VIETNAM OUST DIEM, REPORT HIM AND NHU SUICIDES; SHARPER FIGHT ON REDS VOWED

The South Vietnamese Government had fallen in a swiftly executed coup. The Army, led by generals friendly to the United States, had ringed the Presidential palace and captured both Diem and Nhu when they fled. The report of suicides was untrue; both men had been assassinated. Washington accepted the new situation with equanimity.

> WASHINGTON, Saturday, Nov. 2—The Administration welcomes the coup d'état in South Vietnam, assumes that its policies helped to bring it about and is confident of greater progress now in the war against the Communist guerrillas.
>
> There were, of course, no public statements to this effect even after the success of the coup appeared certain this morning. Officials denied any involvement in the military plot and are likely to deplore the deaths of President Ngo Dinh Diem and his brother Ngo Dinh Nhu if reports of their deaths are confirmed.
>
> It is conceded here, however, that the United States Government had created the atmosphere that made the coup possible. This has been done by President Kennedy's public denunciation of President Diem and by constant pressure from Washington for changes in his regime.

While the situation in South Vietnam had been worsening in early 1963, a lull had crept into East-West relations. The significant news was not in what Washington and Moscow were doing, but in what they were not doing. Thus, they did not enter into new realms of cooperation, but neither did they upset the fragile truce in Berlin or Cuba. They did not reach agreements on disarmament or the control of the United Nations, but neither did they exchange angry recriminations over their failure to do so. Kennedy had said that the world was at the brink of disaster during the Cuban missile crisis at the end of 1962; now it appeared to be in a hiatus.

The first fruit of this interlude came in Geneva. The Times reported:

> GENEVA, June 20—The United States and the Soviet Union signed an agreement today to establish a "hot-line" emergency communications link between Washington and Moscow to reduce the risk of accidental war.
>
> The direct cable connection for transmitting teletypewriter messages in times of international tension could be hooked up within 90 days, a United States source said.

Kennedy did not overplay the significance of the hot line. He called it a "limited but practical step forward in arms control and disarmament" and hoped that "more encompassing steps will follow."

A month later a major step in the American-Russian détente was announced. The Times said:

U.S., SOVIET AND BRITAIN REACH ATOMIC ACCORD THAT BARS ALL BUT UNDERGROUND TESTS; SEE MAJOR STEP TOWARD EASING TENSION

MOSCOW, July 25—The United States, the Soviet Union and Britain concluded today a treaty to prohibit nuclear testing in the atmosphere, in space and under water.

The historic document was initialed at 7:15 P.M., Moscow time, by W. Averell Harriman, Under Secretary of State for Political Affairs, Soviet Foreign Minister Andrei A. Gromyko and Viscount Hailsham, British Minister of Science.

A communiqué said:

"The heads of the three delegations agreed that the test ban treaty constituted an important first step toward the reduction of international tension and the strengthening of peace, and they look forward to further progress in this direction."

The next night Kennedy spoke to the nation in what he called a "spirit of hope." He called the treaty a "shaft of light cut into the darkness of cold war discords and tensions," but nevertheless "not the millennium."

"It will not resolve all conflicts, or cause the Communists to forgo their ambitions, or eliminate the dangers of war," he said. "It will not reduce the need for arms or allies or programs of assistance to others. But it is an important first step—a step toward peace—a step toward reason—a step away from war."

The treaty, the first major East-West agreement since the decision that ended the four-power occupation of Austria in May 1955, provoked conservative criticism in the United States. There were fears that it gave the Russians a military advantage, misgivings that the Russians had technical information that surpassed ours, suspicion that they might be able to cheat on nuclear testing. Nevertheless, on September 24 the Senate ratified the treaty by a vote of 80 to 19.

The test ban agreement was followed by another small link in the détente.

KENNEDY AUTHORIZES WHEAT SALE TO RUSSIANS TOTALING $250,000,000; SENATE TO CONSIDER WIDER TRADE

WASHINGTON, Oct. 9—President Kennedy approved today the sale of $250 million worth of wheat to the Soviet Union.

The wheat—150 million bushels—will be sold through private commercial channels at the world price for cash or short-term credit. It will be for use only in the Soviet Union and Eastern Europe. This ruled out wheat to Cuba and Communist China. . . .

In what amounted to a summation of his views on the wheat deal, Mr. Kennedy said:

"This particular decision with respect to wheat sales to the Soviet Union, which is not inconsistent with many smaller transactions over a longer period of time, does not represent a new Soviet-American trade policy. This must await the settlement of many matters.

"But it does represent one more hopeful sign that a more peaceful world is both possible and beneficial to us all."

The wheat deal provoked another swirl of criticism about the President. His detractors cried that he was helping to lead Khrushchev out of his economic difficulties and becoming so enchanted by East-West rapport that he failed to recognize the Communist challenge. The criticism grew in intensity two days later when Soviet armor detained an American convoy on the autobahn outside West Berlin. A week later Kennedy rebutted his critics. The Times reported:

BOSTON, Oct. 19—President Kennedy strongly defended today his efforts to improve relations with the Soviet Union but pledged to keep the nation ready to meet any new Communist challenges.

Steps like the treaty banning all but underground nuclear tests and the pending sale of wheat to the Russians, the President said, were directed to the "single, comprehensive goal of convincing the Soviet Union that a "genuine and enforceable peace" would be beneficial to them as well as the rest of the world.

He was determined, nevertheless, to maintain the nation's strength, Mr. Kennedy told an academic convocation at the University of Maine at Orono, because major tensions

Oct. 8, 1963: the President signs the nuclear test ban treaty, as members of Congress and the Cabinet look on.

would remain while the United States and the Soviet Union had "wholly different concepts of the world, its freedom, its future."

The nation, he contended, should "recognize both the gains we have made down the road to peace and the distances yet to be covered."

As Kennedy moved toward an easier relationship with Khrushchev, he was encouraged by the bitter ideological split between the Soviet Union and China. Ironically, he faced a schism in the Western Alliance, too. He had spoken of the "interdependence" of the United States and Europe. He had called for a "United Europe," which would be both a political and an economic union. He had anticipated a "concrete Atlantic partnership" between such a Europe and the United States; this was his Grand Design.

As a first step he had hoped that Britain would join the European Common Market, but de Gaulle vetoed the entry. De Gaulle also rejected Kennedy's concept of a centrally controlled nuclear deterrent

for the North Atlantic Treaty Organization. He insisted on an independent French nuclear force as part of his dream of organizing Western Europe under the leadership of Paris. De Gaulle also declined, as did the Chinese Communists, to sign the nuclear test ban treaty.

In 1963, the cracks in the Western Alliance were apparent. Few of Kennedy's policies had been able to mature fully. Yet his convictions and his direction were unmistakable. He stood for the unity of the Western world, for international control of national disputes, for toughness against the Russians—but only to achieve more lasting settlements—and for the right of all nations to be independent. Kennedy summarized his approach in a speech at American University on June 11, 1963: "This generation of Americans has already had enough—more than enough—of war and hate and oppression. We shall be prepared if others wish it. We shall be alert to try to stop it. But we shall also do our part to build a world of peace where the weak are safe and the strong are just."

SPACE

On April 12, 1961, a Moscow radio announcer broke into a broadcast and said in emotional tones: "Russia has successfully launched a man into space. His name is Yuri Gagarin. He was launched in a sputnik named Vostok." In 89.1 minutes Major Gagarin had made a complete orbit of the earth; he was the first man to go into space—and he was a Russian. At a press conference that same day, Kennedy candidly admitted that the United States was behind in space efforts. "The news will be worse before it is better, and it will be some time before we catch up," he said.

Less than a month later the first American rode into space. The Times said:

U.S. HURLS MAN 115 MILES INTO SPACE; SHEPARD WORKS CONTROLS IN CAPSULE, REPORTS BY RADIO IN 15-MINUTE FLIGHT

CAPE CANAVERAL, Fla., May 5—A slim, cool Navy test pilot was rocketed 115 miles into space today.

Thirty-seven-year-old Comdr. Alan B. Shepard Jr. thus became the first American space explorer.

Commander Shepard landed safely 302 miles out at sea 15 minutes after the launching. He was quickly lifted aboard a Marine Corps helicopter.

"Boy, what a ride," he said, as he was flown to the aircraft carrier Lake Champlain four miles away. . . .

The near-perfect flight represented the United States' first major step in the race to explore space with manned space craft.

Washington was elated. Kennedy called the flight a "historic milestone" and shortly after committed the nation to landing a man on the moon before the end of the decade. A wave of enthusiasm swept the country and Alan Shepard became its first astronaut hero.

A few months later, Captain Virgil I. Grissom of the Air Force was rocketed aboard a Mercury capsule on an arching flight that took him 118 miles into the sky and 303 miles out into the Atlantic. The suborbital flight was not a complete success, however, because the $2 million capsule sank into the ocean and Grissom was forced to swim to safety.

Project Mercury was the first step in a program that sought to place an American on the moon by 1970. Project Gemini, the second step, involved two-man spaceships, which would attempt to rendezvous in space with other orbiting vehicles and fly for as long as two weeks on training missions. Project Apollo, the moon landing itself, would use three-man space craft that would be powered by an enormous Saturn rocket.

From its inception, Apollo had critics. They noted that the program would probably cost $20 billion, 10 times what was spent to develop the atom bomb in World War II. Some scientists, too, attacked the program, saying it was a stunt and wasteful of talent. However, D. Brainerd Holmes, who guided the moon project, said, "If we do not make these efforts we will not be first on the moon, we will not be first in space, and one day soon we will not be first on earth."

Kennedy, therefore, pushed the program. Often he was helped by the stimulus of a Russian space spectacular. Shortly after Grissom's flight, Moscow radio reported that Major Gherman S. Titov had orbited the earth more than 17 times in 25 hours 11 minutes. Clearly, the Russians were holding the lead in space exploration. The following winter the United States took another step into space, but it still lagged behind the Russians:

GLENN ORBITS EARTH 3 TIMES SAFELY;
PICKED UP IN CAPSULE BY DESTROYER;
PRESIDENT WILL GREET HIM IN FLORIDA

CAPE CANAVERAL, Fla., Feb. 20—John H. Glenn Jr. orbited three times around the earth today and landed safely to become the first American to make such a flight.

The 40-year-old Marine Corps lieutenant colonel traveled about 81,000 miles in 4 hours 56 minutes before splashing into the Atlantic at 2:43 P.M., Eastern standard time.

He had been launched from here at 9:47 A.M.

The astronaut's safe return was no less a relief than a thrill to the Project Mercury team because there had been real concern that the Friendship 7 capsule might disintegrate as it rammed back into the atmosphere.

There had also been a serious question whether Colonel Glenn could complete three orbits as planned. But despite persistent control problems, he managed to complete the entire flight plan.

Pinning the Distinguished Service Medal on Colonel John Glenn Jr., first American to orbit the earth, Feb. 20, 1962.

In contrast to the Russian flights, which were largely launched in secret, the American ventures were conducted with a great deal of publicity at Cape Canaveral, Fla., which was later renamed Cape Kennedy. Millions of Americans had watched Glenn on television; after his flight he was a popular hero. Kennedy telephoned him after he landed to say excitedly, "Listen, colonel, we are really proud of you, and I must say you did a wonderful job." When Glenn came to Washington to speak to a joint meeting of Congress, The Times reported:

WASHINGTON, Feb. 26—This normally blasé capital put up its umbrella and stood in a chilling downpour today to offer its unabashed admiration to the first American to orbit the earth.

Lieut. Col. John H. Glenn Jr. was cheered up Pennsylvania Avenue to the Capitol by thousands and thousands of drenched spectators in a demonstration of human and national emotion such as Washington rarely gives.

Shortly after Glenn's flight, Kennedy proposed a cooperative program of space exploration with the Soviet Union. The program involved weather satellites, radio tracking stations for space ventures, a mapping of the earth's magnetic field and joint projects in space medicine and communications. Kennedy repeated his proposals for cooperative ventures in direct overtures to Khrushchev and through the United Nations; at the conclusion of Project Mercury, Kennedy suggested that East and West join in the pro-

BELOW: With Wernher von Braun (right), the President inspects a missile-launching mechanism at Cape Canaveral. RIGHT: Watching a Polaris missile firing from a nuclear submarine off the Florida coast, Nov. 16, 1963.

gram to place a man on the moon. Like most of the other proposals, it was spurned; only comparatively modest agreements were reached on space.

In May 1962, Lieutenant Commander Scott Carpenter matched Glenn's feat by completing three orbits. But three months later the Russians mounted their most impressive spectacular—simultaneous orbital flights. Major Andrian Nikolayev sped around the world 64 times in 94 hours 35 minutes. His partner, Lieutenant Colonel Pavel Popovich, orbited 48 times in 70 hours 57 minutes.

Two months later, Commander Walter M. Schirra Jr. was sent aloft for 9 hours 14 minutes. The headlines said:

SCHIRRA ORBITS EARTH SIX TIMES, LANDING NEAR CARRIER IN PACIFIC AFTER ALMOST FLAWLESS FLIGHT

The 39-year-old astronaut had traveled 160,000 miles, twice as far as the two Americans who had orbited before him. The American space voyage concluding Project Mercury was made on May 15, 1963:

COOPER MANEUVERS TO A BULLSEYE LANDING WITH MANUAL CONTROL AS AUTOMATIC FAILS; 'I'M IN FINE SHAPE,' HE SAYS AFTER 22 ORBITS

CAPE CANAVERAL, Fla., May 16—Maj. L. Gordon Cooper landed safely in the Pacific today after a magnificently executed 22-orbit flight.

The closing phase of the flight was highlighted by a dramatic descent from orbit during which the astronaut guided himself to safety by manually controlling his capsule when his automatic controls failed.

The Russians followed the Cooper trip with another stunning coup—twin orbits by a male and female astronaut. Junior Lieutenant Valentina V. Tereshkova became the first woman in space with a journey of 48 orbits. Lieutenant Colonel Valery F. Bykovsky established a space endurance record by orbiting the earth 81 times in 54 minutes less than five days.

It was apparent that the Soviet Union had a considerable advantage in rocket power. But it was equally apparent that the United States was ahead in some other aspects of the space race. From Nov. 29, 1961, to Dec. 21, 1963, the National Aeronautics and Space Administration put 25 consecutive satellites in orbit. Unlike the Russians, the Americans were racking up an impressive total of successful satellites sent aloft on scientific missions, including the Tiros weather satellites and Telstar communications satellites.

ENTERTAINING AT
THE WHITE HOUSE

Americans have looked to the White House for guidance, inspiration and enlightenment—seldom for cultural uplift. But by the summer of 1962 a story in The Times could say:

> The palpable love affair between the White House and a jade called culture shows signs of reaching an impassioned peak this year. With Robert Frost's participation in the inaugural ceremony heralding the romance and three command performances at the Executive Mansion cementing it in recent months, the extraordinary liaison between politics and art has been attracting comment abroad and speculation at home—particularly in the cultural wasteland of Washington itself.

Actually, Washington offers magnificent art galleries and splendid opportunities for hearing chamber music. But until John F. Kennedy, neither the city nor the Presidents had been publicly associated with a purposeful pursuit of culture. Other Presidents, for instance, had watched Shakespeare outside the White House on the lawn; Kennedy brought him inside. The Times reported it this way:

> WASHINGTON, Oct. 4—Theater in the royal tradition was introduced in the White House tonight and was royally applauded.
> The blood scene from "Macbeth" and four other Shakespearean excerpts were performed on a specially built stage in the lofty East Ballroom for the President and Mrs. Kennedy and 100 guests at a state dinner in honor of President Ibrahim Abboud of the Sudan.

Later, Kennedy wrote to the man who staged the scenes, congratulating him on a "very exciting performance" and expressing his and Mrs. Kennedy's pride in "our American theater." The stage that was built—a three-tiered platform with a red velvet backdrop—could be collapsed and stored when not in use. Performers had appeared at the White House before in brief recitals, but the introduction of the stage meant that, for the Kennedys, the play could truly be the thing. In time the stage was used by ballerinas and bassos, Elizabethan instrumentalists and sopranos—a fair cross-section of the performing arts. And with the artists came the guests. For the first time there was a steady traffic to the White House of notables in the arts. Carl Sandburg came, and so did Gian Carlo Menotti. Leonard Bernstein was entertained, and so were George Balanchine, Ralph Richardson and Elia Kazan.

A month after the Shakespeareans, Pablo Casals appeared at the White House. The visit was an artistic, even a diplomatic, triumph. The Times reported:

CASALS PLAYS AT WHITE HOUSE;
LAST APPEARED THERE IN 1904

WASHINGTON, Nov. 13—The intimate sound of chamber music was heard tonight in the White House. Pablo Casals, Alexander Schneider and Mieczyslaw Horszowski played

The Kennedys welcoming the Shah of Iran and his empress at the White House.

Mendelssohn, Schumann and Couperin before a distinguished audience of musicians, diplomats and art patrons.

The concert, played in the East Room, followed a state dinner given by President and Mrs. Kennedy for Governor Luis Munoz-Marín of Puerto Rico.

There has been music in the White House since Thomas Jefferson appropriated $428 for a pianoforte, but tonight's was one of the few occasions where a program of serious music has been attempted. The occasion also transcended mere music-making.

Casals, who had last appeared at the White House for Theodore Roosevelt, had sworn never to give concerts in any country that recognized Spain's Franco. But the cellist had agreed to the appearance to show his admiration for Kennedy. Not since Jefferson, who played a violin, had a long piece of serious music been heard in the White House. In the past, musicians had been asked to limit themselves to light pieces, preferably not more than five minutes in length. In the audience that night were Samuel Barber, Aaron Copland, Norman Dello Joio, Menotti, William Schuman, Roger Sessions, Virgil Thomson, Bernstein, Eugene Ormandy and Leopold Stokowski.

A few months later, when Igor Stravinsky was in Washington to conduct the Washington Opera Society, he, too, was invited to the White House for a small, private dinner.

In March 1962, Kennedy further established an image of artistic patronage by appointing August Heckscher as a special consultant on the arts for the White House. He was to survey the relationship between the arts and the Government in general and act as an intermediary between the White House and Federal and private agencies. By Executive order, Kennedy also created the country's first President's Advisory Council on the Arts.

Jacqueline Kennedy, of course, played a significant role in shaping the President's—and the nation's—tastes during the Kennedy years. Under her guidance, the Cabinet sponsored poetry seminars, a series of concerts for youth was presented and some of the more esoteric arts reached the White House. The Times told of one of them this way:

WASHINGTON, April 30—The poetry and music of Elizabethan England echoed in the White House tonight after a dinner for a monarch of a modern era.

Performing against a backdrop of velvet, Basil Rathbone, the actor, and the Consort Players of New York presented a program fit for the Grand Duchess Charlotte of Luxembourg.

The offering that night was by six instrumentalists who performed on instruments from Shakespeare's time. Mrs. Kennedy requested, among other numbers, selections by Christopher Marlowe, Shakespeare, John Donne and Robert Herrick. The President, in his only request, asked Rathbone to recite Henry's speech before the battle of Agincourt from "Henry V."

Among the artists themselves, an appearance at the White House lent a special sort of status; the summonses were extended only to those of excellence. Thus Grace Bumbry, Roberta Peters, Jerome Hines and Isaac Stern appeared, and so did the American Ballet Theatre and Jerome Robbins' "Ballets: U.S.A." One by-product of the Kennedys' appreciation of the performing arts was that the White House received a great many unsolicited offers from performers who simply wanted to appear before the President and his guests. A story about this in The Times began:

WASHINGTON, June 2—Command performances at the White House have become almost as sought after as those phenomena of political Americana, postermasterships.

From all over the country these days, the mail pours in: from glee clubs and prodigies, symphony orchestras and modern dancers.

Everyone, it seems, wants to get into the act with a one-night stand for President and Mrs. Kennedy and their guests.

Perhaps the most celebrated intellectual event at the White House during the Kennedy Administration was the dinner tendered to 49 winners of Nobel Prizes. The guests sat in the State Dining Room and the Blue Room, and the evening lasted much longer than had been planned; it was so much of a family reunion that no one wanted to leave. The Times reported the story this way:

Entertaining the Nobel Prize winners and others.

49 NOBEL PRIZE WINNERS
HONORED AT WHITE HOUSE

WASHINGTON, April 29—Much of the cream of scientific America gathered at the White House tonight for a dinner honoring Nobel Prize winners.

The gathering, outstanding in modern White House entertainment, culminated in the first public reading of an unpublished work by the late Ernest Hemingway, winner of the Nobel Prize for literature.

As guests for their biggest dinner, President and Mrs. Kennedy brought together 49 Nobel laureates who live in the Western Hemisphere and 124 other scientists, writers, editors and educators. There were only a few politicians and statesmen present.

The President described the dinner as "probably the greatest concentration of talent and genius in this house except for those times when Jefferson ate alone."

The guest list also included seven Pulitzer Prize-winning writers, including the President himself, and two politically controversial scientists—Dr. Linus C. Pauling and Dr. J. Robert Oppenheimer. Pauling had left a picket line outside the White House to attend the dinner; he had been protesting the use and development of nuclear weapons. Oppenheimer, one of the men who had helped to develop the atom bomb, had been denied a security clearance by the Atomic Energy Commission in 1954.

Besides the life at the White House, the Kennedys found other ways of applauding culture. For instance, they attended the opening performances of both the Opera Society and the National Symphony Orchestra. Kennedy also took a public stand in favor of building a National Cultural Center in Washington. August Heckscher commented, "He cared about the life of the mind; he cared for excellence in all fields."

OVERLEAF: Preparing to greet French Minister of Culture André Malraux.

DEATH

The New York Times.

LATE CITY EDITION
U.S. Weather Bureau Report (Page 56 , . . .)
Cloudy, windy, chance of showers
today and tonight. Cold tomorrow.
Temp. Range: 62—54; yesterday: 64—51.

VOL. CXIII. No. 38,654.   © 1963 by The New York Times Company.
Times Square, New York 36, N.Y.   NEW YORK, SATURDAY, NOVEMBER 23, 1963.   TEN CENTS

KENNEDY IS KILLED BY SNIPER AS HE RIDES IN CAR IN DALLAS; JOHNSON SWORN IN ON PLANE

DALLAS, Nov. 22—President John Fitzgerald Kennedy was shot and killed by an assassin today.

He died of a wound in the brain caused by a rifle bullet that was fired at him as he was riding through downtown Dallas in a motorcade.

Vice President Lyndon Baines Johnson, who was riding in the third car behind Mr. Kennedy's, was sworn in as the 36th President of the United States 99 minutes after Mr. Kennedy's death.

Mr. Johnson is 55 years old; Mr. Kennedy was 46.

Shortly after the assassination, Lee H. Oswald, who once defected to the Soviet Union and who has been active in the Fair Play for Cuba Committee, was arrested by the Dallas police. Tonight he was accused of the killing.

Oswald, 24 years old, was also accused of slaying a policeman who had approached him in the street. Oswald was subdued after a scuffle with a second policeman in a nearby theatre.

President Kennedy was shot at 12:30 P.M., central standard time (1:30 P.M., New York time). He was dead at 1 P.M. and Mr. Johnson was sworn in at 2:39 P.M.

Mr. Johnson, who was uninjured in the shooting, took his oath in the Presidential jet plane as it stood on the runway at Love Field. The body of Mr. Kennedy was aboard. Immediately after the oath-taking, the plane took off for Washington.

Standing beside the new President as Mr. Johnson took the oath of office was Mrs. John F. Kennedy. Her stockings were spattered with her husband's blood.

Governor John B. Connally Jr. of Texas, who was riding in the same car with Mr. Kennedy, was severely wounded in the chest, ribs and arm. His condition was serious, but not critical.

The killer fired the rifle from a building just off the motorcade route. Mr. Kennedy, Governor Connally and Mr. Johnson had just received an enthusiastic welcome from a large crowd in downtown Dallas.

Nov. 23, 1963: The President's office in the White House, filled with his books and personal objects, stands empty.

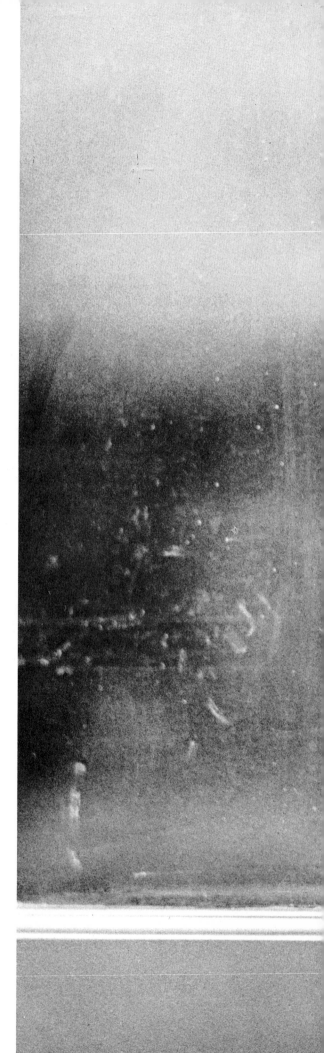

The New York Times.

VOL. CXIII...No. 38,657. © 1963 by The New York Times Company.
Times Square, New York 36, N. Y.   NEW YORK, TUESDAY, NOVEMBER 26, 1963.   TEN CENTS

KENNEDY LAID TO REST IN ARLINGTON; HUSHED NATION WATCHES AND GRIEVES; WORLD LEADERS PAY TRIBUTE AT GRAVE

Foreign dignitaries leaving the White House to walk to St. Matthew's Cathedral.

316

OPPOSITE: Mrs. Kennedy with her children, the President's brothers, and other members of his family, as the coffin is carried from the Cathedral. OVERLEAF: The family at the graveside.

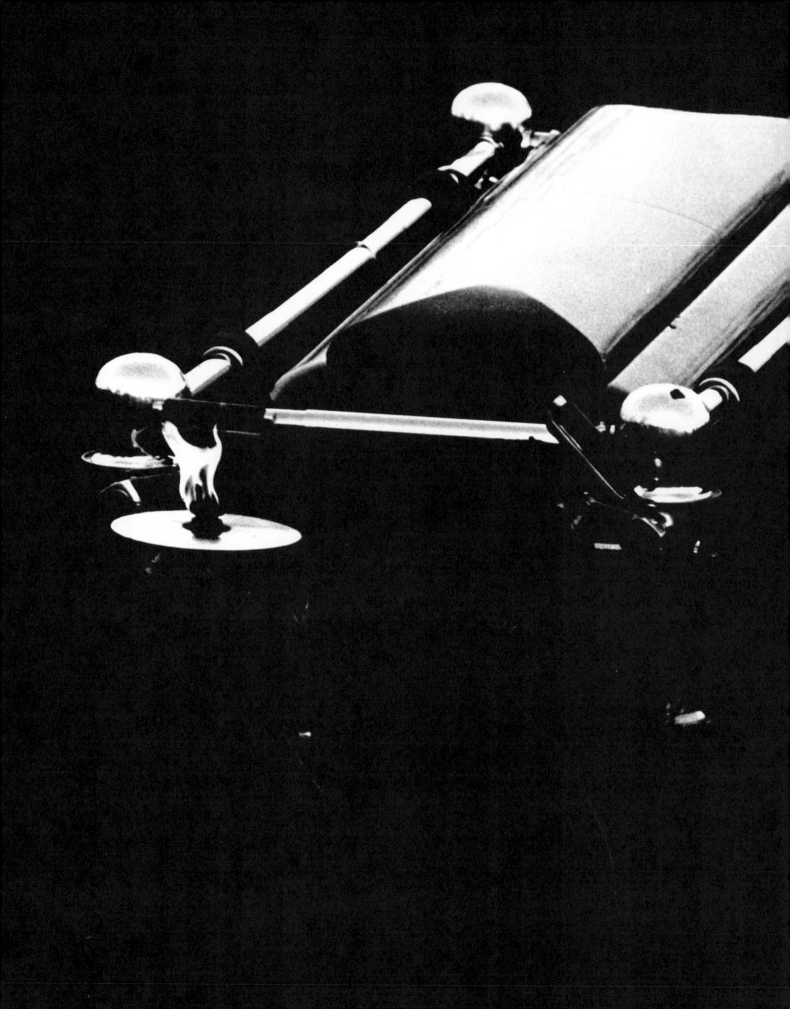

CHRONOLOGY

May 29, 1917	Born in Brookline, Mass.
1930-1931	Attended Canterbury School, New Milford, Conn.
1931-1935	Attended Choate School, Wallingford, Conn.
1935 (summer)	Studied at London School of Economics.
1936 (fall)	Entered Harvard.
June 1940	Received B.S. degree cum laude from Harvard.
Aug. 1, 1940	"Why England Slept" published.
September 1941	Commissioned in United States Navy as ensign.
Aug. 2, 1943	Commanded PT boat sunk by Japanese destroyer in South Pacific.
June 11, 1944	Awarded Navy and Marine Corps Medal and the Purple Heart.
Aug. 12, 1944	Brother, Joseph P., Jr. killed on Naval air raid against Belgian coast.
January 1945	Released from service with rank of full lieutenant.
1945	Worked as reporter for Hearst newspapers.
Nov. 5, 1946	Elected to House of Representatives.
Nov. 4, 1952	Elected to United States Senate.
Sept. 12, 1953	Married Jacqueline Lee Bouvier.
Oct. 21, 1954	Operated on for recurrent back injury.
Jan. 2, 1956	"Profiles in Courage" published.
May 6, 1957	Received Pulitzer Prize for biography.
Nov. 27, 1957	Caroline born.
Nov. 4, 1958	Re-elected to Senate.
Jan. 2, 1960	Announced candidacy for the Presidency.
July 13, 1960	Nominated for President by the Democratic National Convention.
Nov. 8, 1960	Elected President.
Nov. 25, 1960	John F., Jr. born.
Jan. 20, 1961	Inaugurated as the 35th President of the United States.
Aug. 7, 9, 1963	Patrick Bouvier born prematurely and died.
Nov. 22, 1963	Assassinated in Dallas, Texas.
Nov. 25, 1963	Buried in Arlington National Cemetery.

Nearly a year after his death, visitors still thronged to the grave of John Fitzgerald Kennedy.

Index

(Page numbers in italics refer to captions for photographs)